Your New
Baby

Insider Secrets to Save Thousands on All Your Baby's Needs

By
Eva Marie
Stasiak

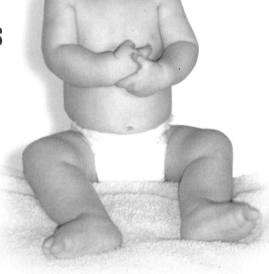

Atlantic
Publishing

Your New Baby: Insider Secrets To Save Thousands On All Your Baby's Needs

ISBN-13: 978-1-60138-138-5 ISBN-10: 1-60138-138-7

Library of Congress Cataloging-in-Publication Data

Stasiak, Eva Marie, 1978-

Your new baby: insider secrets to save thousands on all your baby's needs / by Eva Marie Stasiak.

p. cm.

Includes bibliographic references and index.

ISBN-13: 978-1-60138-138-5 (alk. paper)

ISBN-10: 1-60138-138-7 (alk. paper)

1. Mothers--Finance, Personal. 2. Infants--Care--United States--Costs.

3. Child rearing--Economic aspects--United States. 4.

Family--Economic aspects. I. Title. II. Title: Save thousands on all your baby's needs.

HG179.S8116 2008

332.0240085--dc22

    2008003795

ART DIRECTION & DESIGN: Meg Buchner • megadesn@mchsi.com

COVER PHOTO: Silas Joseph Buchner, 6 months old

Printed in the United States

Table of Contents

Foreword   11

About the Author   15

CHAPTER 1
The Baby Friendly Budget   17

The Secondhand Secret 18

Creating Your Baby-Friendly Budget 19

Get Your Figures 20

Step One: What Does It Cost You to Live Now?.................... 22

Step Two: Determine Your Income... 22

Step Three: Eliminate Unnecessary Expenses....................... 23

Step Four: Create a Monthly Budget for Baby...................... 25

Step Five: Savings 25

Step Six: Become a Smart Shopper 27

    What Should I Do with My Credit Card?....................... 28

    Little Money Savers that Add Up.................................. 29

    Secondhand Shopping and Free Stuff........................... 29

Planning for Healthcare Costs.. 30

Step Seven: Planning for Your Baby's Future 32

CHAPTER 2

While You Wait, Preparing for Your Baby 37

Necessity One: Feeding Your Infant....................................... 38

    Breast-feeding.. 38

    Formula 39

Necessity Two: Diapers 42

Necessity Three: Clothing.. 46

Necessity Four: Infant Car Seat... 49

Organization 52

CHAPTER 3
Baby Showers and Registries 55

Registering for Your Baby Shower..56

    Basic Registry Items..60

The Baby Shower...63

CHAPTER 4
Facts of Life 67

Breast-feeding..68

Formula 72

Bottles and Nipples...74

Bottle Warmers and Sterilizers.............................77

Baby Food and Cereal..81

Pacifiers, Burp Cloths, and Bibs............................84

Diapers 88

Other Diapering Needs and Products......................90

    Diaper Rash Ointment..91

    Booty Budder Recipe 92

    Baby Wipes...93

    Diaper Bag...95

    Diaper Pail..98

Baby Carriers 100

Clothing 104

Helpful Hints: What Not to Buy 106

What Works Best in Baby Clothing 108

CHAPTER 5
Keeping Baby Clean and Healthy 115

Keeping Baby Clean 116

Keeping Baby Healthy 122

    First Aid Kits and Thermometers 122

    Fever Reducers 125

    Humidifiers and Other White Noise 126

    Tummy Troubles 127

    Dental Hygiene 130

Protect Your Baby from Common Colds and Germs 130

CHAPTER 6
Safety in Common Places 135

Car Safety 136

Safety in Your Home 139

    Outlets 140

Wires and Electrical Cords.. 141

Sharp Objects 142

Poisonous Products and Cleaners 144

Cabinet and Drawer Locks 145

Baby Gates 148

Baby Monitors 153

CHAPTER 7
The Nursery

159

Paint 160

Baby Furniture 160

Bassinets and Cribs... 161

Changing Tables 169

Rocking Chairs, Gliders, and Ottomans 172

Decorating and Final Touches.. 174

Rugs, Big or Small.. 175

Curtains and other Window Treatments 176

Photos, Pictures, and Framed Art.............................. 177

Lettering and Names 180

Finishing Touches.. 181

CHAPTER 8
Items that Can Break the Bank   185

An Appropriate Vehicle.. 186

Highchairs 188

Strollers 190

Portable Playards 198

Bouncers, Jumpers, and ExerSaucers 201

Swings and Walkers... 207

CHAPTER 9
Fun Stuff and Playtime   211

Toys for Babies Less than One Year Old 212

Books, Music, and Videos 215

Scrap Books and Baby Books... 222

CHAPTER 10
Enjoying Baby and Budget Together   223

Works Cited.. 228

APPENDIX
Money-Saving References 229

Product Manufactures 230

Clothing & Apparel.. 231

Decorating & Bedding... 235

Diapers & Related Items 241

For Mommies 245

Furniture... 250

In the Bathroom.. 258

Music & Movies.. 259

Nursing.. 260

Nutrition & Feeding 262

On the Go Gear.. 263

Safety & Childproofing 270

Toys & Books.. 272

Web Sites for Gently Used Baby Items.............................. 273

Children reinvent your world for you.

—Susan Sarandon

Foreword

Congratulations on your pregnancy! As you anticipate the joys of parenthood and daydream about coos 'n' giggles and hugs 'n' cuddles, there is also planning you must do. One question that I often am asked from expectant parents is "how much will having a baby cost?" The answer is… a lot. From diapers and formula to car seats, from cribs and strollers to insurance and medical care, your expenses are about to increase dramatically. Having a baby will most likely be the biggest investment you ever make.

According to the United States Department of Agriculture, it is predicted that the average family will spend a total of $250,000 raising one child for 18 years. However, this estimate cost does not include sending your child to college. Additionally the findings show that the average yearly costs increase with each birthday. Being a mother of two children, on a fixed income, I understand how these figures can be extremely overwhelming and scary. However, there are ways to prepare and reduce the total costs. If you become a smart shopper, know your options, plan ahead, and prepare for family life, you can literally save thousands of dollars.

When I was pregnant with my first daughter, no one I knew had any baby items such as a crib, a stroller, or even hand-me-down clothes to share. They either needed the items themselves, or had already loaned them to someone else. Everything I needed had to be purchased, and being a first-time expectant mother, I had no idea of the sheer number of things I would need to buy for my new baby, neither how the costs would add up. I remember walking into a local baby store and then walking right out after seeing just a few of the listed prices. There were so many choices and options; some were expensive and some not. It was the total package that when all added up would certainly break my bank. How was I going to afford all this? It was that question that forced me to go home, take another look at my finances and begin to plan out a budget.

In *Your New Baby: Insider Secrets to Save Thousands on All Your Baby's Needs*, Eva Marie Stasiak does an excellent job showing new parents how to create a budget and plan for the expected as well as the unexpected costs you will incur — an important step in becoming a parent. A budget will help keep your finances in order and give you a better understanding of what you can afford for your new baby and the type of life style you will live.

Aside from creating a budget, you will learn how to become a smart shopper. A smart shopper knows how to find sales, looks in local consignment shops for second-hand items, and buys in bulk when she can. She will spend Sunday afternoons clipping coupons and signing up for baby product giveaways and free product samples. Shopping smart will save you money on formula, diapers, and other baby products.

Another way to save money and reduce your costs is by having a baby shower. A baby shower is a fun and exciting way for family and friends to celebrate and welcome your new baby into the world. Either you can plan and host your baby shower, or you can have a friend host it for you. Either way, you will be showered with gifts and much-needed items for your new addition, and it is a way to reduce your bottom line. In *Your New Baby*, Eva will show you how to select a store, create your baby registry, and choose items to put into your registry. It is in the decisions you make when selecting items for your registry that will help you reduce the initial costs of baby items. The last thing you want to do is fill your registry with items that are not necessary. You will be able to purchase other items and more later with all the money you have saved from using the tips you learn in this book.

Your New Baby will be a valuable tool that will replace your worries and allow you to enjoy your pregnancy and the first years with your new baby. Eva will show you how to use the resources you have to save money on baby needs. She shows how to shop for secondhand baby items as well as how to find free baby stuff. You will learn that by breast-feeding your baby, you will literally save thousands of dollars on feeding costs. If you should choose to bottle-feed your baby, Eva also gives advice on the products you will need to buy and how to save money when shopping for items such as formula, bottles, and accessories. She also covers topics such as purchasing health insurance, healthcare, saving for college, and what to when a life emergency strikes.

Expecting a baby almost always instills fears in new parents. There are so many issues to think about, items to buy, and planning to be done. Many expectant parents visit Baby Corner and post on our message boards about worries of their financial ability to bring a new life into this world. It is a scary thought, especially if you are living on a fixed income. By using the tips provided in this book, you will learn how to be a smart shopper and a better planner, and you will be amazed at just how much you will be able to afford for your new baby. By purchasing *Your New Baby: Insider Secrets to Save*

Thousands on All Your Baby's Needs, you have already made a good financial decision, that of wanting to learn how to get the most for your money so you can offer your new family a more enjoyable life. Your bank account will thank you.

Warmest Wishes,

Elizabeth Geiger
Editor, Baby Corner
205 Doris Avenue
Vestal, NY 13850
editor@thebabycorner.com

Elizabeth Geiger is a mother of two children and currently lives near Binghamton, New York. She has been a work-at-home mother for ten years offering information, advice, and support to expectant and new parents through her online Web site, Baby Corner.

Since 1998, Baby Corner has been providing information, advice, and support to expectant and new parents.

*With articles, interactive tools, and a supportive community for parents to connect with others, Baby Corner is a top destination for expectant and new parents. For more information visit **www.thebabycorner.com**.*

About the Author

Eva Marie Stasiak is a Colorado native who resides in Littleton with her incredibly supportive husband and young daughter.

Eva has been writing since graduating from Fountain Fort Carson High School in 1997 and decided to pursue a freelancing career in 2005. Since then, she has ghostwritten articles about children, mothers, health and fitness, wellness, hypnosis, cross stitch, and other crafts. Eva's crafting articles have been published on **www.ThriftyFun. com**. She has also published her poetry in various magazines and anthologies, including *The Best Poems of the '90s*. Eva was also the recipient of two Editors' Choice Awards for poetry in 1997.

Eva continues to make contacts and attract new clients through **www.elance.com**.

While still in high school, Eva was certified in Early Childhood Development and Education, and in 2001, she received her BA in

Journalism from the University of Northern Colorado. In her free time, Eva serves as president of the H.O.P.E. Babysitting Co-op, reads everything she can get her hands on, and enjoys her amateur love of photography.

Dedication

This book is dedicated to my loving and encouraging husband, all my remarkable family members, and especially to my beautiful, spirited, and spunky daughter, Monika.

The Baby-Friendly Budget

The word "budget" is often feared and hated by many people. Parents and parents-to-be are no strangers to the fear and foreboding that thoughts of creating a new (often tighter) budget bring to mind. Forming a budget that works for you can be a tedious and time consuming job that is often not enjoyable. It is also commonly thought that the idea of a baby-friendly budget is nothing more than a myth. This is not true; there is a simple and easy way to prepare a budget for your baby, no matter what your income may be. The difficult part of budgeting is maintaining that budget while acquiring all the products you will need for your new family.

The Secondhand Secret

Before we jump into the dissection and contemplation of your finances and budget, let me reveal some secrets that often do not occur to many expecting moms and dads. First, new products are good; they are brand new, and no one has used them. Everything from the pretty packaging and delicate ribbons and bows seems to whisper that these items are special, just for you and your baby, used by no one else, and created exclusively for your precious infant. The harsh reality is that new baby items are expensive. It is also worth noting that millions of those cute little baby shoes were mass produced by a machine, and none were created exclusively for your baby. This is a thought that often helped me out of the "brand new" dilemma when I was pregnant and a bit emotional.

When my husband and I found out we had our little surprise on the way, I was excited at the idea of purchasing all the adorable baby items every woman wanting to be a mom dreams about. It was not long before I realized that my dreams of shopping for the baby rarely included accurate totals at the cash register. I was sad to say we needed to find a new way to acquire all those baby gadgets and gizmos. All brand-new items just would not work with the amount of money available to spend on our upcoming family addition. Gently used and secondhand items were our savior. The secondhand stores, online auctions, and garage sales offered a large variety of items that were useful, nearly new, and, at times, brand new with tags still attached.

Most secondhand or gently used items are already mom-tested and approved, and they are often inexpensive. Secondhand boutiques and shops all carry a good selection of baby clothing, accessories, and necessities that are perfectly good, even after they have been used for a short time by another baby and mom. In fact, babies grow so fast that most gently used items have been used for only several months before they can no longer be used for the same child.

Do not turn away free or gently used less-expensive items because you want your baby to have the best. The best that your baby will get will be his family having the means to support him and enough stress-free time to love and play with him without worrying constantly about how you will afford the $200 designer nursery mobile. Money can cause a good deal of stress for new parents. Having a budget will help you feel confident in affording the items you need and knowing when you can afford the items that are nice to have but not ultimately necessary.

Quick TIP

There is nothing wrong with buying used, accepting free, and spending less on new and used items whenever you can. Love is the most important thing your baby will need, and it is free.

Creating Your Baby-Friendly Budget

Creating a budget that will keep your cash flow in the positive and allow you to purchase the things you need is a simple task of addition and subtraction — the money you will have minus the money you must spend on bills and savings. What is left is the money you will be allowing yourself to spend on the new items you need and want to purchase for your baby. However, there are a few decisive steps you need to consider to create a successful, baby-friendly budget. Those steps will be gone over in detail in the following paragraphs; however, first you will find it helpful to have a schedule to apply to the following chapters.

If you have received this book as a gift or purchased it yourself, you may be either already expecting a new baby or are planning to conceive a baby in the near future. If your mother-in-law gave it to you and you have not so much as mentioned a baby, someone is trying to tell you something. The schedule for your budget should be flexible; if you are pregnant already, you will want to start your budget immediately. If you are thinking about becoming pregnant, you will have an advantage financially if you start your baby-friendly budget now, as this will reduce worry and stress, making your life a bit more relaxed and likely making it easier to conceive.

The schedule for your budget is simple — start early. During or before pregnancy, save as much as you can, and purchase your items as they are needed. Do not feel like you need to run out five minutes after deciphering the code on your pregnancy test and purchase everything that comes in miniature sizes. In the chapters to follow, you will find out when you need to purchase most things for your baby. Until then, the rule of thumb will be to relax and stick to your budget and concentrate on saving and getting the necessities of life for junior.

Get Your Figures

Because a baby-friendly budget will often be a strict budget to follow, you will want to begin with all the correct figures. This means you will need to take into account differences in income before and after your baby is born. For instance, many parents have two incomes prior to their infant's arrival and only one after the baby is born. Another situation to consider is whether the mom is planning on returning to work. What is the loss of wages during the time she chooses to take off, both before and after the birth of your child? Your household income may have some changes. Whether this is for the first three months after your baby is born while mom and baby adjust and recover, or whether the loss of the second income will be permanent, is a vital piece of information you will need to consider. If you are planning on returning to work, you will want to consider child care costs. These will vary depending on where you live, but for an infant, the cost of child care will range from $1,000 to $3,000 a month.

Another common mistake in budgeting for a new family member is not recognizing costs that will ultimately occur, whether they are stated in your budget or not. The most common of these costs include a change in vehicle if necessary (if your current vehicle is not family-friendly), prenatal vitamins, doctors' appointments, hospital bills, pediatric appointments after the baby is born, and any unexpected health costs due to complications. Of course, many parents will not have to worry about some of these expenses, but it is wise to be prepared for all situations rather than finding yourself pulling out the credit cards to pay for some hefty, unexpected expense.

You might be thinking that you could not possibly plan for the unknown. Most pregnant women would not want to predict that there could be a problem. Adding to your family is unpredictable; however, you can be more prepared than you might think.

Babies are a pure joy but an expensive addition. To begin your baby-friendly budget, try to prepare yourself mentally. When you first look at the money you will have available to spend on baby products, it may seem small, but you are going to be preparing for the bigger picture in case there are unexpected expenses along the way.

Quick

The Seven Steps to a Baby-Friendly Budget

1. Determine Living Costs
2. Determine Your Income
3. Eliminate Unnecessary Expenses
4. Create a Monthly Budget for Baby
5. Savings
6. Become a Smart Shopper
7. Plan for Your Baby's Future

Step One: What Does It Cost You to Live Now?

The first step in preparing your budget is to make a simple list of what it costs you to live without your baby. What is the flow of money in your life right now? This is best done before you conceive, but if you are already pregnant, it is not a step you can skip. As you create your list of expenses, be sure to include everything you can think of. It is often easiest to start with the bills you pay on a regular basis — car payments, fuel, insurance, phone, cable, water, energy, groceries, membership dues, Internet, and mortgage or rent. Once you have all your monthly bills written down, along with the amounts they are on average, move on to what you spend each month on other things. This will include such things as doctors' appointments, dining out, shopping, medications, and any other spending habits you might have. These are often the little things that add up. Many people do not even realize they are spending this money until they check the bank account and see that there is much less than originally thought. After you have written down all your spending habits and monthly bills, you will need to add them up and see how much money you are spending each month. It may be surprising, but do not panic.

Step Two: Determine Your Income

Now that you have all your expenses accounted for, you will want to add up your household incomes. This will include all the money that comes into your bank account on a regular basis. Usually, this is much easier and requires much less math than totaling up all the expenses. Subtract your expenses from your income, and that magic number will be your baby budget. Babies cost about $10,000 in the first year. Do you have enough?

Step Three: Eliminate Unnecessary Expenses

Again, do not panic. If your budget is not looking good at this point, there are steps you can take to improve it. Start to look at the things you can eliminate from your monthly expenses, especially from your nonessential spending habits. Nonessential spending habits are the trips to various restaurants, shopping malls, coffee shops, and other expenses that can be altered. Many people spend more than 30 percent of their paychecks on dining out alone, which is much more costly than grocery shopping. Any items you can eliminate, no matter how small, will add up. Of course, eliminating the cost on paper is not enough; you have to stop getting that latte every morning if your new budget is to work.

When toning your budget to make it more family friendly, there are many places you can look to cut costs that might not occur to you. The most common areas to slim down are in phone, cable, and Internet services. Before planning a family, many adults like to have the more luxurious service plans in these areas of life; however, if you find that you do not watch many of the movie channels included in your cable package, consider downgrading to a more reasonably priced package. This will work the same for Internet. How much of a difference will it make if it takes two extra minutes to get online? It could make a difference of $15 to $30 each month, saving you $180 to $360 each year. Many people these days also seem to be able to survive on cell phones alone, some completely eliminating the home phone altogether. If these are options for you, then they will add to your baby budget. However, take caution not to cut expenses that you will just end up adding back later. If you cut an expense and then decide you must have that particular feature back, be sure to put it back onto the expense area of your budget. If you can cut down the amount of money you spend on your phone, cable, or Internet services, you may save anywhere from $15 to $100 a month, and if you can live with fewer features on all three, even better. Every dollar will add up in the end. No savings is too small.

Adding money to your baby budget can also come in the area of your automobiles. As you start to plan for your new bundle of joy, which is going to cost around $700 to $800 a month in the first year, you will need to look at your transportation anyway. Do you have a child-friendly car? Does it have a back seat? Will a car seat fit in the back seat? Is it easy to get a child seat in and out of the back seat? If any of these questions are answered with a no, then you might need to consider a new form of transportation. While you consider this prospect, you can also take money-saving points into consideration. What vehicle will get better gas mileage and allow for safe transportation of your family? Look for a lower payment (with a child in tow, the last thing you need is leather seats). If you are in a position in which you will need to change the vehicle you drive, and even if you are not, you can save a bundle of money by shopping smart in this department. Low-gas-mileage cars with the bare necessities will likely lower your monthly expenses in several budget areas, which include the car payment, insurance, and gas.

When a life-changing event takes place, such as discovering you are pregnant, looking at the interest rates of your home loan can save you money. Be cautious here, though. Taking a second mortgage out on your home should be done only if the savings are adequate. If interest rates are not lower or you have not paid enough of your loan off up to the point of taking the second mortgage, it can create a financial pitfall. It is best to talk to a financial advisor about your reasons for this before you take any action. Many soon-to-be parents can become less reasonable about whether this is beneficial when they see the amount of money that can come from taking out a second mortgage. Keep your goals in perspective. If a second mortgage will hinder you in the long run, look to cut costs elsewhere.

Cutting costs to add to your budget now does not have to be as drastic as changing vehicles or taking out a second mortgage on your home. You can cut costs in many different areas of your life that you might have never considered before now. Simple things such as dining out less often, packing a lunch, making coffee instead of stopping at the coffee shop every morning, shopping for sale items instead of brand names, or taking the bus instead of filling your gas tank every three days can all add up to big savings in the end. The point is to see where you can save money and how much you can save. Then take another look at the revised budget you have made with the savings included.

Step Four: Create a Monthly Budget for Baby

On average, you will want to have a minimum of $600 to $800 to spend on your new baby's needs each month in the first year of her life. This amount of money can come from two different sources. It can be saved over time, or you can adjust your budget so that you have the funds available each recurring month. Adjusting your budget to have this monthly money available is not possible for some families. If you can do it, test it before your infant arrives. This will ensure that you are sticking to your budget and give you a bit of extra money during your pregnancy to start acquiring all the essential items you will need, including paying for prenatal pills and doctors' appointments.

Step Five: Savings

Saving money to contribute to your child's first year of life is not a new concept. Many couples who have not yet conceived a child start planning their family by first starting a family savings. Much of the money that can be saved ahead of time will be spent either during pregnancy or in the first year of your baby's life. However, building your savings before your little one arrives is also a good way to build her future savings as well. The idea is to put whatever money is unspent at the end of each month into a separate savings account for emergencies, unexpected costs, and your child's future.

Case Study: Julie Skelton

Julie Skelton is the wonderful mom of baby Pete, who is one year old. While Julie and her husband did not come up with a formal budget for their new family, she does admit that she now wishes they had; having a baby is more expensive than Julie and her husband had anticipated.

She also shared her views about how she purchased items and how she might have done things differently. "In the beginning of purchasing items for my baby, I would ask friends what brand they had and whether they were happy with it, especially with the infant and toddler car seats. Above all, price and quality are my main concerns. I have realized brand name and high price is not always the best."

While Julie did receive a Boppy pillow, clothes, and a bassinet as hand-me-downs from other mothers, family, or friends, she now wishes in hindsight that she would have been less worried about receiving used items for her baby. "If I could pass along any piece of knowledge to new parents, I would say accept gently used items from friends. I wanted everything new for my baby, and I realize now that this is not a top priority, as long as it is safe."

When asked what she would change about her first year of motherhood if she could change one thing, Julie offered this advice.

"I would relax about being on a schedule. I was so concerned about that, even when he was just a newborn. Babies make their own schedules, and they change all the time. Wait until they are a little older to have a nap schedule and regular bedtime."

Enough about the future for now; you will learn more about that in a bit. You may be still focused on the immediate cash flow and how to stretch those dollars you worked so hard to squeeze out of your everyday living and bills. There are many ways to save for your baby. The first and most productive is going to be cutting costs, as you have already read about. This is the most effective because you will not just save this money once; it will be saved every month, and with 12 months in a year, it will add up faster than you realize.

Step Six: Become a Smart Shopper

Aside from cutting costs, you will be able to save a good sum of money just by becoming more thrifty and spending conscious. Until now, you probably had your favorite brands and the usual products that you reach for simply out of habit. If you are serious about being able to afford a new family member, your next task will be to forget about brand names and "favorites for no reason." Favorites for no reason are simply those products that you favor and you have no idea why. Do not worry; nearly everyone does it, and most people do not even realize they do. Many of these favorites are born from habit. You choose them simply because you have always used the products and it has never occurred to you to try a less-expensive brand.

You might be thinking that saving a dollar on macaroni and cheese will never get you far; however, if you stop to consider the number of items that go into your grocery cart every week without notice of price, only brand, you will be able to easily see how this can add up over time. Many consumers do their grocery shopping once a week and purchase more than 50 items on each of their shopping trips. If you consider that half of those items could easily be replaced with less-expensive brands, with an average savings of one dollar per product, each shopping trip would begin to save you at least $25. With 52 weeks in a year and a minimum savings of $25 each week, you are going to save $1,300 in a year.

Of course, you might save more or less each week, depending on sales the store might be having and the items you need. Do not eliminate the brands you purchase for known reasons unless you consider the reason to be unimportant in the end. If you usually purchase a certain brand of cereal because of the nutritional content and being healthy is important to you, you might not consider changing this buying pattern. You can still look for the same nutrition in a less-expensive brand, but in the end, if you are merely purchasing the less-expensive items and not using them, you will have failed in your efforts to save money. By purchasing items you do not use, you may end up spending more money to replace the products you are not using. Paying attention to prices instead of brands when you shop for groceries or anything else will help you create good money-saving habits that will eventually become second nature.

What Should I Do with My Credit Card?

Your next strategy for saving money, related to becoming a smart shopper, is much simpler than checking prices and searching for less-expensive brands — although it will apply to you only if you are a credit card user. Stop using your credit card. It is a simple idea that takes some getting used to and plenty of restraint for many people. If you take a moment to remember the interest rate of your favorite credit card, you can simply add that amount on to every purchase you make with it and multiply it by the number of months it will take you to pay it off. You are not saving money. Even if you are using your credit card only to shop fantastic sales, you will simply be paying the bank instead of the store where you purchased all your sale items. Using your credit card can be a budget killer. It is not an effective way to save money.

It is not necessary to cut up all your credit cards. You simply need to apply some rules to their use. If you cannot follow rules, cut all the cards up but one. If you have to cut up your credit cards and only keep one, keep the one with the lowest interest rate. It is a good idea to always have one credit card in case of emergency. An emergency does not mean that Babies "R" Us is having a season-end sale. Credit card spending while on a budget should be limited to true emergency situations, such as unexpected health costs, emergency room or hospital visits, and unavoidable car repairs. Have a credit card for those true emergency situations but not to pay bills or go shopping with. Make this a rule set in stone. If you have to, leave your credit cards at home when you go shopping. This goes for the checkbook, too. Taking only the amount of money you have budgeted for that expense to the store with you will keep you focused and on target with your budget.

Little Money-Savers that Add Up

Avoid having to pay late payments on your bills, shop at stores you know the layout of so you do not meander through the areas where you do not need anything, and, whenever possible, shop cheap. Secondhand stores and garage sales are good ways to save on baby clothes and maternity clothes. There are certain items you will want to purchase brand new, including your crib and car seat, as that is the safest and most responsible thing to do. However, maternity clothing and baby clothing are good items to buy at secondhand shops and garage sales.

Secondhand Shopping and Free Stuff

Shopping secondhand is a good idea because it saves you money. Most maternity and baby items are in good condition, even if they have been gently used for a brief time. Most maternity clothes are worn for only three to six months before mom has outgrown them, and the same goes for infant clothing. Often, you can even find maternity and infant clothing brand new with tags still attached because of the overabundance of these items as gifts to new moms. Many moms and most babies simply do not have adequate time or enough days to wear everything that has been given to them throughout the pregnancy and rate of growth they will experience. Buying maternity and baby clothing secondhand is one of the best decisions you can make. Your money will go further, and you will be delighted by the deals you can find on practically new clothing. There are many other items you can purchase used as well, and they will be covered in the appropriate areas as you progress through the chapters of this book.

Planning for Healthcare Costs

Budgeting for your new little boy or girl will not only include clothing and life's necessities; you will need to plan for the short-term future of mom's and baby's needs. Short-term future health costs will include prenatal appointments to measure mom and baby's health and growth as well as expenses for labor, delivery, and postpartum care. If you do not have health insurance, you will need to make some decisions about how you will pay for these expenses. They are not optional; you must take care of your body while you are pregnant, and you must deliver your baby in a safe and healthy environment. There are a number of hospitals that will allow you to make small payments over time. Checking with your nearby hospitals is important so you can determine what will be best for you and your family for healthcare and financial circumstances. There are other options for labor, delivery, and postpartum care for you and your baby. These can include home birth, birthing centers, doulas, and midwives. All these different types of facilities and care givers will cost varying amounts, and some may not be covered by insurance plans. The choice of where and what methods you will use for the delivery of your baby will largely depend on your beliefs and preferences.

Many insurance plans require you to pay only minimal co-pays for your doctor's visits and will cover most of the hospital costs for the duration of your stay, making you responsible for only a small percentage of the total hospital costs. Costs of other types of labor, delivery, and postpartum care and services might or might not be covered by your insurance, and you should verify what costs you will be responsible for should you choose an alternative type of care. No matter how much your insurance might cover, some coverage is better than none.

As an expecting parent, it is your responsibility to educate yourself on what is and is not covered by your specific insurance plan.

Start by speaking to a representative using the 800 number usually found on the back of your insurance card. When you call, have a list of questions so you can get all of them answered in one call, if possible. These questions should include coverage of your obstetrician visits, hospital stays, and emergency services pertaining to your delivery, any pregnancy complications, health coverage for your new baby, and what your deductibles will be for mom, baby, and the various doctors you will visit.

After you have obtained all the payment and coverage information, you will have the ability to form a medical budget to add into the savings and budgeting you are already doing. Not every pregnancy, delivery, and baby will have the same medical needs, and your costs may vary. In establishing a medical budget, you will at least be able to save part of the money you will need when delivery day comes. If there are unexpected costs or things that do not go according to plan, which is not unusual, most hospitals and doctors' offices will allow you to be on a payment plan for the remainder of your balance. Some hospitals and doctors' offices will even let you start to pay early for the services you will eventually receive that are not covered by your insurance. The labor and delivery of your baby will be a major cost, and it is wise to be prepared for it. You will be coming into the first days of your child's life, and adding undue stress about money is a silly thing to do when, with a little planning and self-control, you can prepare yourself as much as possible by saving as much as possible.

Saving money for the unexpected is hard to do. There seems to always be something you need or want or just do not think your baby can live without. The truth is, if it is not food, diapers, a small amount of clothing, and a safe car seat, in most cases, your baby will be able to survive without it for the first few months of life. Keep yourself focused on the things you need. Set in your budget a specific amount of money to be put into savings each payday. This is the money you will use for unexpected costs, medical expenses, and future savings.

Step Seven: Planning for Your Baby's Future

Finally, in the area of budgeting, you will need to start to plan for the far-off future of your child. This is a must whether you have already conceived your child, are still trying, or even if your baby has recently arrived. Understandably, the idea of college when your infant is still in mommy's belly seems a bit ridiculous to many; however, the time will arrive faster than you know, and it will be expensive when it does. There are several ways for you to get an idea of how much you will need to save for your child's education beyond high school; this takes into account that the average cost of college per year is now around $18,000 with room, board, and books. The easiest way to obtain a ballpark figure in savings will be to multiply this amount by the current rate of inflation. You can also try to predict which colleges your child may be interested in and estimate costs from figures in tuition, books, and room and board for those specific schools. Your baby will likely attend college for four years, so multiply your ballpark by four and start saving.

College is a fantastic expense that will plague you and your child for many years if there is no planning put into place early on. The cost of college goes up every year. Because of this, it is safe to say that, even if you cannot save everything your child will need for college, what you save can benefit you both as the time comes nearer. Talking to a financial advisor to see what types of college savings plans might be best for your family at the time will be a wise decision. Some of the many choices you will have will include savings accounts, trust funds, CDs, Section 529 Plans, Roth IRA accounts, and mutual funds.

All these different types of savings plans will have different points of interest to different parents, and this is often a personal choice to make. Many couples seek the help of a financial advisor, which is a good way to learn in detail about each type of savings plan and which will be the best fit for your family and your finances. If this seems like too much to take in right now, start with a simple savings plan that you can deposit a small amount of money into each payday or when you have extra funds. Savings accounts are a way to start because you still retain the freedom to access the money whenever you might need it, in case of emergency. Once you have the chance to educate yourself on the other types of savings options or have met with a financial advisor and feel you are ready to make a decision on a new type of account, you can transfer your baby's savings into any of the other types of accounts at any time. You will want to assess your options and make a decision before your little one is not so little anymore.

Budgeting is a heavy topic and, unfortunately, it is the best way to begin a book about shopping for your baby. For, without a budget, you might feel that there is no limit set on the amount of money you should spend in a given period. If you are like most working families, there are limits that should be in place, and being sure you understand your limitations is a healthy way to start your family. We have covered a large amount of overwhelming information in this first chapter. To give you a less intimidating outlook on budgeting for your baby, here is a simple summary list of what you are going to need to complete a comprehensive and secure budgeting plan.

- Make a simple list of what it costs you to live now, without your baby.

- Determine your household income.

- Eliminate excess expenses you can live without.

- Create a budget that will include $600 to $800 monthly for baby's needs.

- Create a savings account and deposit a set amount each payday for unexpected costs and surplus medical costs.

- Become a sale-oriented shopper, not a brand-oriented shopper.

- Stop using your credit cards.

- Shop secondhand stores and garage sales and accept free baby items that do not compromise safety.

- Meet with a financial advisor to plan for your child's future.

After you have completed the above list, you will begin to see your budget take shape. You will compose a budget of what it costs you to live now. You will then go through your bills carefully to see where you can eliminate expenses that are not necessary that you would prefer not to pay for. Next, set up your savings account and find a comfortable amount to deposit each payday which will help with medical costs at delivery time and other unexpected or emergency costs. Finally, you will need to train yourself to shop smart. Stop spending unnecessary money on things you do not need and do not use and on brands that are simply overpriced. In doing all this, you will want to be strict about keeping on track with what your goal is — being able to afford an addition to your family. You will also need to keep a balance of flexibility in mind, as there will always be little surprises in store while you are waiting and after you have had your precious baby girl or boy.

Case Study

Tranquil Massage
www.tranquilmassage.biz
bryn@tranquilmassage.biz
Ph: 303-717-5016
Bryn Rath, Certified Massage Therapist/Owner

Bryn Rath is a mom and businesswoman who is very proud of her two children, ages four years and six months. Bryn was a wonderful participant in the Case Studies for this book and had a wealth of knowledge and advice to offer all our parents reading; whether you are expecting your first or your fifth, Bryn's information rings true with most.

Throughout the Case Study process, Bryn shared a bit of personal information and offered a good way of considering the idea of budgeting for a new baby. "We did not have a budget that worked, and now we wish we had paid more attention to all the costs that were coming. Your budget needs to be flexible because of a variety of unforeseen costs that may come up. A flexible budget could have saved us from blowing money on things that were later unnecessary.

"We bought several packs of cloth diapers, pins, and plastic pants with the intention of using cloth diapers full time. We took everything out of packages and washed and put them away, never to use them again. Cloth diapering was not feasible for us and wasted money that could have bought the disposables. I wish we had been more realistic with our new expenses."

When asked about determining factors when shopping for items for her baby, Bryn said, "It depends on the item. I would say originally I was motivated by what things looked like — if it matched our style. Price was a factor for most items we purchased. Over time, we learned to ask around to get other parents' advice, then to consider quality, price, and general usefulness. Brand name was really never an issue."

Along with budgeting experience, Bryn had some great advice that she learned after becoming a mom.

"The most valuable knowledge that I have learned (as a parent) is that I needed to give up the want for things to be perfect. The house might not be as clean, the clothes might not be hung perfectly (or at all), and I will make mistakes in my parenting. The important thing is being with my baby and doing what feels right and comfortable for my family. I listen to advice and stories from other moms but only try what makes sense for us. Nobody is perfect, and that is okay; our imperfections are what build our character. So my house is messy, but it also looks like a home for two little boys.

"I would also pass along to new parents to relax and breathe. Take time for yourself to collect, calm, and center yourself. If you can not physically leave the house, go to your bedroom and shut the door. Couples need to also make time to be together without the new baby to reconnect and relax. We are fortunate to have all of our parents and my sister close who are willing to watch our kids when we need a date night. But if we did not have the family close — we would find parents-night-out programs or babysitters because we firmly believe in the importance of being together as a couple, not just 'mom and dad.' Do not feel guilty to be away from your child.

"If I could change anything about the first year of life of my children, it would be to worry and plan less and play and cuddle more. They grow too quickly to waste the day worrying about the best laundry detergent, newest educational toy, or theories on how to get your kids to sleep. I wish I had just spent more time holding them because the first year goes by so fast. I personally would still work because I love my job and needed the time away, but time not working would have been spent doing more family things."

Chapter 2

While You Wait, Preparing for Your Baby

Now you have your budget in hand and you are ready for the fun to begin. Shopping for your baby can be fun and satisfying. It can at times be overwhelming, but for the most part, baby shopping is one thing that parents can do to start to feel prepared mentally and physically (meaning you will know you have the physical, material items you need for your baby). While you are waiting patiently for nine months for your daughter or son to arrive, buying the things your baby will need will not only be helpful in that you will have them when the time comes, but you will likely feel more mentally prepared for what your baby will need. You will never know entirely what it is to be a parent through shopping, but you will start to get acquainted with the items that can help you as you journey through life with your new child.

There is a long list of things to prepare for while you are waiting for your infant to arrive. It is important to know what it is your child will need once she arrives. This list is relatively short and will include food, shelter, clothing, and diapers.

Necessity One: Feeding Your Infant

For many parents, food for your infant will be easy, as the most popular form of feeding infants all over the world is breast-feeding. Breast-feeding your child will save you a good amount of money. After all, breast milk is essentially free.

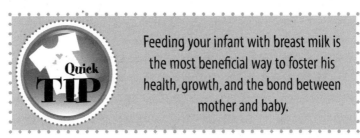

Feeding your infant with breast milk is the most beneficial way to foster his health, growth, and the bond between mother and baby.

For now, I will focus on the financial points and facts of what you will need for feeding your infant. There are costs that are going to be associated with both breast-feeding and formula-feeding your baby. There are hidden costs that you might not be aware of in both areas. Later, in "The Facts of Life," we will reveal more detail about feeding your baby, including points to consider when making the decision to breast-feed or formula-feed.

Breast-feeding

There are a few necessities you will need to purchase if you are planning on breast-feeding your baby. You will need some packages of breast pads to save any embarrassment when you are running late with feedings, nipple ointment to keep yourself comfortable, and possibly a breast pump for expressing milk and saving it for later feedings. Nipple ointment and breast pads are relatively inexpensive and should cost you no more than $100 every six months. A breast pump, on the other hand, will be a bit more costly. Most breast pumps will range anywhere from $70 to $300, depending on the type of pump you need. Manual breast pumps will be less expensive, and professional electric breast pumps will cost anywhere from $150 to $300. When making the decision to purchase manual versus electric, take into account how often you will need to pump and how much time you will have to do so. If your budget is already tight and you will most likely have the option of pumping whenever you like and for however long you need, a manual pump will be sufficient. If you are planning on returning to work or have other reasons that you would need to pump quickly and often, the expense of a professional electric pump may be well worth it.

Formula

Formula is one of the things you should have on hand before your infant is brought into the world. You probably will not need more than two packages of formula if breast-feeding goes well for you, but it can be a lifesaver even for a fully functioning, breast-feeding mother. Formula can be expensive depending on the decisions you make for your child. The key here is to pick what you think is the best choice nutritionally and stick with it. Changing formula once your baby is accustomed to one brand or recipe can mean big troubles for mom, dad, and baby. Babies' digestive systems are sensitive, especially in the first three to six months of life, and changing the formula you use can upset the balance in an infant's system. Many of the different brands of formula will contain the same basic ingredients; however, if the amount of each ingredient varies, it can cause upset stomach, excess spit-up, and more gassiness or colic. This is one area of shopping in which it is good to stay brand specific. That being said, you do not have to choose the most expensive brand; you can use a less-expensive brand and save yourself money from the start.

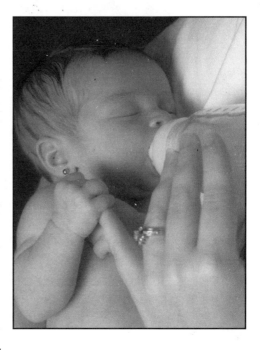

Enfamil and Similac are two of the most popular brands of infant and baby formula; however, you should not get hung up on a brand name just because it is a popular one. Be sure to check the nutritional contents of other, less-expensive brands and compare them to the leading brands before making your purchasing decision. Most single containers of about 26 ounces of powdered formula will cost between $25 and $32 apiece. If you are planning on using only formula or mostly formula, you will be purchasing one to two 26-ounce cans of powdered formula each week. Powdered formula is the least expensive way to purchase baby formula. But, if necessary, there are liquid formulas as well, which will cost you $1.50 more per day.

On a side note for supplementing breast-feeding with formula: You will want to have at least two bottles and infant size-one nipples in your home. If you are using formula alone, you will want to have at least four sets of bottles and infant nipples to ensure there is always a clean set on hand when you need it. These can be used with formula or for feeding your infant breast milk that has been pumped. There is no telling when you may need a bottle, but the fact is that, sooner or later, you will likely need at least four bottles and nipples. Having a few bottles and appropriate-sized nipples in your home will keep you prepared in case any number of things happen: Mom gets stuck in traffic, mom needs a night out, mom needs to sleep, or health factors prevent mom from breast-feeding for a short time. If you do not have a bottle and a nipple and mom is unavailable, dad or the babysitter will have a hungry and cranky baby on their hands. We will reveal more about how to choose a bottle and nipple that is right for you and your baby in "The Facts of Life" chapter.

The hospital we were at when we discovered we would need to supplement our daughter with formula happened to supply us with Enfamil. This was good in that our daughter loved it, but it was toward the higher end of the price range. We made the drastic mistake of trying to change formulas to save money, which ended with me covered in baby vomit and our daughter being highly irritable, gassy, and just plain unpleasant for about two weeks. From this lesson, we learned where to purchase the formula she was already accustomed to for less money. I became a coupon collector and registered myself and my mother on the Enfamil Web site. I also was an eBay account holder and found that I could safely purchase formula from online auctions. The only caution here is to be sure the cans of formula you bid on are not expired, all formula is still sealed, and there are no punctures in the packaging.

Many moms will stock up on formula when they find good sales, but then they find themselves left with an excess stock once baby moves on to the wonderful world of cow's milk, cereal, and baby food. There were many times I would purchase a lot of ten to 12 cans of Enfamil formula for $50 to $60. If I were to spend $50 at the grocery store on the same formula, I would have been able to bring home only two cans of formula, so I was saving an good amount of money. Whenever I would bid on formula in an online auction, I would insist on receiving a picture of the formula in the packaging; being sure that, if there were any problems once I received the package, I could return it; and vigilantly checking the cans of formula for punctures or breaks before opening or using it. If you have ever looked at a can of powdered baby formula, you know that it is easy to tell if it was tampered with, punctured, or previously opened. I would estimate that over the course of our daughter's infancy, we saved nearly $1,200 purchasing formula from online auctions. You can also find formula coupons for sale online — just be sure that your savings from the coupons will be more than what you purchase them for.

No matter what brand of formula you choose for your baby, go online and look for the manufacturer's Web site. Enfamil and Similac both offer a new mommy coupon club that is free. You simply register on the company's Web site (listed in the Appendix), put in your address, name, and due date, and watch the coupons start to flow into your mailbox. These are not little coupons for $0.25 off; they range from $2 to $9, which is helpful when you are spending nearly $40 a week on formula alone. Once you start to receive coupons for anything, not only formula, save them no matter what the expiration date is. Many establishments will accept baby-related coupons from manufacturers after the expiration date has passed. This is because many of the manufacturers will still pay the retailers for your product purchase. They would prefer to keep you, as a customer, happy and coming back for their product rather than turn away business over a few dollars here and there.

Another helpful hint in registering for formula coupons is to have a friend or your mother register, too. They can mail you the coupons, and you can double your savings, especially when your baby moves from breast milk to drinking formula alone. Of course, breast-feeding your infant is going to be the best money saver.

Necessity Two: Diapers

The next necessity on your list of things to stock up on while your belly grows is diapers. Most moms these days use disposable diapers; however, you still have a choice. There are many different cloth diapering companies that will supply you with almost all the products you will need to use cloth diapers. Some cloth diaper companies will even pick up and launder your diapers weekly. Do not get too excited; you still have the grand responsibility of getting the "baby poo" out. Due to health concerns, most take only soiled diapers, not full diapers. This is a decision that should be made before baby arrives, as diapers will be the most used and costly thing you will be purchasing for the first few years of your baby's life. We will spend more time on the pros and cons of cloth versus disposable diapers later. For now, you should look at the financial side of this dilemma to determine whether you have the option of one or the other.

On average, you will need to plan for about 65 diapers a week. This figure can vary depending on the size of your child's appetite and bladder.

The least expensive way to go when diapering your baby is cloth diapers; this means taking care of the monumental pile of laundry yourself. The cost of the cloth diapers you will need ranges from $100 to $300. There are many different varieties of cloth diapers, and the cost per diaper can range from $1.15 to $32.50. The cost of your cloth diapers alone will depend on what type you decide will best suit your infant's needs.

Having your cloth diapers laundered by a home pickup service will cost somewhere between $700 and $1,500 a year. You will also need to factor in the cost of diaper covers, which have recently replaced those loud, scratchy plastic pants that were once so popular. The cost for diaper cover-ups is not extremely high, but it does add around $100 to $300 to your bottom line each year. This is going to be a three- to four-year ordeal, and each year your baby will continue to grow, making it necessary for you to continue to purchase different sizes of diaper covers.

To make an informed decision, you need to add up the costs to your yearly bottom line using cloth diapers. If you are using cloth diapers and washing them yourself, you can expect to spend somewhere in the area of $300 to $600 each year. If you choose to have them laundered by a service, you can add another $700 to $1,500 on to that total, giving you the wide range of $1,000 to $2,100 each year. If you decide to use cloth diapers, you will need to have about 65 on hand when you arrive home with your baby to be well prepared.

The addition to your yearly bottom line for disposable diapers will be in the vicinity of $350 to $650. If you have a trash company that bills you per the amount of garbage you require to be picked up, be sure to add that cost into the equation, as it will vary depending on where you live and what waste disposal company you use.

If you choose to use disposable diapers, you will need to be prepared when you come home with your new baby. This sounds a bit frightening, I know, but there is nothing worse than wasting good sleep time running to the convenience store to purchase a package of overpriced diapers.

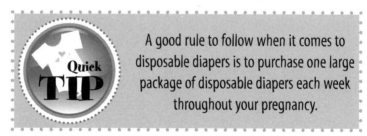

Quick TIP

A good rule to follow when it comes to disposable diapers is to purchase one large package of disposable diapers each week throughout your pregnancy.

Now the next question: What size? You likely will not need 36 packages of newborn-sized diapers. Babies do go often, but they also grow quickly.

It is generally suggested to have two or three large packages of newborn diapers on hand when baby comes home. You might need the smaller size for longer, but until you know how big your baby will be, it is tough to predict. Some retailers will not accept returns of unopened diapers. You should have two to three packages of newborn-size diapers, ten size-one diaper packages, and whatever else you purchase in size two. If you can purchase one package a week throughout your pregnancy, you should end up with 30 to 38 packages of diapers.

The buying one package a week during pregnancy strategy is a good idea for baby wipes, too, as you will be using them for the greater part of three years. You can never have enough baby wipes. Through personal experience, I have learned that, not only do I use them for bottoms, but I also tend to use them for a variety of other things: sticky hands and faces (mine and my child's), spit-up on my shirt, unidentified goo on my daughter's clothing, runny noses, when there is not a scrap of toilet paper in our house, cleaning public changing areas, and even once to check the oil in my car when a strange light came on. Wipes are to a mother as toothpicks and duct tape are to MacGyver.

As far as coupons for diapers and baby wipes, you can register on many name-brand Web sites for coupons just like with formula. However, any brand of wipes will do. Stick to the less-expensive ones, as they are all about the same. Registering on various name-brand sites means you will receive coupons only for the products you are requesting so that your mail box will not be overwhelmed with random coupons for things you are not interested in shopping for.

Now you have the two most basic needs for your new baby taken care of — at least for a little while. You will be able to feed your child and you will be able to keep her bottom clean and comfortable.

Case Study: Monica Padden

Monica Padden is a proud and busy mom of three kids. Owen is nine, Lyla is seven, and Ottilia is nine months old. Monica has learned much through her years of parenting and had some helpful information.

When asked about her favorite baby and parent-friendly items, she listed the Baby Bjorn, the Soothing Glider, and Avent bottles. Monica's two oldest children, Owen and Lyla, both had colic she feels was emphasized because of the generic bottles she used with them. Monica feels that the Avent bottles she purchased for approximately $4 a bottle were instrumental in preventing colic with her third child, Ottilia, and adding to the comfort of her baby. Both the Soothing Glider and the Baby Bjorn were great for soothing her baby and keeping her hands free while other business needed to be attended to.

When purchasing items for her children throughout the first year of their lives, she mainly tried to focus on how long her baby would need the item and if she felt they would enjoy using the product. Monica and her husband did not develop a budget for their expected family, and in hindsight, she wishes they had. When she is shopping, she tries to focus on quality and price of the item; however, brand name does affect her decision to a point. "Yes, I tend to still use Similac formula instead of the store brands," she admitted.

When it came to helpful advice, Monica said, "Try not to plan how things are supposed to go. I learned to take each day as it comes. I find myself taking it hour by hour, or even minute by minute, especially during the 'rough times.'"

Necessity Three: Clothing

Now, as cute as babies are in all their bare-bodied glory, you will want to have clothing for those special occasions when you venture outside the home or have company over to visit your new little angel. This is a tricky area for many expecting parents and especially new mommies. Baby clothes are so adorable and tempting that passing up 500 outfits on your first trip to the baby superstore can seem nearly as hard as passing up the double-pickle pizza and ice cream at 2 a.m. during your third trimester. It is hard, but it is possible. If you do not trust yourself to stick to your budget, you should consider shopping online where temptation is less obvious or taking only a preset amount of cash with you to the store. Yes, it is a good idea to leave the checkbook and credit cards behind when you go shopping for your baby, especially for his clothing.

Most babies will not need a large amount of clothing for the first three months of life. What you need for your baby will ultimately depend on the climate where you live and the season in which your child is born. Our daughter was born in the winter months, which meant it was necessary to have a few extra warm outfits, whereas if she had been born in the summer, I probably could have survived with onesies alone.

When your baby comes home from the hospital, you should plan on having about ten onesies, three to four sleepers, a warm hat (often the hospital will provide you with one), seven shirts, seven pants, and seven pairs of socks. Be sure to take the time to launder all this clothing so it is ready for your baby to wear when you get home from the hospital. Baby skin can be sensitive to the dyes used in clothing, and the last thing you will want to do in the first week after the birth of your baby is laundry. It is likely that you will not need to use many of the items right away; however, it is good to know you do not have any laundry awaiting you after delivering your baby. If you can afford to purchase only the above items, it will be enough clothing to get you through week to week and allow you to stay within your budget. If you can afford more without going outside your budget, you certainly can indulge in a few more adorable outfits, but do not go crazy; there is still a great amount of shopping to cover.

If you are like many other new parents, you might want to have a cute outfit for pictures and to bring your baby home in. This is not necessary, but it is nice. As you shop for your baby's clothes, keep in mind the season that you are due in, and purchase clothing that is climate appropriate. Another good reason to limit the amount of clothing you buy for your baby is that many people awaiting your baby's arrival will purchase at least one outfit for him or her regardless of whether you need it or not. Baby clothing is expensive, especially if you decide to purchase new clothes. The average cost of the items listed above when purchased new will be about $350. This is if you come out only with the clothing mentioned above. You can reduce this cost or afford to purchase more clothing simply by shopping at secondhand or gently used shops and boutiques or, if you are able to shop in the summer months, looking for garage sales.

Do not remove store tags from clothes. Returning baby items that you will not need is acceptable even if they were gifts.

If the clothing is too small or you do not think you will need it, you can often exchange it for items you will be able to use. Your close friends and family will prefer it if you have the things you need rather than a lace-covered, itchy dress that is dry-clean only and which will sit in your baby's closet for a year before you sell it at a garage sale with the tags still on it. As for people you do not see on a regular basis who give you items you may not need, they will likely never know that you were not about to dress your child in corduroy and polka dots for the first three months of his life and exchanged the gift for a practical pair of baby sweat pants and a onesie.

Necessity Four: Infant Car Seat

Now comes the one big-ticket item that you absolutely must have before you leave the hospital, especially if you plan on driving home. Most hospitals will not let you leave with your infant unless you have an approved infant car seat properly installed in your car. To save yourself some worry come delivery day, purchase your infant's car seat and base early, but not too early. Many people will receive the base and car seat as a gift at their shower.

The key here is to have your shower early and, if you do not get the car seat or car seat base you have registered for, you will need to buy it before you go to the hospital. You will also want to allow yourself enough time to learn how to properly install the seat base in your car. Most infant car seats are not too complicated, and once you have the base installed, you will likely not have to remove it unless you are switching vehicles. If you can afford to do so, it is nice to purchase two bases so you have one in each vehicle that your baby may be riding in at any given time.

Getting proper instruction on installing your infant car seat or any child car seat must be done and is relatively easy; just be sure not to put it off too long. Fire stations will install and teach you how to install your child car seat for free. They are also available to check your installation to be sure it is correct and safe. Call your local fire station to see what days and times they do car seat installations or car seat checks. Get this done at least one month prior to your due date, as babies often come early, and there is no predicting when your baby will make her grand entrance into the world and be ready for her first ride in the car.

The cost of your car seat will vary depending on the brand you decide is best for your baby. Some of the most trusted and popular brands in infant car seats include Graco, Evenflo, and Safety 1st. These brands are trusted by many parents for quality, price, and safety and are, for the most part, in the middle price ranges. Average costs of infant car seats and bases range from $90 to $250. Aside from price, you will want to look for safety, size, quality, and ease of installation.

First and foremost is safety. Be sure there are no recalls out on the car seat you plan to buy before you purchase it, after you purchase it, and the entire time you are using it. (See Appendix for resources.) Recalls on all types of products seem to come out of nowhere these days, and it is important to know that there are no malfunctions with safety equipment you will be using on a daily basis. All infant car seats are tested and approved by government standards, which means a new car seat will be a safe one for your child. Even though all car seats currently manufactured pass safety tests, part of making your child's car seat safe lies in the installation. If you install any car seat incorrectly, it can be unsafe, unreliable, and unpredictable. The best suggestion for installing your car seat is to get help from your local fire station.

You will want to check the size on any car seat you are thinking of purchasing to be sure it will fit in your car correctly and safely. Most retailers will allow you to take the displayed car seat out to your vehicle with an associate to be sure it fits properly. Not only should you check to see that it fits safely in your car or truck, but you should also be able to remove the carrier without too much trouble. Bumping and banging your infant carrier every time you remove it or put it into the car will often wake your infant or startle and alarm him. Quick and easy access is going to be a big convenience in keeping your stress levels in check while running errands with your new baby in tow.

Case Study: Aimee Stauth

Aimee Stauth is a wonderful mom of two: Tevin is two, and Brynlee is one year old. She is a stay-at-home mom who works very hard to keep her two kids happy and to balance a little of her own time to get to the gym and de-stress.

Aimee admits that her main struggle when purchasing items for both her children was with what car seat would be the best value for the price. "We wanted the safest model, but we could not spend a fortune on brands like Britax. So we 'settled' for the Evenflo but have been so happy with that decision. We just tried to weigh safety, ease-of-use, and cost, which is hard when your child's safety is at stake."

To be sure she was getting the best for the right price, Aimee said, "For items that were more than $50, such as car seats, I did a great deal of research through Consumer Reports. For anything less than $50, I read user reviews online and spoke with friends who had made similar purchases."

Along with taking the time to conduct strict price comparison for expensive items, Aimee and her husband also made a family budget before becoming pregnant.

"We did have a budget before I became pregnant. We found it very useful because it allowed us to continue spending what we were comfortable spending on things like entertainment while keeping us in line with our desires to save for retirement and college tuition."

Quality is a big deal in infant and child car seats. This is an item that may be put to use several times a day for the next six months to one year. Infant seats will last you up to a year, and then you will need to move your child into a child car seat that can last up to four or five years. If you purchase a low-quality car seat, you will often find that it is uncomfortable for you or your child. There can be any number of complaints with infant car seats from tearing, fraying, uncomfortable or chafing materials, installation difficulties, and even difficulty cleaning (cleaning is a common woe for parents with toddlers, as many parents are surprised to discover a variety of snacks and other gooey items tucked into every crevice of the car seat).

 **Quick TIP**

Once you have purchased these four things — diapers, formula, clothing, and a safely installed infant car seat — you will essentially have everything your baby needs to survive when you come home from her birth.

There are other things that are nice and seem necessary, but in reality, diapers, clothing, formula, and a car seat are the four most important things to have in your home or vehicle when you and your baby finally arrive home.

Organization

Once you have the four necessities and whatever else you might be able to afford before delivery day, you will want to keep organized. I cannot tell you how many times I purchased an item just because I was not sure whether I had it or not. The result of this was four sets of fingernail clippers, a variety of baby shampoo that I am still using three years later, nipples that fit brands of bottles I never even purchased, and more rattles than 100 babies could use. Keeping your new and used baby items organized will keep you from spending money on things you might not need or already have plenty of. Most pregnant women are nesters, and therefore, organization is not a problem.

To keep organized without having to spend hours doing so, have a place for all the items you will buy on a regular basis. Find a place to keep all your diapers, formula, wipes, and bottles. Knowing where these items are will be helpful once your son or daughter arrives, and it will let you know at a glance how much of each you have on hand. You might decide to keep diapers in the nursery closet and formula in a kitchen cabinet — just be sure to keep like items in the same place. Another tip for organization is to keep the items you decide you want to return in the trunk of your car. Throughout your pregnancy, you are going to receive gifts, as well as purchase some items, that later you might think better of. If you are given or purchase an item you decide you no longer need, want, or that you have already, return it for something you need. This adds up and is like shopping for free.

Keeping these items in the trunk of your car with the receipt will give you plenty of time to return them. You will be able to stop whenever you are in the neighborhood of that particular store and exchange the item at your convenience. Finally, about getting yourself organized, keep a list around of what you need and, as you receive or purchase these items, simply mark them off your list. This will save time and money, as well as give you a sense of accomplishment as you get closer to a fully checked list. Keep this list in your purse or glove compartment so it is easily accessible whenever you are doing some last-minute (budgeted) shopping.

If, like most of us, you do not have unlimited money, it is important to realize in what order your baby's needs should be addressed for you to feel prepared. If you can purchase only the items listed in this chapter, you will have what you essentially need for your baby's first three months of life. If you have more in your budget, you will want to also consider purchasing a place for your baby to sleep and a way to tote him along on walks or in stores. There are many other items that would be nice to have before your bundle of joy arrives, and we will go over these items. There will also be suggestions as to when it is best to have each item, if your budget allows.

The items in this chapter are those that will cover the most basic needs for you and your new baby. If you cannot afford any more, be satisfied that you will have just as healthy and happy of a baby as anyone else, whether you have a fancy, vibrating bouncy seat or not. Do not fret over what you cannot afford; there is always the baby shower, which is a fine, festive event that anyone having a baby should take full advantage of.

A little-known fact that many parents-to-be do not realize is that babies do not care what they have, do not have, what brand it is, where it came from, how old it is, or who drooled on it last.

Baby Showers
and Registries

The baby shower should be a mandatory holiday in every country of the world for expecting parents. There is nothing more exciting than having together those who care about you and your baby, celebrating the life that is on its way. And, of course, buying your baby the things she will need. The fact is that, even if there were no such celebration, people would still buy you gifts on learning you are pregnant. There is some drive in people, especially women, to purchase baby products, clothes, toys, and furniture for any reason that can be justifiably defended. I received gifts not only from family and friends who were invited to my baby showers, but also from mere acquaintances, coworkers, neighbors I had never met (or told I was pregnant for that matter), and strangely, some people we still are not sure we know who they are. The bottom line is, baby showers are fun and good for your bottom line.

Registering for Your Baby Shower

Before you have a baby shower, you will need to take on the daunting task of registering for all your baby needs. When I was pregnant, I thought that this was going to be fun and exciting. On the contrary, it took my husband and me a total of four trips to the baby superstore to complete our registry for one baby. This was largely due to poor planning and a complete lack of knowledge about what we would need. The best advice you can receive about registering for your shower is to be prepared, know what you need and want, and walk the aisles of the baby store strategically. Hopping from aisle to aisle and scanning the things that are most exciting will get you confused and frustrated only.

Registering for your baby shower should be done as soon as you are up to the task. Many moms and dads will wait until after the first trimester, as that is often the most challenging time of pregnancy (apart from labor) for mom. Once your morning sickness, severe tiredness, and cranky hormones are all under control, you should begin to prepare for the adventure of registering for baby shower gifts. The sooner you can complete your registry, the sooner people will have the ability to see what you need and want and get thinking about what they would like to contribute to your new family. Most expecting parents will register in the fourth month of pregnancy because mom will have regained a little energy, and if you are finding out the sex of your baby, you will likely know by the fourth month, unless you have a discreet baby. If you have decided to be surprised about the sex of your infant, you should still register. Do not let this lack of information stop you; there are more than enough neutral items that all babies need for you to complete a baby registry.

In your baby shower invitations, include a registry card or list of stores where you are registered.

When the time comes to register for your baby shower, the first thing you should do is decide at which store or stores you would like to register. There are a variety of different stores that have baby registries, some of which include Babies "R" Us, Target, Wal-Mart, JCPenney, Pottery Barn Kids, and Felicite Registries. You can register at one or several different stores, and this will all depend on what you need, want, and like. Some baby stores, such as Babies "R" Us and Target, will print out registry cards that say where you are registered and list your registry number. These cards are free, convenient, and easily slipped into the envelopes of your baby shower invitations.

The business-sized cards are easy to make if the stores you decide to register at do not offer them or charge for them. If the store charges for the registry cards and you do not feel you have time to make up your own, purchase one sheet, which may be less than a dollar, and make copies of your own at home or work. The registry cards are not a necessity but are useful since you will want this information in your shower invitations, especially if you do not want to write the information in each invitation. If you decide to make your own, you will need only a computer and some business cards for printing. Design your cards however you like, or visit sites such as **www. vista.com** to design baby registry cards; however, you will have to pay for this service. If you design your own registry cards, include your name, sex of baby if known, registry number, and due date. All this information will be helpful to anyone who wants to shower your

unborn infant with welcoming gifts, whether the people can make it to your baby shower or not.

Most stores that have baby registries will also supply you with a complete list of the things you will supposedly need for your baby. These lists are often composed of nearly every type of item the store sells and can seem overwhelming. The best thing to do with the baby registry list is to pick one up before you plan on registering and go through it, deciding what you will need or want and crossing out what you do not want to register for or no longer need.

Taking the time to decide on the things you will need before registering will save you what I like to call the "baby boxing bout." This is the common argument that erupts in the middle of the baby store when you and your significant other start to disagree about the things you need and do not need to register for. Registering for your baby is stressful enough, and you do not need to add to it by arguing about brands of formula in the middle of Babies "R" Us. It sounds quite petty, but it does happen. Some of the hot topics for baby registry arguments include:

- **Pacifiers:** Do you want to use them or not?

- **Pack 'N Plays or playpens:** One parent sees an extraordinarily useful item, while the other sees only dollar signs.

- **Clothing:** Set a limit so you do not get carried away.

- **Brand names:** Go with brand names for safety and health, not for clothing and disposables.

- **What items will you need more than one of:** Bottles, nipples, pacifiers, diapers, formula, wipes, diaper rash cream, and so on.

Now you should have the stores you would like to register at, the list of what you and your spouse feel you need to register for, and an idea of the task that is before you. If you are organized, registering for your baby shower is not that hard and can even be fun.

When you go to the store where you will be registering, you will first need to get a scanner from the customer service desk or inquire about how the store's registry works. Someone should be happy to help you and show you exactly how to scan or enter the items you want into the store's database, as well as the quantity, and how to remove the items you accidentally scan or decide you do not want. After you have had your short training lesson in how to register, which should take only about five minutes, you will be free to roam the store, scanning all the items you are hoping to receive from family and friends for your precious baby.

However, randomly roaming the store is exactly what you should not do. It is best to start at one end of the store and work your way through the aisles strategically. Start at the front, back, left, or right – whichever you prefer – and walk each aisle so you have to do it only once. This will help, as you will soon discover that you will move through itemized shelves. You will have the chance to select all the furniture you want at the same time and all the feeding items you need at the same time.

It is perfectly acceptable to go back to a store and add or subtract to your registry. Some stores also allow you to do this (or register completely) online.

Having a list or strategy will make you less likely to forget something important. This is exactly what happened when a close friend of mine and her husband registered. They were so relieved when the exhausting experience was over until they went home and realized that they did not register for a car seat, a car seat base, or a stroller. My friends had skipped this aisle, as they could not make a clear decision and were disagreeing quite a bit. They decided to come back to it after they both had time to think about it. My friend ended up returning to the store at a later date to add these items to the registry.

Register for everything you do not have and need, everything you want, and everything you are pretty sure you will use. You can register for any items you think you will need for the immediate care of your baby or for the future. Do not be afraid to register for a potty training seat or clothing that is larger than zero to three-month sizes. Print out a registry list and go through it thoroughly.

Basic Registry Items

When you register be sure to include:

- furniture (crib, bassinet, changing table or dresser, glider)

- feeding accessories (breast pump, nursing pillow, bottles, nipples)

- formula, cereal, baby food

- diapers, diaper rash cream, wipes

- strollers

- car seat, car seat base(s)

- clothing such as onesies, sleepers, socks, pants or shorts, shirts, dresses, bibs

- Pack 'n Play or playpen

- linens for crib and playpen

- décor items such as lamps, rugs, window coverings, storage, hamper, wall hangings, shelves

- sling

- play mat

- bouncer, jumper, swing, stationary entertainer

- monitor

- baby gates

- humidifier

- toiletries such as nail clippers, first-aid kit, brush/comb, colic drops, thermometer

- diaper bag

- diaper pail and refills if required

- receiving blankets

- toys for zero to 12 months

- bathing accessories (shampoo, soap, bathtub, bath toys, lotion, washcloths, towels)

- books, journal, baby book

- baby music or heartbeat CD to soothe baby

- photography (yes, you can register for photography packages)

You may not need all this, but if you would like it, your baby shower is the most likely place you will get it without having to purchase it yourself.

It is good to register for a wide variety of items because this will often mean you will have a wide variety of prices on your registry. Many people who will be shopping from your registry will do it one of two different ways. The first is that they will already have something in mind that they would like to get you and your baby, and they will use your baby registry to check to see which brand, style, and how many of that item you registered for. For example, your mother may already have decided that she would like to buy the car seat for her grandchild. She will use your registry to discover that you chose the Graco infant car seat and stroller set. Grandma will then have the option to purchase the whole set, which would include the infant seat, base, and stroller that the infant carrier fits into, or simply purchase the carrier and the base, leaving the stroller on the registry for someone else to possibly purchase.

The second way that people will shop is by price. Do not be offended by this; they will simply look to find the most they can get for you that fits in their budget. For example, most friends will have a set price in mind, usually between $25 and $75. Having a registry makes shopping easy. They can browse through the list online or print it out at the store and locate either one big item or several small items that are still available on your registry. It does not matter how your friends and family decide to shop for the things on your registry; having a baby registry will make your life and those who wish to shop for you and your baby much easier. Following the above steps should make registering much less stressful and a good deal more fun.

One last baby registry hint that I discovered when I was pregnant is that, if you are the kind of person who cannot wait to see what you may be getting, you can often see online what has been purchased from your registry. This will not spoil the surprise as far as who has purchased the item for you, but it will let you know what is on its way. As people shop from your registry, the number of items that have been purchased will be listed. This is so others will not purchase double or triple of what you need, but it can be fun to snoop. If you like to be surprised, do not view your registry after you have sent out your baby shower invitations.

The Baby Shower

Once you have completed your baby registry, you are ready for your baby shower. Planning a baby shower is most often done by a close friend or family member. You can plan your own; however, it is likely that someone close to you is planning on taking care of this for you. Planning your baby shower can be inexpensive, especially if others do it for you. You simply need to provide them with the names and addresses of those you wish to invite and settle on a day that is good for you and your

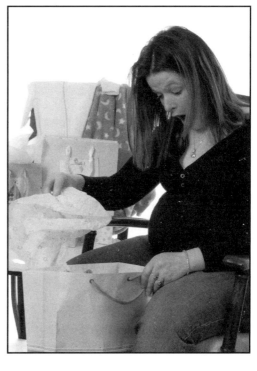

hostess. The baby shower that is planned by a close friend or family member is most often free for you, aside from possibly having to purchase thank you cards.

If you plan to throw your own shower, you will need to buy invitations or use an Internet invitation, which can be done for free through services such as **www.evite.com**. Other expenses involved in the baby shower might be food and beverages, a cake, decorations, and thank you cards. Costs for these items can be as minimal as you like. Decorating for your own shower can be free if you decide not to decorate or use things you already have. If you decide to purchase decorations, they will most often cost between $25 and $50. You will want to account for refreshments and snacks for your guests as well, which again, you can fit into your budget as money allows. Finally, you will want to have thank you notes or cards to send out to all your family and friends that purchased you gifts or came to your baby shower to help you celebrate. Most baby showers will cost anywhere from $100 to $200. If you use your imagination for decorating and go easy on the refreshments, you can easily spend less than $100 on your own baby shower if you choose to plan it yourself.

After you have planned your baby shower, whether you have decided to do it yourself or someone has graciously offered to host this event for you, you should stop to remember why you are having a shower in the first place. A baby shower is not an event strictly meant to receive gifts. Yes, it is nice that most people will want to bring gifts to your shower for you and your baby. But your baby shower should be viewed as a time to sit back and relax. Let your friends and family pamper you a bit; your body is working hard to support a life that will soon come into your own life full force. The baby shower is a celebration of the life that is coming and a celebration of the mother who is supporting that life with her own. Enjoy your baby shower. Have fun with your close friends and family and do not worry about what you are or are not getting. The time will come when you will have everything that your baby needs.

One last thing to remember for your baby shower and all your other shopping needs — purchasing items secondhand is a good idea. If you want to be sure that your friends, family, and acquaintances know that you are not opposed to receiving hand-me-downs, gently used items, or consignment store purchases, let them know. You can tell people you are close to or you can add it into your baby shower invitations. Most people will still purchase you new items; however, those who truly want to give the most for their dollar will look at quality used items.

Case Study: Amy Dorman

Mommy-to-Be & Lil Me Boutique
7600 E. Park Meadows Drive Lone Tree, CO 80124
www.mommy2b-lilme.com
E-mail: mommy2b-lilme@comcast.net
Ph: 303-649-BABY (2229)
Amy Dorman, Retail Shop Owner

Amy Dorman is a busy and accomplished businesswoman and mother of four who opened her own boutique in 2004. Mommy-to-Be & 'Lil Me Boutique uses the tag line "consignment with a twist," which refers to the mix of new, handcrafted, and gently used items offered in her store. The most popular items purchased in her store include maternity and children's clothing and all types of baby gear. Most of the gently used items are sold with a 35-50 percent savings over purchasing the same items new.

Amy does not offer anything diaper related used, such as cloth diapers or diaper covers, mostly for hygienic reasons. However, her store does carry swimwear that is very gently used or new with tag on. Other great products that you can find in secondhand shops and consignment stores include furniture, shoes, clothing, decorating items, toys, and maternity clothes.

In Amy's Case Study, she was asked not only about her successful retail business, but also about her personal experiences with parenting and shopping for her children. Amy was very thankful for many of the baby gifts she received from friends and family. The most useful gifts she received were a $250 gift certificate to her local grocer from her husband's employer and a medical-grade electric double-breast pump.

Finally, Amy shared with me that the most valuable piece of knowledge she has learned as a parent is "to prioritize" and that her children's "health and well-being is the most important thing. Nothing else is earth shattering."

Make sure you send out thank you notes for your baby shower gifts. Some Web sites, such as **vistaprint.com**, allow you to create customized note cards with your own photos and also offer free printing deals if you join their e-mail list.

Samples of homemade thank you cards and shower invitations

Chapter 4

Facts of Life

Bringing a baby into your lives means several things. The first, and most important, is that you will be changing your lives forever. You will feel everything more vividly. You will want to do only the best for your child. This can be both frustrating and wonderful. Getting the best for your baby will almost always be your most pressing concern. Therefore, having the right resources to get the most important things for your baby's life will be instrumental in your preparation for parenthood. This chapter should help you identify those products, items, and accessories and then fit them into your budget so you can get them in the timeliest manner possible. In this chapter, you will learn about essential products that will be the most useful for you and your infant, how to make decisions among the different options of particular products, and when it will be essential to have these items.

This chapter will include a more in-depth look at food and diapers for your infant and how to choose which options are best for your family and life style. We will also discuss different styles and types of bottles, nipples, sterilizers, bottle warmers, and the options available in these products, as well as what you might and might not need for your life style and infant. Baby food and cereal will be important to have as well; you will find a brief description of how to choose these items and what the costs of baby food will be. You will learn about bibs, pacifiers, and burp cloths, including where to find them and how much you should pay for such items. Finally, you will learn more about diapers — both cloth and disposable — and diapering accessories that you might consider purchasing or registering for. We will cover the things you will need or that might be helpful for you to have if you can fit them into your budget. Keep in mind the budget you have set for yourself and use that to determine whether you are able to purchase some of the items that might not be essential for you or your baby.

Breast-feeding

The choice to breast-feed your baby can not only save you (literally) thousands of dollars, but it is also the best nutritional choice you can make for your child. Breast-feeding your infant will give her an adequate amount of antibodies to build the best possible immune system and has all the natural, nonprocessed ingredients that she will need for a healthy infancy and first year. Every baby needs to have adequate amounts of certain nutrients, and breast-feeding your baby will save you the time of fretting over what amounts of each ingredient you believe your little one needs. The idea of giving your child the best nutrition possible is a good reason to breast-feed your baby. Combined with the money and time you can save, this makes breast-feeding come in at the top of the list of good things you can do for your baby.

In the second chapter of this book, we discussed the costs of breast-feeding your baby. If you spend the median cost for breast-feeding your infant, you will spend about $300 to $500 to feed your infant if you use only breast milk for the first year of his life. This estimate includes the minimal costs of breast pads and nipple ointment, which most breast-feeding mothers will need, as well as the average cost of a breast pump. Breast pumps can cost anywhere from $70 to $300, and, if you purchase a good-quality breast pump, you will need to spend this amount only once, even if you are planning on having more children in the future. Whether you decide to breast-feed or formula-feed your baby, the items and accessories will need to be on hand when you return home from delivering your baby.

Quick TIP

Purchasing formula alone without breast-feeding your infant will cost on average $1,200 for the first year. Aside from the money breast-feeding saves you, the time you save will be even greater.

Breast-feeding your infant means that you will not only be relieved of the expense of buying formula on a regular basis, you will also be relieved of the immediate need to purchase many bottles and nipples. After the first year of life, most babies will convert to cow's milk, and you will no longer have a need to purchase formula.

Breast-feeding will save you time because you will have fewer bottles to wash, less formula to mix and prepare, less time at the grocery store, and less time packing and unpacking your diaper bag with bottle-feeding necessities. The time you will save in cleaning bottles and nipples is simple — the more time your infant spends feeding at your breast, the fewer bottles and nipples you will be using. This is the same concept for the time you will spend preparing and heating bottles for your baby. This might not sound like much time, but if you have to wake every two hours each night to feed an infant, the few precious minutes it takes to prepare bottles can add to life-saving minutes of sleep for many moms. If you are breast-feeding your baby, the baby's meals will already be prepared every time he is ready to eat. If you are formula-feeding your infant, you will need to prepare a fresh bottle every time he is hungry. This can take from two to five minutes, depending on how efficient your bottle warmer or microwave is and how well you function on little sleep.

Some women have no choice but to make formula the primary feeding source for their infants. Our baby was able to access and use a small amount of my breast milk; it was still necessary to come down to the kitchen for each feeding to prepare a fresh bottle after our daughter was done breast-feeding. By the time I was finished breast-feeding and bottle-feeding our daughter, I had come up and down the stairs twice and had to get my wits about me enough to correctly prepare a clean, properly heated and mixed bottle of formula every two hours for the first three months of her life. This can be challenging in the middle of the night. If you are breast-feeding, you will always have your baby's food source, you will never forget it, and it will always be warmed and ready to go with little effort on your part.

Finally, you will save time by breast-feeding your little one by spending less time at the store purchasing formula and less time looking for deals on formula. Formula is expensive. Finding the best deals at the right stores, clipping coupons, and figuring out how much formula you will need week to week is a time consuming process when you have an infant on your hands. This was not a task I enjoyed, although once I found the right stores with the right coupons, the weekly process of purchasing formula started to be less consuming. Still it would have been much easier to know that the entire recipe of nutrients for our baby was already mixed, prepared, and ready, not to mention attached to my body.

Many mothers choose to breast-feed their babies for the first six to nine months of life, and some choose to breast-feed well beyond the infancy of their children. However, there are circumstances that prevent some mothers from breast-feeding for this length of time or at all. Some moms also choose not to breast-feed their child because they must return to work or have other challenges with breast-feeding that make the entire process more stressful for mom and baby than it needs to be.

Case Study: Ashleigh Hindman

Belle's and Beau's
6150 S. Tower Road, Aurora, CO 80014
Ph: 303-693-6715
Ashleigh Hindman, Kindergarten Enrichment Teacher

Ashleigh Hindman is a caring and nurturing mother to her little boy, Kaden, who is now two years old. She is also always around kids from infant to school age and has a great deal of experience with infants. When asked to give her top two favorite baby-friendly items, she listed the Medela Single Deluxe Breast Pump and the DEX Products brand snapping bib.

The electric breast pumps by Medela are one of many consumers' favorites; the model Ashleigh used was about $70 and can be battery or electric powered. Though it was not the most expensive or top-of-the-line breast pump Medela makes, it was very easy to use and just goes to show that you do not have to purchase the most expensive product to get great results. The Medela Single Deluxe Breast Pump saved Ashleigh time and worked well for the entire time she was breast-feeding Kaden.

The DEX Products brand bib is a soft plastic snapping bib that has proved to be a lifesaver that Ashleigh uses for all meals with her son. This is the bib they also use at the school Ashleigh teaches at, and the bibs are very affordable at approximately $2 each. The bib snaps at the bottom to create a crumb catcher and does catch almost anything that falls from her son's mouth.

When it is time to clean up, the bib can be removed with all the food still trapped in the crumb catcher, which can then be unsnapped and wiped clean with a wet washcloth. Ashleigh's exact words about this bib were, "The best bib ever."

When asked about what a new mom should know, Ashleigh offered this advice. "Breast-feeding your baby is not as natural and easy as it looks, but give it a chance because it is one of the most amazing things you will experience."

Formula

The decision not to breast-feed your baby does not make you any less of a mother. Breast-feeding is a personal choice, and it must be made with both you and your baby in mind. Before I was a mom myself I was always a proponent of breast-feeding, and I still believe that it is the best thing you can do to support your child in health and in bonding with Mom. However, there are circumstances that will prevent good mothers from being able to supply their new babies with breast milk, and I speak from firsthand experience.

When my husband and I found out I was pregnant, I had visions of holding our baby close and bonding for nine months through the intimate act of breast-feeding. By the time our daughter was two days old, it was brought to our attention by our nurse that there was a problem and she was not getting a sufficient amount of breast milk. This explained a good deal, including the loss of an entire pound of weight in the first two days of her life — she was born 6.1 pounds, and by the second day, she weighed only 5.1 pounds. It also explained why I felt as though I had lived 100 years of life in those first two days, as I could not figure out why our daughter would not stop crying. I would feed her (as instructed by every book and La Leche League counselor I spoke with), hold her, change her, burp her, and still she was not happy. She was hungry.

I was exhausted, and our daughter seemed satisfied enough after feedings, so the idea of hunger never occurred to us. This was an unexpected expense; formula was needed from day two of our daughter's life. I was still able to breast-feed her in small amounts, but she had to be supplemented with a bottle of formula at each feeding every two hours.

There are many reasons that some new mothers decide to use formula to feed their babies instead of breast milk. There is the possibility that you are not able to breast-feed due to a physical limitation, lack of milk production, health concern, or infection. The likelihood of this is low; however, the possibility is there, and it is real. The best advice for difficulties in breast-feeding is to get help as soon as you can if you are having problems and would like to continue. If, after investigating the problem, you find that the only answer is to supplement your baby with formula or move to feeding with formula alone, accept this and move on. Some moms find that breast-feeding is just not something they can handle. As wonderful as many mothers-to-be think breast-feeding will be, there are some mothers who simply cannot get comfortable with the feeling. This does not mean they love their child any less; it is simply a physical limitation that can occur for some women.

If any of these instances occur for you, you will need to be prepared to formula-feed your child to some extent. You might be required only to supplement your child with formula while you continue to breast-feed as much as possible, or you may need to make the decision to feed your infant only formula. Either way, you can still be a wonderful, caring, loving, and compassionate mother. One of the preparations you should make in case any of these situations should arise is to research and pick a formula you would use when you might not be able to breast-feed. Get the facts, find out what ingredients are in each brand you are considering, and then make a decision based on nutritional value, quality, quantity, and price. All infant formulas found in grocery or baby stores are FDA approved and will benefit your baby's health. Talk with your selected pediatrician and hospital or other healthcare providers to get their opinions on what brands of formula would be best for your baby.

 Powdered formula will be the least expensive type of formula you can purchase. If you are feeding your infant with formula alone, you will spend the greater part of the first year of your baby's life purchasing two 26-ounce containers of formula each week.

Formula is an expensive endeavor. As revealed in Chapter 2, formula will cost anywhere from $25 to $32 for one 26-ounce package of powdered formula. On average, you will spend anywhere from $2,000 to $2,500 on formula in the first year of your child's life. This is a large amount of money that can be an unexpected expense. Do not forget that there are resources available to you, including WIC, if you are eligible, and coupons that can save you a large amount of money over time and can be used by anyone who takes the time to find them. One simple and quick way to locate good coupons is to contact any manufacturer via the World Wide Web to inquire about coupon programs and special offers. Some of these resources are available in the Nutrition & Feeding section of the Appendix.

Bottles and Nipples

Baby bottles and nipples will be another aspect of feeding your baby you will need to be prepared with when your baby arrives home from the hospital. There will no doubt be a time in the first year of your infant's life that you will prefer to bottle-feed your baby. This is a factor whether you choose to breast-feed your baby or not. There will ultimately be a time when you will either stop breast-feeding or need to rely on a bottle due to health constraints, scheduling problems, or just plain lack of sleep.

Bottles come in nearly every shape and size. There are bottles that are angled, made of plastic, use bags, are different sizes, and even are easy-to-hold shapes. The type of bottle you choose to use for your baby will mainly depend on what your baby will drink from. Many babies will drink from any bottle or nipple, as long as there are nutrients flowing from it. However, there are some babies who are a bit more refined in their selection of where their milk or formula flows from. The number of bottles you will need will largely depend on how often you will need them and how quickly you can clean them.

Quick TIP

Do not purchase a large amount of bottles in advance. Get acquainted first with what your baby will prefer.

Bottles that reduce the amount of air that your baby swallows are the most popular. These will include the angled bottles and those that function with a bag design, otherwise known as disposable bottles. The most trusted brands of bottles include Avent, Evenflo, Playtex, and Gerber. Avent bottles and nipples will be the most expensive of these four brands but are highly recommended by moms and claim to have the most infant-friendly nipples on the market. Other pluses of the Avent feeding systems are that you can purchase them in disposable, semi-disposable, and non-disposable styles, making your selection and preferences easy to obtain. The downside of the Avent feeding system is that it is one of the more expensive bottles and nipple sets on the market. An Avent bottle and set of nipples will have an average price of $15.

Other competitors, such as Evenflo, are just as loved by many mothers, including me, because they are less expensive and offer a comfortable feeding system for most babies. The Evenflo bottles and nipples are in the mid-price range, as far as bottles and nipples go, with an average price of $6 to $8 for a set of three bottles and various size nipples. The Munchkin Healthflow brand of bottles are even more reasonably priced, and although they are less known, seem to have just as much success among users as many of the more expensive brands. Finally, on the lower end of the price range, you will find Playtex and Gerber bottles and nipples. These brands can be found in almost every store that carries baby products, including your local grocery store or department store. The nipples of the Playtex and Gerber bottles are a little smaller and therefore are good for smaller babies, as long as the flow of liquid from the nipple suits your baby's suckling and eating style.

Many moms find that it is more the nipple than the bottle that their baby is fussy about. After all, the actual bottle is merely a container for the fluid that your baby is drinking. The nipple is the item that will be delivering the fluid to your infant, and it needs to come 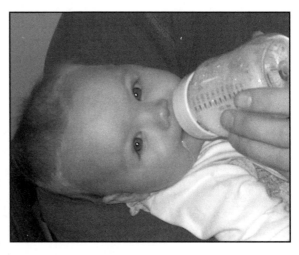 in a comfortable speed and be made of a comfortable material that is easy to manipulate and easily dispenses formula or milk. Avent claims that their nipples are shaped more like the breast and are the most colic-reducing nipples in the baby-feeding industry, which reduces the amount of endless crying some infants will experience after eating. The Avent nipple is loved by many mothers in many places; however, the nipple is big and, for smaller babies, this can be a problem. Our daughter was small, and because she was bottle-fed from the second day of her life, the Avent nipples were much too big for her tiny mouth to manipulate. As she grew, the Avent bottles and nipples were successful; however, in the first months of her life we used the Evenflo bottles and nipples, and I cannot say that I preferred one over the other when price came into the picture.

When it comes to choosing a bottle and nipple for your son or daughter, consider their age and size before you purchase a mass quantity of either. You will want to eventually purchase enough bottles and nipples so that you do not have an endless amount of dishes to do; 10 to 12 bottles and nipples will be more than enough. My advice would be to purchase one set of bottles and nipples from the brand that you believe will suit your infant the best. Give the bottle and nipple a trial run after you bring baby home; monitor whether your baby is getting the food quickly and easily from the nipple and whether the bottle is too big or uncomfortable for you, or, depending on the age of your baby, for your baby to hold.

You will also want to observe that the fluid being expressed from the bottle is not coming out too quickly; if it is, you will need a smaller or firmer nipple. Once you have found the bottle and nipple that suits you and your baby the best, shop secondhand stores, garage sales, and online auctions for the type of bottle you want, especially if it is one of the more expensive brands. Bottles and nipples can be sterilized easily in boiling water or the dishwasher, and purchasing these items secondhand is not a health concern. I would suggest having at least one set of bottles and infant-sized nipples on hand when you bring your baby home from the hospital.

Bottle Warmers and Sterilizers

Bottle warmers and bottle sterilizers are not a necessity. They are nice to have if you believe you will use them, but there are other ways of warming your infant's food and cleaning the bottles and nipples he uses. Some parents will use these items endlessly, while others will decide they were a waste of money.

For bottle warmers, the question of whether you will use this item will mainly depend on how many bottles you will need to warm during the first year of your baby's life. If you will be breast-feeding your child most of the time, you may not need a bottle warmer. If you will be preparing formula for your baby on a regular basis, a bottle warmer is nice to have.

One of the advantages of bottle warmers is that they come with specific directions for heating bottles with specified amounts of liquid in them. They can be safer than the stove or microwave and prevent burns.

Some bottle warmers are manufactured to fit baby food jars as well and include timing directions for different types of foods and cereals. All these things can be done with a warm pot of water on the stove or in your microwave — it simply takes a little time and experimentation to find out the proper times and settings.

Most bottle warmers are suggested for heating bottles and baby food, as microwaves heat foods with different consistency unevenly. When you heat a bottle in your microwave, for instance, the concern is that the upper half of the fluid absorbs more of the heat than the lower portion. This can burn your baby's mouth if you forget to shake the bottle well after heating it. Stove-top heating warms most items evenly throughout; however, once you get an item too hot on the stove, it can take some time to cool it down enough to be comfortable for your infant to drink or eat. These are concerns that you can easily overcome, making the bottle warmer nonessential. However, if you feel that a bottle warmer will benefit you, it can be relatively inexpensive.

There are options in bottle warmers that range from $10 to $40. The lower-priced models are just as good as the more expensive ones. The lower-priced bottle warmers include brands such as DEX and Prince Lionheart and mainly include on-the-go bottle warmers, which will keep bottles warm while you are out and about with your infant. DEX offers a $9 automobile bottle warmer that plugs into a power source in your car, and Prince Lionheart offers a bottle warmer that warms the bottle at your convenience, wherever you may be. Both of these bottle warmers can easily be found for $12 or less.

The next price range you will find is $15 to $20, and there are many brands to choose from. We used the First Years Quick Serve Bottle Warmer by Learning Curve. This bottle warmer was only $18 at Babies "R" Us, and we used the warmer at least ten to 15 times a day for the greater part of two years. It was consistent and never broke or caused any problems. In fact, there was a point in time when I realized that I could plug the bottle warmer into the outlet of our upstairs bathroom. I kept a small amount of formula in the same area and, before bed, I would add the right measurement of formula to an empty bottle, saving it for later. When our daughter awoke in the middle of the night for feedings I would have to add only water and heat the bottle, which could be done while I breast-fed her for a short time. The bottle warmer made our lives much easier and less stressful, especially in the middle of the night. These are not the circumstances for most moms, and so purchasing a bottle warmer is strictly a matter of whether you feel it will help you and be worth the $20.

There are more expensive bottle warmers that can range all the way up to $40. Spending this amount of money on a bottle warmer is unnecessary. The Avent Express Bottle and Baby Food warmer is one of the more expensive models you can find. It does all the same things that the lower-priced models do, with the exception of having a timer you can set to heat for longer times if you wish. I would not recommend spending this much money on a bottle warmer; however, if you are tied to the name Avent, you may feel it is necessary. The less-expensive bottle warmers and the First Years model we used will fit Avent bottles. If you decide to purchase a bottle warmer, you will likely not need it until you have stopped breast-feeding your baby. For most moms this will not be until your baby is six to nine months old.

Bottle sterilizers are in the same gray area as bottle warmers. You do not need to have one; however, if you choose to have one, it can make cleaning your bottles and nipples environmentally friendly, quick, and easy. Sterilizers and steamers are meant to be used after you have cleaned your bottles by properly washing them. They are used to kill all bacteria that may be left in or on the bottles and nipples and can also be used for breast pump cups and tubing. However, it should also be said that you can use your  dishwasher for this purpose, as well as steam bags, which can often be used up to 20 or more times before throwing them out. A bottle steamer or sterilizer is going to be most used if you need to wash four or more bottles a day and are committed to being environmentally friendly.

We did not use a bottle sterilizer or steamer, and I have yet to find a mom who raves about them, which tells me most moms probably rely on their dishwasher for this job. The positive side to the steamer or sterilizer is that it will kill bacteria in less than eight minutes, after which you need to clean the steamer itself. You can also kill bacteria on your bottles and nipples by boiling them on the stovetop for eight minutes, after which you can simply dry out the pot you used and put it back in the cabinet. However, if you are interested, you can find various bottle steamers and sterilizers at most baby stores. The prices for these items are often between $30 and $50. Again, this is an item you would not need until you

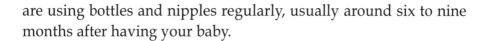

are using bottles and nipples regularly, usually around six to nine months after having your baby.

Baby Food and Cereal

Around four months into your baby's life, you will enter into the terribly messy yet wonderful world of feeding your baby food. Baby food and cereal will seem like a relief on your expenses if you have been feeding your baby formula. If you have been breast-feeding your infant for the previous four months, buying baby food and cereal will add a little expense to your budget but nothing too alarming.

Most pediatricians and nutritionist suggest that you start your baby out slow when it comes to introducing her to "solid" foods. First, you will begin with rice or oat cereal, and you will not try any other new foods for two to three weeks. Once your baby has mastered the consistency of cereal, everything is staying down, and you know there are no allergies or strange reactions to the cereal, you will be able to move on to another type of cereal or to your first jar of baby food. Most rice or whole-grain cereals will cost in the range of $1.50 to $4.50 for what will be a small eight-ounce box of cereal. This box may last two to three weeks, so the added expense will not be much.

This is the same for baby food. After you have trudged your way through the different types of cereals, including rice, whole-grain, and multi-grain cereals, you will be ready to introduce solid baby foods to your child. Solid food is a misleading statement; I have yet to find a jar of baby food that appears to be solid. However, it is termed solid food, and the introduction of these foods will work much like the cereals. You will begin with one food and usually stick with that food for three to five days before introducing a new food to your baby's diet. Introducing new foods to your infant slowly is done for two reasons. The first reason is your baby might have allergies that you have yet to discover. Introducing foods one at a time will give your baby's body time to react to each new food, letting you know if it is a food that agrees with him or not or if an allergy might be involved. The second reason you will introduce foods slowly to your baby is to let his system acclimate to the new happenings. Until you start cereal and other foods, your baby has likely consumed only breast milk and formula. The need to adapt to digesting new properties will take time, and too much variety can create a cranky baby with an uncomfortable tummy.

New foods can cause gas, diarrhea, tummy aches, acid reflux, and other symptoms, so taking it slow is in your and your baby's best interest. Baby food is inexpensive, especially when you are going to need only a few jars a week for the first two or three months of the journey into solid foods. Most baby foods will range from $1 to $2.50 per jar; often, you can find even better deals with coupons and in-store sales

for $.25 to $.50 a jar. For baby food and cereal, the upper range of the price bracket will be found in organic baby foods at specialty stores, and the lower range will be baby foods that you can often find at your local grocery store, such as Gerber (which offers a wide variety of Kosher products) and Earth's Best (which offers all organic products). You will not need to have baby foods or cereal in your home until your baby is around three to four months old. Before this, all your baby will need is breast milk or formula.

Case Study: Jill Cartwright

Jill Cartwright, mother of Ally, an adorable one-year-old little girl, participated in my Case Study and provided some very helpful information for parents when it came to baby food and a wealth of knowledge about how to find out what is in your baby's food.

"Speaking as a parent of a child with food allergies, some of the most useful items that I received were credit-card-sized index cards with reference to food labels. A friend who purchased them off the Food Allergy and Anaphylaxis Network Web site gave these cards to me. This is by far one of the best and most reliable Web sites for food allergy information. Since my daughter is allergic to so many different foods, these cards gave me a reference when deciphering food labels. For example, before all of this, I had no idea that 'casein' as a listed ingredient could mean that the product contains milk. Since the cards are the size of a credit card, they easily fit into my wallet so that I always have them with me when I am grocery shipping and am unsure about a particular food ingredient."

In addition to Jill's experience with a daughter that can eat very limited ingredients, she learned a great deal about grocery shopping for baby foods; if you are interested or concerned about products, allergies, or ingredients for any reason, Jill has some very helpful suggestions.

"In regards to food shopping for a child with food allergies, I have found that the best place to go is the local grocery store that I have been shopping at for years. I went to 'specialty' food stores (and still need to for a few items) but found that I still had to read every label and still had a limited selection given the allergies that my daughter has. It took some time, but I was able to find a fair selection of foods at a much better price by shopping at the regular grocery store.

The first few visits are the most tedious, and I found myself in tears in some of the aisles. But each visit got so much easier and quicker. I still had to call some manufacturers, and I got a good sense for which manufacturers really care about their consumers and responsible food labeling. Honestly, I would recommend every mom to read labels, not just those with children with food allergies. Knowing what you are providing in terms of your child's nutrition is so important."

Finally, this advice that Jill shared with me to pass along to my readers is something that I never really considered too much, and I am thankful I met and spoke with her.

"My advice for all parents is to recognize that every child is different. Be conscious of other people's children when putting together things like play groups. Never just offer another child something to eat or drink without first checking with the parent or guardian.

"If I could change one thing throughout the first year of my daughter's life it would have been worrying less. As a new mom, we worry about every little thing (at least I did). I realized that while I was worrying so much, I was missing how much fun it was. And the worrying did not add anything to our lives except stress. Kids are amazingly fun, so enjoy every minute."

Pacifiers, Burp Cloths, and Bibs

There is no argument that you will need burp cloths and bibs. Everybody's baby burps and spits up from time to time. Some babies do this more than others, and you will find that you will use your burp cloths for many different reasons. You will use them for their intended purpose most, throwing one over your lap or shoulder to catch whatever mystery substance is propelled from your baby while you are burping him after a meal of breast milk or formula. If you are like many moms, you will also use burp cloths to clean baby's face and to wipe up spills and other messes.

Burp cloths can be found in every baby store, including secondhand and thrift stores, and will range in price. If you are able to find used burp cloths that are in fairly good condition, you might spend only $.25 to $1 on each cloth. If you choose to purchase your burp cloths new, there is a wide range of prices. Usually, new burp cloths are sold in sets of three or more, and the price can range from $4.50 to $15 for each package. The lower-priced burp cloths will do fine in almost any case. They are soft and absorbent, and many come in colorful prints that will help hide the messes your baby makes or stains that will not come out.

Quick TIP

The most important things to look for in a set of burp cloths will be that they are soft, comfortable, and a good size for how you will use them the most.

As for how many you will need, that depends on your laundering habits. It is good to have at least five to seven, and many moms will prefer to have many more than this because they are used so often. I would suggest having ten to 15, if your budget will allow. This is an item that you will want to have a few of on hand when you come home from delivering your baby, as they will be needed nearly each time you feed and burp your infant.

Bibs are a wonderful invention and will save many of those cute ensembles you or your family and friends have bought for your baby. Bibs, as most moms-to-be know, protect your baby's clothing or skin from the foods and liquids that your child will inevitably spill, drool, spit, and splash all over the front of herself. Bibs are often received in large quantities at your baby shower because they are cute, and many display humorous messages across the front. Bibs are a bit overpriced in my opinion, simply because they are cute. You can find many free bibs from other mothers and for good prices at garage sales. Some may be stained, but your baby is only going to add to the artistic food display on the front.

Thrift stores and secondhand stores will have bibs in large quantities much of the time and price them low, around $.50 a bib. New bibs will often be sold in sets, much like burp cloths, usually three or more to a set, and cost anywhere from $9 to $20, depending on how many are in the package and how cute the catchy sayings on them are. Bibs are an item that you might want to have one or two of when you come home; however, it is not necessary, as you will mainly be using burp cloths until your baby starts to eat cereal and baby foods. By the time your little one is four months old, you should have at least five to seven, which will be enough to realistically get you through one week of feeding without having to do laundry.

Preferences on pacifiers differ. Some parents believe that pacifiers are unnecessary, and others believe that babies need them for self-soothing. Depending on your view of the pacifier, you might want to purchase some, and you might not. If you have your baby in a hospital, the hospital will often provide you with one infant pacifier; however, getting more  than one pacifier from the hospital can be challenging. Purchasing a pacifier for your child will seem like an easy task until you show up at the great wall of pacifiers in the store, where you will find that you can spend hours trying to decide which brand, design, and shape will be best for your baby. One of the most popular brands of pacifiers are NUK because the sizes it offers for the different ages of babies are appropriate for the mouth size of those ages. They are often made of soft plastic that is easy for even infants to manipulate with their tiny mouths.

Having a pacifier for your baby is not negative or harmful. Pacifiers help babies to self-soothe through the action of sucking, which is the only way an infant knows how to soothe himself. Many parents have been told in the past that pacifiers will compromise the alignment of your child's teeth; however, most orthodontists do not agree that there is much danger of harming the growth of teeth unless your child is still using a pacifier when he has reached an age where his permanent teeth are coming in. The main frustration with pacifiers that you will eventually have to worry about will be getting your toddler to give his up. Pacifiers are not an item that many children part with easily. Because of this, if it seems that your child does not want or need a pacifier to keep him happy, then bypass the pacifier. If you do use a pacifier and feel that your baby needs one, try to break the habit early. After six to nine months of age, there is no need for a pacifier, as your baby should have learned some self-soothing behaviors by the age of five or six months old. Some babies will simply give up their pacifiers on their own; however, do not rely on this and continue using one if it is unnecessary.

Pacifiers come in many shapes and sizes and can be found both new and used.

Quick TIP

If you choose to buy a used pacifier or have received hand-me-downs from other moms, this is completely safe. You will simply want to sterilize them as you would any pacifier that you would purchase from the store.

Sterilizing your pacifiers or any other items that will go into your baby's mouth can easily be done with boiling water. Boil the items for a minimum of eight minutes, and then allow them to dry and cool completely before giving them to your infant. New pacifiers may be sold in pairs or singles and can be found for $3 to $8 at any store that sells baby items and products. Having a pacifier on hand when you arrive home is convenient, but do not forget that the hospital will often provide you with one. This may suffice until you can find the right size and fit of pacifier for your baby.

Diapers

Diapers are a necessity, and you will need them from the moment you arrive home until your child is three to four years old. Babies need comfortable diapers that will fit right and be the right choice for Mom and Dad. Most people think of disposable diapers when diapers are mentioned; however, you do still have a choice as to whether you would prefer cloth diapers or disposables. In Chapter 2, the wide range of money that you will be able to spend on diapers alone each year was revealed: $350 to $650 for disposable diapers, $300 to $600 for cloth diapers if you choose to launder them yourself, and a surprising $1,000 to $2,100 for cloth diapers with a laundering service.

Of course, there are other factors you might want to consider when deciding what materials you would like to cover your baby's bottom in. There are noted differences in the effects of cloth and disposable diapers on several things: potty training, environment, and laundry. For some parents, there is no other consideration; price may be the only determining factor.

Choosing between cloth and disposable diapers is a personal decision, and there are positives and negatives to both. First, you should take into account all the good and bad points of the cloth diaper and the disposable diaper. You will find many books and people that will want to discuss the politics of the environment and how the cloth diaper benefits the environment. There is no question that cloth diapers are better for the world we live in, but this is a decision that should be based on what is best for you as a parent and for your new baby. Cloth diapers are better for the environment, and disposable diapers are often better for the parent. It depends on how much time, patience, and energy you have.

Quick TIP

Cloth diapers are considered better for potty training your child later in life. Because cloth diapers are less absorbent than disposable diapers, they are less comfortable when wet, making your future toddler think twice about clinging to his diapers when you are tired of changing them.

Newer disposable diapers, created to help potty train toddlers, allow the child to be more aware of wetness but are not as uncomfortable as a cloth diaper. Cloth diapers will absorb only a small amount of liquid; even potty training diapers are made with moisture-absorbent gel to help keep the baby's skin dry, which helps to prevent irritation, chaffing, and diaper rash.

Purchasing cloth diapers that will be reused once laundered will save you a good deal of money; however, there are other things to consider when it comes to the diaper dilemma and choosing cloth over disposable diapers. Who is going to wash all those dirty diapers? Laundering your own cloth diapers will by far be the least expensive thing you can do as far as money. Time and energy, on the other hand, will be short once you factor in all the hours spent de-soiling, washing, drying, and folding your baby's cloth diapers. You could use a cloth diaper service, but most cloth diaper laundering services are not cheap. Another reason that cloth diapers might not be the best choice for you would be that they are not as efficient at protecting against leaks; there is no gel in the cloth diapers that absorbs the way disposable diapers do. The lack of moisture absorption can also add to the number of diaper rashes your infant will experience.

Disposable diapers are going to be less environmentally friendly, yet much more convenient. They are more reliable in protecting against leaks, but often children who wear disposable diapers potty train slower than those who wear cloth diapers. Disposable diapers come on most occasions with one cost: purchasing never-ending packages of diapers for three to four years. However, once the diaper is used, you simply throw it away. There is no mess to dispose of or to try to eliminate from the diaper, and there are many different types of diaper pails now made to suppress any smells that may try to escape into your home.

 There is only one hidden cost with disposable diapers, and that is if your trash company charges you extra for more than a specified amount of trash.

There you have it. Make a decision based on your budget and your life style. If you are considering using cloth diapers, you should check with several diapering companies in your area as to their prices, because many services will vary. The estimates provided in this book cover the pricing of most diapering agencies I have found; however, there are many available, and picking one without reviewing their pricing could be a costly mistake. If you decide that cloth diapers are not for you, and disposable diapers are going to work best for your life style, your family, and your baby, look into purchasing them in bulk if possible, as the prices will be much more reasonable than at most local grocery stores. There are positive and negative points to both cloth and disposable diapers. Carefully consider these and make an educated decision based on budget and preference.

Other Diapering Needs and Products

Making a decision between cloth and disposable diapers does not end the battle with diapering needs. There are other products and items that you will need: diaper rash ointment or cream, baby wipes, a diaper bag, and possibly a diaper pail.

Diaper Rash Ointment

Diaper rash ointment is relatively inexpensive; you will need only to have one tube or container on hand at any given time. Some moms, myself included, will find it more convenient to keep two containers around — one in the house and one in the diaper bag — but this is only if it is affordable. I know that diaper rash ointment does not sound like it would drain your bank account, but keep in mind all those little expenses you are cutting to stick to your budget. This can be one of those areas if you do not need the extra tube for your outings.

Diaper rash is a nasty little infection that comes with most baby bottoms. I have yet to meet a mom who has not had to deal with diaper rash at one point or another. The main defense against diaper rash will be to keep your baby's bottom as clean and dry as you can at all times; change diapers regularly and bathe your infant on a regular basis as well. However, it is good to have at least one tube of diaper rash cream in your home when your baby comes home with you. Diaper rash tends to sneak up on you silently, and then, once your baby is afflicted, you will find that your baby becomes not so silent.

The cost of diaper rash cream or ointment will vary depending on the brand or type of product you purchase. The lower-priced diaper rash creams fall between $3 and $5. Some of the most trusted brands include Desitin, Aveeno, Boudreaux's, Triple Paste, and organic brands such as Babybear Shop and Nature's Baby Organic Diaper Cream. The lower-priced brands are the creamy styles of Desitin and Aveeno. These also come in a thicker ointment that costs slightly less; however, the $1 to $2 difference is worth having a cream that is easy to apply rather than a sticky and greasy ointment that can ruin clothes. The next step up in price for diaper rash control will be Boudreaux's and Nature's Baby, falling between $8 and $13. Finally, you will have the most expensive brands, which all have five-star reviews most places you look. These include Triple Paste and Babybear products, which may be found in stores that specialize in baby products or online. The Triple Paste and Babybear brands, depending on where you find them, will range from $20 to $40.

One thing to watch when you are purchasing diaper rash cream and comparing prices is how much ointment or cream you are getting for your dollar. All these brands work and get the job done, but, depending on your preferences and baby's needs, one of the more expensive brands might suit you better, especially if diaper rash is a constant and painful problem for your baby. The Triple Paste and Babybear diaper rash creams often come in larger sizes and tend to last longer, which may factor into your purchasing decision.

One thing I have found throughout the first three years of our daughter's life is that there are many tips and secrets handed down from other mothers which you should consider before you rush out and purchase a more expensive remedy. One of the best secrets I learned from another mother is what my husband and I refer to as "Booty Budder." This is not the actual name of this diaper rash ointment recipe. I do not know what it is called or whether it even has a name. It is safe, and it was suggested by a close friend's pediatrician.

Booty Budder Recipe

- 2 Tablespoons Desitin Creamy Ointment

- 2 tablespoons Maalox

- 2 teaspoons Lotrimin AF

Mix together and store in an air-tight container. Apply generously to baby's bottom at any sign of diaper rash or as a preventative measure.

We used this recipe whenever our daughter had a severe diaper rash and while she was teething to prevent diaper rash. Because I too was skeptical, here is how the ingredients work to help your baby's bottom. The Desitin Creamy Ointment soothes and helps to heal the diaper rash. The Maalox helps draw the acid from baby's waste out of the skin, which reduces the pain associated with the diaper rash. This is the same thing Maalox does in your stomach: It soaks up the acids that cause heartburn and other stomach troubles. You can use any flavor of Maalox you like, but be warned that the mint will make your baby smell minty. The final ingredient is Lotrimin AF, an antifungal cream that is found in the foot-care aisle of most grocery and department stores. Because it is an antifungal cream, it will help keep the diaper rash from getting infected, as well as heal and eliminate yeast infection in the diaper rash. We used this "Booty Budder" cream many times, and it is for application on baby's bottom alone. In most cases, even when our baby had a diaper rash so severe that her bottom would have open sores, the "Booty Budder" would heal the diaper rash within 24 to 48 hours. Although I and many of my close friends and acquaintances swear by this homemade recipe, be sure to always check with your pediatrician before using any new products with your infant.

Baby Wipes

Another item that your baby's bottom will require more often than diaper rash ointment or cream will be baby wipes. In the first three months of your baby's life, you will likely use a 200-count box of baby wipes each week. You will be changing 12 to 14 diapers every day. If you use two wipes each time to thoroughly clean your infant, you will have used 196 wipes every seven days. It may sound a bit repetitive, but you will need to have at least one box of baby wipes available to you when you come home from delivering your baby.

Baby wipes are much like diapers: You will use them all the time. However, they are different than diapers in that you will use them for many different purposes. Finding yourself without baby wipes can be devastating, whether you are in a public rest room or in your own home. To remedy this situation, you can factor into your budget not only a package of diapers every week but also a package of baby wipes. Baby wipes will not be too hard to factor into your weekly budget, as long as you can designate $3 to $5 a week to them and even less if you shop with coupons or stock up at sales. Purchasing baby wipes in bulk at stores such as Costco or Sam's Club can be beneficial, as the prices are often much better for the amount of product you are taking home with you.

 When purchasing baby wipes, you can save a money simply by purchasing refill packs instead of the tub every time. This will give you 600 wipes versus 200.

Most often, the refill packs are three sets of wipes packaged individually within a larger package, so you will be able to keep them fresh and use them when you are ready.

The only real buying tips when looking for the baby wipes you prefer is to open the first package you purchase and see if the texture is soft and pliable. Your baby's skin will be soft and sensitive, and having a harsh, paper-like wipe can be uncomfortable for your baby, cause rashes and other irritations, and ultimately make your baby cranky. When it comes to baby wipes, I am a fan of Pampers. Throughout the first three years of our daughter's life, there were many times that I purchased all different brands of wipes, including Huggies and many store brands. Pampers baby wipes have proven, in my experience, to be the softest on our baby's skin, to keep their moisture longer than other brands, to contain no alcohol, to be safe for baby's face and hands, and to be easily removable from the package with one hand. The cost of Pampers baby wipes compared with other brands is not unreasonable, usually costing only $1 to $2 more than the generic brands.

Diaper Bag

By this time, you will be stockpiling quite a bit of baby stuff that you will need to take with you when you leave the house with your infant. This leads you to the option of purchasing a diaper bag. Diaper bags are certainly not a must-have if your budget simply will not allow you any extras. Using a large shoulder bag you already own or a backpack is always an option. However, if you can afford to get a diaper bag, it will come in handy while you are roaming about town or visiting friends with your baby. If you cannot afford to purchase a diaper bag — and even if you can and are not particular about what type or how it looks — you can register in the Enfamil Family Beginnings Club and you will receive coupons for formula and a free diaper bag. Although the Enfamil diaper bag is not at the height of fashion (it is a plain-black, over-the-shoulder diaper bag), it is reasonable to carry with you, and free is always fashionable.

There are things you should consider when purchasing your diaper bag. Many moms-to-be will look at this task much like getting a new purse. Just remember when you are looking through all the wonderful designs and styles that, if you would like your husband to take your little darling off your hands for a while, it helps to have a diaper bag that is not hot pink and covered in large, blooming flowers. Depending on whom you will allow to watch your baby, this is a bag that is likely to end up on the shoulder of many different family members and some of your close friends. Dad and Grandpa will appreciate your thoughtfulness when selecting a neutral diaper bag.

The best things to look for in a diaper bag will be pockets, changing pad, zippered removable washable pocket, adjustable and interchangeable straps, and durable material. When selecting a diaper bag, be sure to check out all the pockets and storage areas. You will want to be sure you have enough room for a few bottles, diapers, wipes, diaper rash cream, pacifier (if your baby uses one), change of clothes, formula, baby food, utensils, and snacks. Having a good variety of pockets and sizes of pockets will help you keep your diaper bag organized, which will be a lifesaver when you end up having to change a diaper on a moving bus or in a tiny public rest room.

Save money buy purchasing a diaper bag that has a changing pad included.

After thoroughly checking out how many pockets your candidates have, you will want to purchase a diaper bag with a changing pad included. This will come in handy any time you have to change a diaper. The truth is, you will never know when your only diaper changing option will be on your mom's pure white carpet or in the gas station rest room that is crawling with every germ imaginable. Most diaper bags that come with a changing pad will have a convenient way of storing it in the diaper bag. Be sure it is as convenient to access as it is to store. The zippered removable washable pocket will come in handy for storing items that may leak, such as a bottle, or items you do not want stinking up the other contents of your diaper bag, such as a dirty diaper, when there is no trash container available. Use the zippered pocket for one or the other but not both.

There have been many occasions when I have had no choice but to change a smelly diaper using the back seat or trunk of my car as the changing table. Often, when this is the case, there is also no trash receptacle nearby and, not wanting to litter, I have carried a stinky diaper around in my car until finding a convenient place to toss it away. This becomes a smelly problem if you need to park your car somewhere in the sunshine. If there is still no place to deposit the used diaper, you will return to a rather nauseating aroma in your car. Having a zippered pocket in your diaper bag that seals well will save you stinky car rides and prevent that diaper from rolling under a seat where it may later be discovered only when its smell is so assaulting that you cannot drive properly.

Adjustable and interchangeable straps on a diaper bag are a must-have. Most moms will not mind carrying a diaper bag around much like a purse; however, there are times when you will have your hands full and even balancing a strap on one shoulder will seem impossible. Not to mention, most men do not want to be seen throwing any bag over one shoulder and toting it around like a purse, no matter how obvious it is that it is a diaper bag.

Quick TIP

Having the ability to easily change your diaper bag from an over-the-shoulder-style bag to a backpack-style bag is a small consideration but a good idea. It helps balance your load and frees your hands.

Try to balance a heavy object in the crook of your elbow while holding a purse or bag full of baby needs on your opposite shoulder. You will find that more often than not, the bag on your shoulder will constantly slip down so you are walking uncomfortably and off balance. This is what will happen while you are carrying your baby around and trying to balance a diaper bag on the other shoulder. Being able to properly secure the bag over both your shoulders is not only more comfortable, but also better for your posture and back.

Finally, you will want to be sure your new diaper bag is made of material that will withstand the daily punishment you will be subjecting it to. Diaper bags are used every day and usually more than once a day. Every time you leave your home with your child, you will likely have your diaper bag in tow. It will accompany you on walks in the park, hikes in the mountains, trips to every store and restaurant you frequent, and to all your relatives' and friends' homes. Aside from the many journeys your diaper bag will make, you will also subject it to a number of inhumane abuses. It will be spilled on, stepped on, and thrown carelessly about, and your baby will eventually be old enough to invade the contents on a regular basis whenever it is within his reach. This means he will chew on it, drool on it, and drag it along behind him as he crawls around.

Because of all these abuses that I never imagined when I purchased my diaper bag, I bought the most delicate and silky soft diaper bag I found. I thought that this would be rather fitting for the darling little angel of a girl I was going to have. However, it took only three months for my first diaper bag to literally fall apart at the seams. Our child was not even old enough to abuse the beautiful bag yet. The second diaper bag I purchased was made of a thick canvas material, it was khaki in color (so my husband was not embarrassed to take it out of the house), could be used as a purse or backpack, had a stowaway compartment for the changing pad that came with the bag, and had a removable, washable, dirty-diaper pocket. This was the bag I needed; it worked, and I still use it now that our daughter is nearly three years old. The brand was Eddie Bauer; unfortunately, the same exact one is no longer available, but any diaper bag that has most of these essential properties will ultimately work for you. Do not forget to try the bag on and check all the zippers, snaps, buttons, straps, and Velcro to be sure it all works and is easy to use.

Diaper Pail

If you choose to use disposable diapers, you will likely want an airtight way to dispose of the many stinky diapers your new little bundle of joy will create for you. There are ways to keep stinky diaper smells out of your home without purchasing a diaper pail. The most popular free diaper disposal system is to simply throw dirty diapers directly into the outside trash. This works well during the daytime when you can step outside and work on your three-point shot. However, most babies do not follow a schedule when it comes to diapers that are more than wet; yes, babies poop at night. The last thing you will want to do in the middle of the night is wander outdoors to throw dirty diapers into the trash. You will want to spend as little time awake at night as you must, so having a diaper pail can come in handy. Leaving those dirty diapers around, even the ones that are only wet, can create quite an aroma in whatever room you dispose of them.

I have a few friends that bypassed buying a diaper pail and instead decided that they would bag all dirty diapers in Ziploc® baggies. This is a good idea if you want to keep the smell contained; however, I think you will spend nearly three times the money purchasing the baggies as you will in simply purchasing a diaper pail that does not require refills. When selecting a diaper pail, there are two styles to choose from: the kind that requires specific bags that lock smells in and the kind that can use any type of bag. You will want to look for the latter. There is one specific diaper pail that is rated wonderfully among many parents: the Diaper Champ. The Diaper Champ can be found at Babies "R" Us, Wal-Mart, Target, and other popular stores that carry baby items. This diaper pail is commonly found priced around $30 and can be found for less at secondhand stores. It rates among the top choices because it accepts any type of plastic bag, can be used for disposable or cloth diapers, is easy to clean, has a one-hand flip handle, and contains odors. This is by far one of the best diaper pails you can purchase.

The Diaper Genie disposal system often comes in a close second and is worth the money if you can find one used at a secondhand store. New, the Diaper Genie will cost between $18 and $24; one can usually be found used for $10 to $12. The price of this diaper pail is a bit less, but you will have to add the cost of purchasing refill bags that are specifically made for the Diaper Genie. This diaper pail will hold only up to 30 dirty diapers, making the need to change the bag a common occurrence and which is not a simple task. The Diaper Genie is priced less, but depending on how much effort you want to put into changing the bags and figuring out the refills, it might be more worth the extra $10 to purchase the more convenient Diaper

Champ. Likewise, the Diaper Genie can be found at many of the same stores as the Diaper Champ. Look at them both and compare the functionality to make an educated decision about which will be right for you.

In the end, diapering is a long and exhausting process of decisions that will affect the next three to four years of your life. None of the decisions you will make about diapering will be irreversible, though. No matter what decisions you make, you can always return to the decision-making process if one of your options is not working well for you or your infant. It is hard to predict what the best decisions will be. Changing your mind later might cost you some extra money, but if the need is great enough, changing your mind can be done. Just try to make the best decision you can the first time around.

Baby Carriers

Although it might not sound like a necessity, finding a way to carry your baby around with your other than in your arms can be a challenge for many parents. Some babies like to be held quite often, while others prefer to have more personal space. If your baby is one that does not prefer to be held and can quietly entertain herself while sitting in a bouncy seat or nestled into a safe cove of the couch, then you might want to consider yourself lucky. If your baby is a cuddle bug and wants to be held often, this can be cumbersome, time consuming, and exhausting. It is important to know as a future parent that you will love to hold your baby, but there will be times when putting her down for a bit will sound like a little slice of heaven. Purchasing a baby carrier that will allow you to hold your baby close to you while still accomplishing tasks that need to be done can be a necessity for some parents.

There are a few different types of slings and baby carriers that are useful and will allow you to hold your baby close while still having both of your hands and arms free. One of the most popular is the Baby Bjorn. This carrier is a type of backpack that is worn on the front of your chest. It not only keeps your baby close, but is also comfortable enough for your baby to sleep in or simply stay near Mom while watching all you do. The Baby Bjorn can be used for walks, shopping, and holding your baby while you accomplish chores around your home. The Baby Bjorn is also comfortable for the adult wearing it. It provides necessary support for your back and shoulders and does not require you to hold your baby on your hip while you try to do things one-handed. Another good aspect of this infant carrier is that your baby can ride facing front or facing you, and it has the option of providing head support for babies that cannot yet hold up their own head.

Purchasing gently used baby carriers can save you money. However, be sure to research the model number and check for recalls. You may also want to "try before you buy" to see what type of carrier you prefer. Borrow a friend's or ask at the store.

Case Study: Lori Kindell

Lori Kindell, mother of three daughters ages five years, three years, and three months old, is a huge fan of the Baby Bjorn. In her experience, it has been a wonderful help with all three of her daughters.

Lori received several Baby Bjorns as hand-me-downs from friends, and although they are older models of the carrier, she has still used them daily and likely would have purchased one if she had not received them from friends.

"Since my oldest daughter, Juliana, would not lie down to nap as an infant and wanted to be with me constantly, I used the Baby Bjorn very frequently. I used it to carry her during most outings, when she was fussy and in need of a nap during the day, while cooking dinner, when going for walks, and for many other occasions. I also used it for my middle daughter, Kaelyn, and I currently use it for my newborn, Evie, during outings as well as for some naps."

Another item that Lori has found very useful for her most recent baby, Evie, is the Miracle Blanket. Lori purchased her Miracle Blanket online for approximately $30 and loves the comfort and effective swaddle it ensures for Evie.

"The Miracle Blanket ensures an effective swaddle every time. Since it is lightweight, it is also perfect for every temperature." Because Evie will not sleep on her back unless she is swaddled, the Miracle Blanket has been used at bedtime and during naps. It gives her comfort and a good resting period, and it gives Lori peace of mind that she may have a few minutes to herself during her baby's nap.

When shopping for her newborn daughter, Lori most often looked to Babies "R" Us or Target for the everyday, useful items she would need and online for specific or unusual items so she could compare prices. Her first concern when shopping for baby products is quality, closely followed by convenience.

When I asked Lori for a piece of motherly advice to share, she gave me a few pieces of knowledge that could come only from an experienced mother of more than one child.

"Children do not come with instruction manuals. They are all incredibly different. What works wonderfully for one may not necessarily work for another. As a parent, you need to be flexible and creative. Parenting books are incredibly helpful, but at the same time, they will never give you all the answers you crave. Only experience through trial and error with individual children can do that.

"Everything is a phase when it comes to children. Just when you think you may lose your mind due to some horrid behavioral issue, it will lessen in frequency and intensity and you will breathe a sigh of relief. However, soon after, a new phase that may be equally or even more challenging to deal with will begin. But take heart... Everything is a phase, and remember that this too shall pass."

Other types of infant carriers include slings and other variations of the backpack-style carrier that can be worn on the front of your chest, such as the Snuggly, which is lower in price but does not provide as much head support for infants still mastering the art of holding up their own head. Infant slings are carriers that are worn across the front or side of your body and allow your baby to lie in the folds of soft and comfortable material that adjusts to their posture and cradles them comfortably against your body. Many parents like the way slings fit to their body as well as to their baby's body; however, it is difficult to do some tasks, as the baby is not held as closely and tightly to your body as in the Baby Bjorn. A baby sling is good for walks and outings, such as shopping. It can also be comfortable for you and your infant around the home if you simply want to relax without having to hold your baby in your arms constantly.

No matter which type of carrier you feel will work best for you and your baby, it is a good idea to try them out at the store. Both types of carriers are comfortable for infants; the main concern is which is most useful and comfortable for you. The Baby Bjorn is a good item; however, it is costly, ranging from $80 to $125, depending on the style and where you purchase it. You can find good deals on Baby Bjorns at secondhand shops and garage sales; just try the carrier out to be sure it is in good working condition. Check all the straps, buckles, and buttons for safety, and trust your instincts. Slings are a bit more affordable, ranging from $25 to $80, and can also be purchased used; however, they are a bit harder to find, as they are much easier to wear out.

Clothing

Dressing our daughter was one of my favorite activities. After she came home from the hospital, I spent countless hours changing her from one adorable outfit to another. If a spot appeared on whatever she was wearing, I was quick to discard that piece of apparel in the dirty laundry basket and find my next favorite dress or outfit to squeeze her little body into. No matter how fun it was to dress our daughter up every chance I received, when I have our next child, I will not go to such great lengths to create so much laundry for myself. However cute our daughter may have looked in all the amazing outfits we received as gifts and the few that I purchased for her, she would have been much happier just spending the time staring at the ceiling fan.

Clothing is a tricky subject. All the styles and fun apparel items available will be tempting you for the nine months that you are waiting for your baby's arrival. Plus, there are the massive amounts of clothing you will likely receive at your baby shower, if you have one. What makes baby clothing so tricky? First, you will want to buy more clothes than you will need. Second, all baby outfits have a way of looking gorgeous on the rack, but they might not agree with your baby as much as they do the hanger they are on. Third, babies will grow quicker than you can clothe them, and you might find yourself wondering what you were thinking purchasing all these items.

When buying baby clothes, be sure to wait until after your baby shower to purchase most items. Some of the clothing that you will want or need you can purchase before your shower and as your budget allows, but do not get carried away. Also, babies grow fast, and purchasing secondhand clothes for your baby does not reflect any type of neglect. Your baby will not care whether her clothes are new, used, or free. Spending $40 on a new baby outfit can seem excessive when you stop to consider that she may be in that size for only three months. Would you buy yourself a pair of jeans for $40 if you knew, without a doubt, that you would be able to wear them for only three months? Spending larger amounts of money on special items such as Christmas dress-up clothes and outfits for pictures and other special occasions might be fine, but be sure that your budget will allow it. Besides, some of the cutest baby photos are taken when they are wearing nothing but a diaper.

Secondhand stores and eBay are good resources for holiday clothing or fancy dresses. Most of these items are worn for only a short time and may be in good condition.

For now, you should focus on the clothing you will need when your baby comes home from the hospital, which you read about in Chapter 2. To refresh your memory, you will be best prepared to have at least:

- Ten onesies
- Seven shirts
- Seven pairs of socks
- Three to four sleepers
- Seven pants
- One warm hat

Often the hospital will provide you with a hat, giving you two total.

If you have just these items when you come home from delivering your baby, you will have enough clothing to carry you through each week without having to do excess laundry every night. The approximate cost for the items listed above will depend on where you shop but will likely fall in the range of $300 to $400. It is convenient to have more than this, especially in sleepers, socks, and onesies, as these are the items you will use the most. Our daughter was born in the winter months, and once my constant need to change her clothing had subsided, she lived mainly in her sleepers and onesies. These kept her warm and comfortable throughout the day and night. I discovered it was necessary to dress her in day clothes only when we were leaving the house, which, in the first few months of her life, was not often.

Young infants are most comfortable in sleepers and onsies. If you receive many outfits at your shower in small sizes, you may want to exchange them for larger sizes when the baby would use them more.

Helpful Hints: What Not to Buy

Now you need to know what to watch out for and what not to buy. Baby clothes look good no matter what when they are elegantly displayed in the various different shops and baby stores that you will likely be perusing. I have a few tips that would have been helpful to know before our baby was born.

The first of these helpful hints is that name brands are not important. Your baby will not care, and neither should you; purchasing expensive clothing that will be worn for only a few months — and more likely, only a few days out of those months — is somewhat ridiculous.

However, if you must purchase name-brand clothing, the best way to get it at a semi-affordable price will be to shop secondhand, end-of-season sales, and at outlet stores. Secondhand and end-of-season sales will be the most affordable. Outlet stores will have good prices — and even better ones when they are having a sale.

The second hint that I wish I had known was how to discover comfort for my baby. Nearly all baby clothing is made of soft materials, and so I assumed that it would all be comfortable for our baby. This is not true.

Quick TIP

Think comfort! The types of clothing that I will avoid with our next child will be collared shirts or dresses, corduroy and other coarse materials, anything with elastic around the arms and legs, and tight-fitting clothing.

Collared shirts and dresses can seem adorable; however, the collars that are large and do not lay correctly after washing can become a nuisance. I did not and will not iron baby clothes. The iron is often bigger than the outfit you are trying to press, and it seems pointless to iron something that will be worn only a few hours at the most before it is covered in spit-up or mushy Cheerios® cereal. Collars that do not lay correctly get in the way, disrupt feeding, irritate your infant, and — since clothing with collars usually zip or button at the top of the neck — they can be too tight for more roundish babies.

Corduroy and other coarse materials are uncomfortable for most babies. These types of material cause chaffing and irritation of the soft, sensitive skin most babies have. Other reasons that I would suggest not purchasing stiff or coarse materials — this includes lace, different types of tulle, and stiff underskirts — is that it is difficult for your baby to move about freely in them. Many of these types of materials are restrictive, and as your baby's brain develops more with every physical movement he makes, it is important to give him the ability to move about as freely as possible.

Elastic bands and tight-fitting or binding clothing are found in an assortment of baby apparel, and although these styles often serve a purpose of making clothing fit better, adding to the style of the clothing, or helping to trap body heat within the clothing, they can also hinder your baby's comfort. Before your baby is born, you will not know whether you will have a round baby or a long, thin baby. Elastic bands around the wrists and legs of many types of baby clothing might not affect thinner babies, but they can be uncomfortable and even cut off circulation if the clothing does not fit properly in the areas where the elastic bands are located. Another reason this type of clothing can be uncomfortable is most babies will go through times of thinness and chunkiness month to month. Elastic can irritate your infant and often be bothersome enough to cause your baby to cry and can be a hard problem to locate unless you are aware of it.

A close friend of mine who has the cutest little ball of a baby experienced this firsthand. Her daughter was having a hard time sleeping one night and seemed to be uncomfortable and irritable. When your baby is unhappy, the first things you will look to are often the big things — is she hungry, ill, or gassy; does she have a dirty diaper; or is she tired? The last thing that occurred to my friend was that her pajamas were uncomfortable; it was not until my friend was frustrated and stripped her daughter down that she noticed subtle imprints from the elastic on the wrists of her baby. Once the brand-new, never-before-worn pajamas were removed and she was dressed in a more comfortable pair of pajamas, the little girl went right to sleep.

What Works Best in Baby Clothing

Knowing how much you can spend and what you are not looking for narrows the field of baby apparel a little; however, there is still a ton of baby clothing out there that you might not need or want. Knowing what works best for most babies in clothing will cut your search time in half and save you many return trips to the store to exchange items or spend more money that can be saved if you know what you are looking for in the first place. Baby clothing should pass these standards: soft, comfortable, affordable, and useful. These are going to be the top concerns for you and your infant. The easiest way to stick to these four basics is to purchase clothing that is made of cotton or fleece and that is plain.

Quick
TIP

Clothing with many decorations that have been attached can be uncomfortable because of the stitching that must be used to attach all the bells and whistles.

Prints are a good way to have clothing that is cute but also avoid the extra stitching and other articles that can be bothersome to you and your baby.

In the list of clothing that you will want to have ready when your infant arrives home, onesies and socks are going to be the easiest to pick out. They may be inexpensive and can be purchased separately or in multipacks. Most onesies are made of soft cotton and have prints or catchy sayings or come in solid colors. The prices of onesie packages will depend on how many onesies are in the multipack and can range from $9 to $18. Baby socks are also usually made of cotton and come in multipacks of different colors or white, and depending on the number of socks inside, will range from $7 to $12. The most difficult decisions you will make when purchasing onesies and socks for your infant will be what color and what size. Size is easy; look for the age of your baby on the package.

Pajamas for your infant come in all shapes and sizes, with snaps or zippers, and in gowns, footed, sacks, wraps, and many other styles. The most popular parent- and infant-friendly pajamas are sleep gowns and sleep sacks. An infant sleep gown will be similar to a girl's nightgown, with the exception of having an elastic band around the bottom hem of the gown. This helps to keep baby's feet tucked neatly inside, warm and cozy. Sleep gowns are for girls or boys and will come in patterns that are popular for both sexes.

The main attraction of a sleep gown is that it is easy to change your baby's diaper when he or she wears one to bed — or even all day long.

You do not have to mess with any zippers or snaps in the middle of the night; you simply pull the gown up to expose baby's legs and bottom, change the diaper, and then pull the gown back down. Sleep gowns are a good buy and come in various multipacks of two or more and will cost from $10 to $20. Many parents love the sleep gown. The only negative to a sleep gown is that because the bottom does not fasten shut, if you live in a climate of cooler nights or your baby is born in the winter months, they are not as warm as sleep sacks.

Infant sleep sacks are the best invention ever, in my opinion. Our daughter lived in these little contraptions. Picture a sleeping bag with arms and a hole for your baby's head. Infant sleep sacks are the same idea as a sleep gown with a warmer twist. Most sleep sacks will zip up to the neck and have one snap that secures the zipper in place so a wiggly baby cannot unknowingly work the zipper down in her sleep or while she plays. The zipper is always fastened at the bottom of the sack so you do not have to spend time trying to line it up as you do on your coat. Sleep sacks are good for winter months or cooler climates; they keep your baby warm by fully encasing the body heat your baby produces, keep him from flailing about in his sleep and waking himself up, and are soft and warm. They come in many cute designs and are reasonably priced. Many department stores will offer three-packs of these sleepers, ranging from $15 to $23. You can also search online auctions, secondhand stores, garage sales, and friends for less-expensive options.

Footed pajamas are good as well, especially once your baby starts to crawl and roll around. They work fine while baby is not crawling, but they do not swaddle the baby in any way, so if you have a restless sleeper, you may need to swaddle her with a blanket to keep her from waking herself. Footed pajamas usually have zippers or snaps that keep them closed up tight for warmth. One extra positive about footed pajamas for your infant is that if you are going to be taking your sleeping baby in the car, you can still fasten his infant seat safety restraints; this is hard to do comfortably for your baby with a sleep sack. Footed pajamas can be found in any baby store that sells baby clothing and often come in three-packs or more, ranging from $12 to $23.

Finally, you will need to keep your baby's tiny head warm. Your baby has been used to a warm environment for the last nine months, and keeping her head warm will keep your baby healthy and less likely to catch a cold or other illnesses. Most newborn babies do not have the strength or coordination to pull a good fitting hat off, so your choices are wide open. When looking for a hat, think of what is comfortable to wear since this will be a new experience for your  baby. You can purchase a hat that comes with a place to tie beneath the chin, but in the first two months of life, this is not necessary as long as the hat is good and snug on your baby's head. Most hospitals will send you home with one hat for your baby, which means there is no need to purchase more than one hat to give you a total of two.

Having two hats is convenient, just like anything else; when one is dirty, you will have a spare.

Along with these clothing items you will likely be purchasing, you will want to keep your baby's clothes clean. Most clothing should be washed before you dress your infant in it, and for the first laundering of clothes, Dreft is a good product. Dreft is a baby laundry detergent that is gentle for baby's sensitive skin but strong enough to remove excess dyes and other irritants from clothing, blankets, pillow covers, linens, and all other materials that might end up near your baby's skin. After the first laundering of your baby's clothing, you can use a less-expensive brand of detergent, unless you find that your baby has sensitive skin, in which case you might want to continue using the baby detergent; it is not much more expensive than average detergents and might be worth the few extra dollars if your baby is comfortable and happy.

Aside from cleaning your baby's clothing with a detergent, you might consider how you will get the mashed carrots out of his clothing every other day. Although it is not a necessity, it is a money saver to keep your baby's clothing in respectable condition. Not only will you be able to use clothing kept in good condition for other children if you should choose to have them, you can also sell it at consignment shops when you have decided that your family is complete and will no longer have a use for it.

A good stain remover is always good to have on hand, as you will find that your baby will not know or care how much you spend on her clothing.

Case Study: Andrea Walsh

Montessori School of Central Marin
Andrea Walsh, Lead Teacher

Andrea Walsh is the lead teacher at a California Montessori school and the mother of one adorable daughter.

Her experience with children has grown throughout her career and her own experience of being a mother. Andrea offers some great hints for keeping those cute little clothes clean throughout the months that your baby will be wearing them. When asked what her most parent-friendly product was, she said that the powder form of Oxyclean when used with a hot tub of water and soaked overnight will take anything out. I tested out her recipe for gleaming whites and was even able to get a three-month-old stain of chocolate milk out of one of my daughter's white shirts. It works.

"Oxyclean is a clothes saver. For any stain, place clothing item in a washtub full of hot water with one scoop of Oxyclean, soak the clothing in the Oxyclean water overnight, and wash it in the morning. It takes out everything from red wine to baby poop."

Andrea also offered some heartfelt advice about making that decision to stay home with your new baby or return to work.

When asked what Andrea would change about the first year of her daughter's life, she said, "I would not have worked. I only worked part time, but I feel I missed some of the important things. I did take some time off, but it was not enough."

In light of this, she also offered, "Not everything has to be perfect. It is better to have fun and make memories rather than be the 'perfect mom.' Remember your child's age, as my sister-in-law reminded me — no matter how smart your child is, she is still only one, two, or three years old."

There are many other items that you will see in the stores often that you will want to purchase for your baby. You may accumulate a large quantity of clothing from friends and family, as well as from your baby shower. Most moms who were asked in the Case Studies that you will find throughout this book mentioned that the present most given to them was baby clothing, so do not fret that your baby will have nothing to wear. Covering the basics will give you plenty of clothing for a week's worth of wear, even if you receive nothing in the way of clothing as gifts.

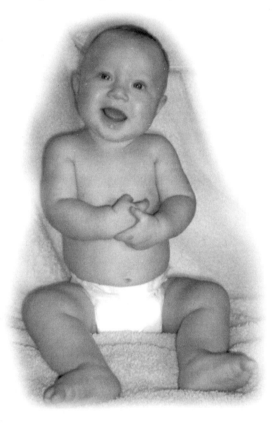

Quick
TIP

Babies cannot read labels and do not care what they wear!

Keeping Baby
Clean and Healthy

Keeping your infant clean and healthy will be two of your main concerns once you gaze into those little eyes and fall in love with him or her. When I was pregnant, I knew in the back of my mind that these would be some of my main tasks in life once I became a mother. Though it was not until she was here and she seemed much more real that I started to get worried about how to keep our baby clean, healthy, and safe. When you see babies, the last thing that occurs to most people is how much trouble an infant can unknowingly get into. The fact is that even though your baby may not realize what he is doing, many times it can be potentially dangerous, unhealthy, or just dirty. Learning how to avoid many messy and unhealthy disasters will be a good way to start out parenthood; looking back, there are so many different things I know now that I wish I had been aware of before our daughter was born. Throughout this chapter, I will share many hints and habits that will help you to keep your baby clean and healthy as well as the costs and where to find the items you will need on a daily basis.

Babies are amazing. They are cute, some are snuggly, and you will always hear about how wonderful they smell. Well, it did not take me long as a new mother to figure out that babies do not always smell wonderful. And I am not just referring to the three-times-daily dirty diaper; babies do a variety of things that will cause not-so-pleasant aromas. Babies need baths so they do not stink. Not only do most babies have a million rolls for dirt, grime, and goo to get stuck in, they are constantly spitting up and drooling something all over themselves. I certainly do not mean to take the cute factor away from your future infant. I am sure you want every person who holds your baby to croon about how good she smells and looks; you certainly do not want to hear that she stinks and looks as if she could use a good scrubbing.

Keeping Baby Clean

Keeping your baby clean will be a continual habit, and you will need a few items to do so properly. The main things for keeping your baby clean that you will want to have on hand when your baby arrives home will include shampoo, baby soap, towels, washcloths, a scalp brush, a place to wash your baby, baby lotion, nail clippers, and infant cotton swabs. All these items are essential for keeping your baby smelling good and looking as clean and cute as she possibly can.

Bathing your baby often brings about visual pictures of a cute little naked baby happily playing with bubbles and cooing at you while you scrub up all his little toes and fingers. The truth is that bathing infants is difficult; they wiggle, squirm, and cry; they are slippery, and most do not enjoy bath time, as it is often cold and a bit stressful for mom, dad, and baby. Infants are not at a stage of life in which bath time is a joyful, fun-filled experience. Because they do not yet know how to play or enjoy their time in a bathtub, they will often not be happy for the bath you have prepared for them. The good news is, bath time for an infant is necessary only once or twice a week. Babies that are less than six months old do not spend a whole lot of time getting dirty. Most of what you will need to wash off of your baby will be breast milk or formula, spit-up and drool and to keep their bottoms nice and clean; also pay close attention to cleaning in all those cute little baby rolls and behind the ears. Babies under six months old will not be rummaging through sandboxes, painting, gluing, making mud pies, or any of the other messy or dirty activities that are often associated with children. Those are later.

Bath time for an infant will require several things — a place to wash your baby, shampoo, a washcloth, and baby body wash. You will want to have a soft towel to dry and warm your infant up in immediately after his bath, as infants lose body heat much quicker than older children and adults.

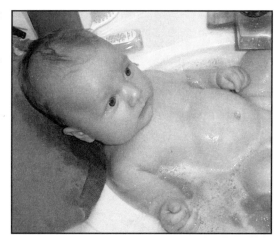

Finding a safe place to bathe your infant that is comfortable for both you and your baby will be your first quest. You will have a wiggly baby that is wet and slippery and who cannot hold her head up without your help. There are several different types of baby bathtubs that are good for washing your baby. Many moms and dads all over the world love them, and many other parents have purchased them and never used them. We purchased one for $35; I used it three times and then sold it at a garage sale for $3. So how do you know if you need one or not?

 Wait until your baby arrives and determine whether he enjoys bath time. If you have a baby that is constantly wiggling and attempting to avoid the bath all together, you might find it easier to wash him in the sink or get into your bathtub with him and hold him while you bathe him.

If you have a baby that enjoys bath time, lies somewhat still while you bathe her, and is not constantly trying to escape, a baby bathtub may be useful. The best infant bathtub for the best price is the Safety 1st Space Saver Fold up Tub. This is a good product that stores easily, fills easily, fits in the sink, dries quickly, holds baby as well as any other tub, and seems comfortable for most infants. It can be found at most department stores and baby superstores for only $10. There are other, more expensive baby bathtubs that do many of the same things as the Safety 1st bathtub. Most of the more expensive bathtubs do not fold up for storage, and fitting many into your sink can be difficult or unsafe. Be sure to check the product information of your baby bathtub if you intend to use it in the sink to be sure it is made for that use.

One of the main points to remember when looking at baby bathtubs is that you should not spend a large amount of money on them. Your infant will be using them for only six to seven months, and then he will be sitting on his own and wanting to have more space to explore in the bath. Confining him to a small tub when he is ready for the larger bathtub you have in your home can often make bath time an unpleasant experience for you both.

Once you have your baby outfitted with a bathtub that works well for you both, you will need washcloths, towels, shampoo, and some baby body soap. Washcloths and towels are easy if you are on a tight budget and do not have many pennies to spare. Use the same ones that you use. There is no set rule for washcloths and towels. The ones that are in your closet already may be just fine for your baby. As long as you have one or two soft washcloths that will not irritate your baby's skin, there is no need to purchase special baby washcloths. The story is the same for towels, if you have at least two soft towels in your home that are big enough to wrap your infant up in to keep her warm in the few moments between getting her out of the bath and dressed.

The hooded baby towels are nice to have but not a necessity if you are on a tight budget. This is a type of towel that is smaller than your average adult towel and comes with one hooded corner so you can dry your infant's hair and head while having her all wrapped up in the rest of the towel. They often come paired with matching washcloths and can range in price from $9 to $30, depending on where you shop for them. You can also find these items at garage sales and secondhand stores at much better prices, more in the area of $4 to $6.

Baby shampoo and baby body soap are another easy purchase. You can find these items in any department store, grocery store, or baby superstore. Baby shampoo is suggested for washing your baby's hair and scalp because it is gentle, and most are made to not sting if they get into your infant's eyes. The same can be said for baby body wash. It is made to be gentle on your baby's skin, and most are not fragranced or dyed. Baby body wash is often easier to use than a bar of soap, as there is less to hold on to and manage while also holding on to your wiggling infant in the tub. Baby shampoo and body soap will last you a long time. Most of these products, such as Johnson and Johnson's, are sold in larger bottles ranging from 18 to 28 ounces and cost between $3 and $6, depending on the brand and type of shampoo or body soap.

There are specialty brands that you can also purchase that will be slightly higher in price; some natural products will cost even more, and this may be worth it to you, depending on your values and budget. Burt's Bees is a popular brand of natural products that offers one-step wash formulas for your infant. The baby shampoo and wash can be used on baby from head to toe and are composed of completely natural ingredients. Burt's Bees products can be found online at **www.burtsbees.com** and in many different department and natural-product specialty stores; a 12-ounce bottle of the shampoo and body wash can be found for less than $10 and leaves your baby smelling like a little coconut.

In the first year I had our daughter, we bathed her two to three times a week, and it took me nearly a year to make it through our first bottle of baby body soap. Shampoo was a different story, but we had a baby with a full head of hair, and she was constantly getting things in her hair, which meant we washed it more than her body.

Other baby care items that will likely go right along with bath time or be best kept in the bathroom will include baby lotion ($3 to $5), baby Q-tip® cotton swabs ($1.50 to $2), infant fingernail clippers ($3 to $5), a comb or brush ($2 to $5), and a scalp brush (free to $4). Many of these items are self-explanatory, even if you have never been a parent before. It is nice to keep these items in your baby's bathroom because these are the many things that can easily be forgotten on a daily, sleep-deprived basis. Taking care of your infant's nails, hair, and skin will be easily done at bath time once or twice a week. If you can get into this habit early, it will save you time and stress later as your infant grows and becomes more active, leaving less time for nail, hair, and skin care.

After our daughter was born, it seemed that I was consistently forgetting to do little things like clean out her ears, clip her nails, and moisturize her skin with baby lotion. I soon discovered that making routines was the best way to keep track of these little things, especially while functioning on only three to five hours of sleep. Training myself to clip our daughter's nails before bath helped me to remember to do this twice a week, which was a good thing, as our little girl was a face scratcher. Both her face and mine at times showed the telltale signs of sharp, unclipped little baby nails. After I clipped her nails, my husband and I would give her a bath — bathing a child together makes things much easier when you have a baby who does not want anything to do with the bathtub. During her bath, we used a soft-bristle plastic brush, often referred to as a scalp brush, with a small dab of baby shampoo on it to clean her hair and scalp; this type of brush will help to remove any dry skin or cradle cap, as well as thoroughly clean your infant's scalp and hair when used with baby shampoo. Most hospitals will give you a child's soft plastic hospital brush, which is perfect for cleaning your infant's body and scalp with soap or shampoo. If your hospital or place of delivery does not supply you with one of these infant brushes, you can find them at most baby specialty stores and superstores for $2 to $4.

Once her bath was done, I would gently clean our baby's ears with a cotton swab and brush her fine baby hair with a small, soft comb. This is also a good time to take care of any medical necessities in the first weeks that your baby is home from the hospital or place of delivery. All babies will need to have their bellybutton attended to, which is easy — just a quick wipe with an alcohol-soaked cotton swab. You should do this daily, and keeping the alcohol bottle out on the bathroom counter will be a good reminder for you. If you have a boy and you have decided to have him circumcised, you will also need to attend to keeping his penis clean and protected. Cleaning your baby's circumcision should be done three times a day, and only the use of warm water is necessary.

When most moms and dads think of bath time for their children, there is often a thought of bath time toys. For the first three to four months of your child's life, bath toys will not be necessary. Most babies are not interested in bath time at this age. Once your baby can sit up and effectively grasp toys and cups, you will want to find some bath toys for him. When we decided our little one was ready for her first bath playtime, I went shopping downstairs in our kitchen cabinets and found a variety of plastic cups and strainers that she was more than pleased with. If you insist on having store-bought toys for your infant's bath time or find that he wants to play and spend time in the water, I would suggest using the dollar store or an inexpensive department store to look for bath toys. Many of the baby stores are significantly overpriced in this area, and you can find more interesting items that are colorful and float at many different stores, such as Wal-Mart and Big Lots.

Keeping Baby Healthy

Keeping your infant healthy often amounts to the simple task of being cognizant of what your baby is trying to tell you each day. The main proponents of keeping your new infant healthy will be to keep her fed, adequately clothed, and clean. However, there are some items and products you should have around your home to keep both of you happy and comfortable.

First-Aid Kits and Thermometers

Among these items, the two most important will be a baby thermometer and a first-aid kit. It is likely that you will not need a first-aid kit until your little one is on the move, crawling or walking about and exploring her environment. Even though most parents do not need a first-aid kit in the first six to nine months, it should still be considered a necessity on your list of things to purchase. When shopping for a first-aid kit, be sure it contains a variety of small and large adhesive bandages, antibiotic ointment, burn-cooling gel, butterfly closures, eye pads, and first-aid tape.

These are all things you will likely not need right away, but if you do need them, it is a wonderful relief that you have them in a nearby cabinet. No house is ever fully babyproofed until you have a baby in it every day. All infants and babies are different. What will interest one will not interest another, and there is likely going to be something in your home that your baby will find a way to endanger himself with. You will never get all the proverbial bases covered. Racking yourself with guilt over them will not make you a better parent, but learning from them will make you wiser. In the next section of this chapter, you will learn about childproofing your home; for now, just be sure to purchase and store a first-aid kit in your home. A good first-aid kit containing all the items above may cost between $12 and $16. They can be found at any department store, baby superstore, and often, the grocery store.

A baby thermometer may be more used in your house than your first-aid kit. There are a variety of different types of thermometers you can choose from, but before picking out the most expensive thermometer on the shelf, you should consider how you will most likely take your baby's temperature. There are four popular ways to get an accurate temperature on your squirmy, wiggly baby.

The first and oldest way of getting an accurate temperature is rectally. Then there is the under-arm method, temporal (forehead) thermometers, and finally, the inside of your baby's ear. The first two temperature-taking methods will require the same type of thermometer, making it a safer bet.

When I became a mom, I never thought I would want to subject our darling little girl to a rectal temperature taking. However, when your baby is sick and will not hold still enough to take her temperature in her ear or under her arm, you do what you have to do. Our daughter hated to have her temperature taken under her arm and in her ear; she would not hold still even for the few seconds it was supposed to take to get an accurate reading. Taking her temperature rectally was the only way to get an accurate temperature for us; she seemed to not even notice I was taking her temperature and was just as demure as if I were simply changing her diaper. I was desperate to get an accurate temperature; our daughter was only two and a half months old and was burning up with a 104.8 fever. We were worried, and the hospital told us it was imperative that we obtain an accurate temperature before giving us any instruction as to what to do next.

Many of my friends hated that I took our daughter's temperature this way whenever it was needed, but when you stop to think about it, it is not a cruel thing to do. Babies do not talk; they cannot tell you if they are hot or cold, what hurts or does not feel good. They simply cry and suffer until you can successfully diagnose them. If your baby will lie still enough to take his temperature under his arm — granted you will likely have to hold him down — wonderful. One of my best friends had good luck with this method; the same is true for the ear thermometers and temporal thermometers. These are often more expensive and can be used only to take temperature in the ear or along the forehead respectively.

Thermometers will range in price depending on what type of thermometer you decide will be best for you and your infant. I suggest a rectal or underarm thermometer; not only are they significantly less expensive, but most can be used for either method of taking your infant's temperature. Most rectal and underarm thermometers are priced around $10. There are some that will range up to $14, but there is no need to purchase the more expensive ones unless you are brand specific or your pediatrician strongly suggests it. Ear and temporal thermometers are a bit more expensive, ranging from $18 to $55 and are less accurate than taking infant temperatures rectally. If you are wary of taking your infant's temperature rectally but would still like to be able to do so if necessary, I would suggest the Especially For Baby 3 Pack Digital Thermometer Set, which can be found in most department stores and baby stores for less than $15. This is a good set that offers you all ways of taking your baby's temperature. There is a rectal thermometer, a digital thermometer for older children and adults, and a pacifier thermometer. All three thermometers have an alarm that sounds when your baby's temperature is above 99.5 or 99.9 degrees Fahrenheit, and they all feature last temperature memory recall.

If you are having a hard time making the decision on thermometers, write down the thermometer names and brands that you are most interested in and call your pediatrician. If you have yet to select a pediatrician for your child, call a few pediatricians on the phone and get a nurse or doctor's opinion on which thermometer would be best for the age, size, and temperament of your child.

Fever Reducers

Once you are successful at finding out how high your baby's temperature is, you will likely need to know how to treat a temperature.

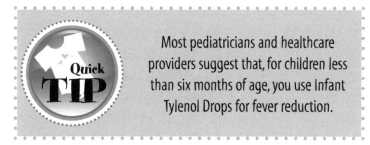

Quick TIP

Most pediatricians and healthcare providers suggest that, for children less than six months of age, you use Infant Tylenol Drops for fever reduction.

After your baby has passed the six-month mark of age, you can also use Infant Motrin for a fever reducer. Both of these medications are FDA approved and can help to lower your infant's temperature and relieve other symptoms experienced while ill. Infant Tylenol Drops can be found at most department stores, grocery stores, and baby superstores, and half an ounce will cost around $5 to $6. Infant's Motrin Drops can be found in all the same places and will cost, on average, $10 for a one-ounce bottle. These are items that you will not use too often, so purchasing one bottle should be sufficient. You should plan to have one bottle in your home soon after your baby is born because your baby can catch a common cold or other illnesses without warning. It is good to have a fever reducer available in case you are in immediate need of one at an inconvenient time. Also, getting a sick baby ready to leave the house can be difficult and result in an unpleasant drive to the store for both of you. When purchasing any type of medication for your baby, whether over-the-counter or not, always be sure to check with your pharmacist or pediatrician on dosage and frequency for your child's age and weight.

Humidifiers and Other White Noise

Other items that you will likely want to keep in your home might include a humidifier, fan, or air purifier. Any of these will serve the purpose of white noise for your baby to sleep soundly to. Depending on where you live, climate and humidity or the lack thereof will determine which of these, if any, you decide to purchase. Although it is true that your baby may be able to live without any of these things, having them in your infant's room will help him to sleep more soundly, are healthy for your baby's breathing, and help to drown out other household noises that can possibly wake your sleeping angel. Yes, there is a way that you can avoid tip-toeing around the house whenever your infant is sleeping. Humidifiers are recommended for those who live in dry regions or warmer climates. A cooling humidifier will add moisture and coolness to the air and will create white noise for your baby to sleep to. You can find a good humidifier priced from $15 to $32. We have used a humidifier for nearly three years and continue to use one, especially when our daughter must be tucked into bed long before any house guests may be leaving.

A fan will create the same white noise and cool the room your baby sleeps in; be sure to purchase a baby-safe fan that will not allow little fingers to come near the fan blades. A $5 fan will work just as well as a $20 fan; the only difference will likely be size and the amount of white noise it produces. Fans alone will dry the air in the room; if you live in a humid region, this might be a good way to cool and dry the air your baby is breathing on a small scale, though humidity is not a concern for your baby's health.

Air purifiers are good for families with allergies. If there is a history of severe allergies in your family, an air purifier might be a good idea. Many come with humidifiers built in and will also produce cooler air and white noise. Air purifiers on average are more expensive than humidifiers and fans alone, but the benefits might be worth the extra money if allergies are a likely problem for your child in the future. Most children do not have sensitivity to airborne allergens until they are two or three years old. A good-quality air purifier will start at $35. Some are expensive, and it is unlikely that you will need a large, expensive air purifier. If you are concerned about allergies affecting your infant, check with your pediatrician about further testing and care.

Tummy Troubles

All babies get sick, eventually, and most babies do not even have to contract a cold to not feel well. Newborn babies have spent the previous nine months in their mother's womb being fed only what their body needs in the way of nutrients directly from Mom's body. There has been no outside contact with what we often consider a baby's primary source of food, whether that is breast milk or formula; this is all new to your baby's digestive system. Many infants have a difficult time processing their food. Whether it is simply the shock of a new source of food or something Mom has eaten, there will likely be times when your baby will have tummy troubles. Babies have indigestion, heartburn, gas, acid reflux, and more often than not, some form of colic. There are several ways to combat many of these woes; the first and cheapest will be to simply watch your diet if you are breast-feeding. If you find that your infant is not feeling well or is extra gassy after feedings, you might want to talk to your doctor about cutting back on spicy foods, dairy, or certain proteins. Other ways to soothe your infant for free will include spending an adequate time after feedings to burp your baby.

Even if your baby is not big on burping, the constant pressure to the tummy and chest and the tapping on his back will help to burst or move any gas bubbles that might be hiding. One of the best ways to burp your baby is sitting him on your knee to burp him. Sit his bottom on your knee and place one hand on his tummy and chest area. Lean him forward so most of his weight is positioned against the hand on his chest and belly. While in this position, your baby should look like he is sitting sort of scrunched-up in the middle with his back slightly

rounded. Then firmly pat his back, just as you would do when you burp him on your shoulder. The extra pressure of your hand and his body weight, combined with the scrunched-up belly, will help to move the extra gas up to the surface and often give you a bigger burp faster than burping him on your shoulder.

If your doctor or pediatrician approves, you can also resort to some fairly inexpensive tummy trouble remedies, such as Mylicon or Gripe Water. Both of these products are suggested for helping to soothe a baby of various discomforts after feedings. These two products are close in price and are touted by moms and dads everywhere to be lifesavers when it comes to tummy troubles with their infants. Mylicon and Gripe Water can be found in many different baby specialty shops, grocery stores, and department stores and are priced from $7 to $9 for half an ounce. Only several drops are required when your baby shows symptoms of discomfort. The main difference between these two over-the-counter remedies is that Gripe Water is an all-natural supplement and Mylicon is not but is recommended by many pediatricians. If your baby's tummy troubles persist, you should speak with your pediatrician, as there might be forces more powerful than mild gas or indigestion at work.

Case Study: Armita Motallebi

Armita Motallebi is a stay-at-home mom with two spunky little children: her daughter is two years old, and her son is two months old. While Armita is trained in Early Childhood Education, she has chosen to stay home with her children throughout the first years of their precious lives.

When I asked Armita about the best advice she has received from another parent, she said, "If your child has colic, use Gripe Water. Moms of babies with colic should also drink peppermint water. Both of these together often will soothe the baby right away. I used both with both my kids."

The most stressful times of the day for Armita and her husband were the nights and not being able to get enough sleep.

"Our solution was to try to take it easy during the day (nap), or change shifts at night with your spouse."

Dental Hygiene

Dental hygiene starts before your baby has teeth. Most pediatricians will tell you that even though your baby has no teeth, she can still build up plaque and other bacteria on her gums. It is important to keep your baby's gums just as healthy as you will want to keep her teeth. Keeping your baby's gums healthy is easy and inexpensive. Toothbrushes for babies consist of a plastic or rubber-like thimble that has a small area of brush-like nubs that usually fit over your index finger. You will need to buy one of these infant toothbrushes as well as some fluoride-free toothpaste. Toothpaste for your infant will last a long time. You will use only a small amount, and brushing baby's gums and teeth once she has some will need to be done only once a day. This can also help while your baby is teething, as many infants find anything to do with their mouths soothing. Gently rubbing your baby's gums with the toothbrush and a small amount of toothpaste will clean away any plaque or bacteria and will help baby teeth to break through the gums when the time comes. Infant gum brushes or infant tooth brushes can be found in deluxe baby care kits or can often be purchased alone for less than $4. Infant fluoride-free toothpaste can be bought at any department store, some grocery stores, and most baby specialty stores for $3 to $5.

Protect Your Baby from Common Colds and Germs

Protecting your baby from colds and germs that are in the air everywhere you go might not occur to you every time you leave your home. There are some simple precautionary steps you can take to help keep your baby healthy. Most pediatricians do not want babies exposed to colds and flus until they are at least three months old, and if you can make it beyond six months, the better for you and your baby. It is inevitable that your baby will at some point catch a nasty bug. To prevent such bugs, viruses, and other means of illness from coming in contact with your baby, there are several things you can do and several products that can add to your success.

First and foremost, do not subject your baby to sickness knowingly. Babies' immune systems are not like adults' or even young children's. They have not had time to build up immunity to certain bugs that you might not catch as easily.

Quick TIP

Most doctors suggest not taking your baby out for the first two weeks of her life. Stay home and adjust to your new family and routines.

Staying home for the first two weeks not only keeps your baby well, but it also forces you to rest when you otherwise might be losing valuable downtime while your infant sleeps. Take advantage of those two weeks. You will have the next 18 years to show off your child to your family, neighbors, and friends. Do not take your baby to a sick person's house or allow someone with an illness, no matter how "good" they feel, to come and visit you and your baby. Mom's immune system will be working overtime to help heal her body from pregnancy, labor, and delivery, so there is a greater chance that she might not catch illnesses that her baby could much more easily contract.

While trying to prevent your baby from random germs that he might come in contact with, do not be shy. There will be a point in time when you are out and about with your baby and a complete stranger will want to peek beneath the blanket, pick him up, or touch his irresistible little hands and face. These are the worst things you can let a person do, whom you do not know. You have no idea when the last time they washed their hands was, what sicknesses they have had or been exposed to recently, or if they picked their nose in the last 15 minutes. Do not be afraid to tell a complete stranger or acquaintance that you are not comfortable with unfamiliar people holding your baby. There is a reason personal boundaries should be respected; if you were minding your own business and a stranger approached you and decided to randomly hold your hand and whisper baby talk in your face, you would probably be uncomfortable with this situation. Defend your baby's personal space.

Items you can purchase that will attribute to keeping your infant healthy and germ-free will include a convertible carrier cover and a shopping cart cover.

A convertible carrier cover fits tightly over your baby's carrier and usually has a zippered or Velcro face opening. These are good for cold climates, winter months, keeping baby asleep while you run errands, and protecting your baby from random strangers pinching her cheeks or breathing all over her while they get a closer look. The zippered or Velcro hole will allow air to move through the material, keep your baby in darkness, muffle outside noise, and keep in warmer air. These carrier covers can be found in many different designs and styles and are available online and at most baby superstores. The average cost, depending on the brand and quality of the cover, will range from $14 to $32. This is a good item to take to the hospital with you if you are due to deliver your baby in the winter months or months prone to precipitation, as it will also keep your baby dry as you make your way to the car.

Shopping cart covers you will not need right away, because in the first three to six months, you will likely keep your baby in his carrier while you shop.

The time when your baby is able to sit up and support himself enough to ride in a shopping cart will likely coincide with teething and other oral fixations. I cannot count how many times I was in the grocery store, happily shopping while our daughter was being content and quiet, only to turn around and discover she was being quiet because she was chewing on the metal handle bar of the shopping cart. Yuck. This is a place where germs and bacteria thrive because it is touched and handled by so many different people. Purchasing a shopping cart cover that is easy to assemble and will cover the appropriate parts of the cart seat will save you many colds and other germs you do not want in your baby's mouth or for your baby to come into contact with.

A good shopping cart seat cover will cost between $25 and $60. The higher end of the price range may cover the entire area of the shopping cart seat that your child could come into contact with as well as having three to six toys, rattles, and teethers attached to the area that covers the shopping cart handle. If you will remember to take and use your shopping cart seat cover, the more expensive styles are well worth the money. The decision about how much you want to pay for this item will need to be determined by whether you will use the item often and how concerned you are about the cleanliness of the shopping carts at your favorite stores. You also have the option of purchasing disposable shopping cart seat covers, but these are still going to cost $11 to $15 for a three-pack, and they are not made of the soft cushioning materials that the nondisposable ones are made of. If you decide that this will be an item you would like to use, once you purchase one, keep it in the trunk of your car so you do not forget it or find yourself without it on the occasions when you make stops unexpectedly.

You will eventually have many thoughts that will cause you concern with keeping your infant healthy and clean. Most of these are random, excess worry, but if they are things you can prevent or avoid, then you should do all you can in your power to prevent them. Your infant will become a magnet for germs and bacteria; babies put everything imaginable into their mouths.

Quick
TIP

Babies orally discover and learn about the things around them; if they are not putting it in their mouths, they will want to touch it, poke it, move it, hug it, or kiss it to learn more about how it feels and what it does. After they touch it, they will put their hands in their mouths.

Do not dismiss your concern over sickness and unhealthy environments as crazy overprotection. You are the only person that your baby can truly rely on to protect him or her — whether you are keeping the baby 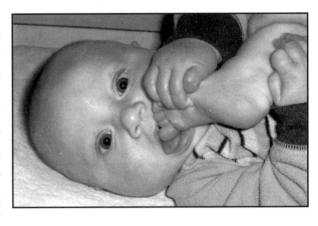 safe while crossing a busy street or keeping him or her from getting the flu by covering their shopping cart seat.

Chapter 6

Safety in Common Places

The health of your baby is closely related to keeping your baby safe. Just like getting his little hands on germs, your infant will also want to get his little hands on everything else he sees. He will at some point want to climb up chairs and shelves, stick something in an outlet, run into a table with his head, and most will at some point in their young lives fall down the stairs. Making the environments your baby is in as safe as possible will save you a good deal of worrying and your little one a good deal of bangs, bumps, scrapes, stitches, and bruises — possibly even a concussion or two as well. Safety for your baby should include all his environments; you need to check that your car is safe, his home is safe, and the homes of those who watch him should be walked through and checked for major safety issues as well.

Car Safety

You already know that you need to purchase an infant car seat and have it installed properly, but what else will plague you in the car? Every baby store or store that sells baby toys will have a wide variety of toys to clip on to different areas of your baby's car seat. Many of these items are made to clip onto the handle of your convertible carrier. These are a waste of money, if you plan on following safe driving rules. When you have your infant in the car and you are driving, the handle of your infant carrier — this is the part that snaps into the base that is anchored by the seat belt — is always supposed to be locked back when the car is moving. This is because if your car was hit, having the handle up would be unsafe. The car seat is not made to protect your baby properly with the handle up and can cause severe injury to your baby if an accident were to occur. Because you should not have the handle up, purchasing toys to hang from the handle to entertain your baby while in the car will be practically useless, unless you plan on using them only when the seat is not in the car, in which case your child will likely be out of the carrier or have many other toys to play with.

 **Quick TIP** Another unsafe car accessory that is offered around every corner of the baby store is baby shades that are not composed of completely soft materials.

The best baby shades to purchase from a safety point of view are the inexpensive plastic ones that stick to the window by way of static cling. They are used much like stickers, and because there are no bars, rods, or other hard hanging accessories, they are safe in the event of an accident. The Safety 1st 2 Pack Sun Shade is good, safe, and best of all, affordable. It can be purchased for less than $3. Although these might look like disposable window shades, they will last as long as you need them to. I use these sun shades; they have been stuck to my windows since 2004 and are still holding strong. These window shades are easy to see through, protect your baby from the sun's harmful rays, and are completely composed of soft material that will not injure your child if it comes dislodged from the window in an accident. I know that there are much cuter and window sun shades for your vehicle, but when you consider what a metal rod could do to your baby if it were dislodged in an accident, most parents agree that this is a place when safety must rate above style.

Finally, you might be tempted to purchase one of the infant mirrors that attaches to your vehicle's back seat so you can see what your little darling is up to while you are in the driver's seat. These mirrors are called by several different names, but the most common is an infant automobile mirror, and they can be helpful if you can find one that is both safe and useful. For the first three to five months of your baby's life, she will be sitting backward, where it is impossible for you to see what is going on, whether she is hysterically crying or being suspiciously quiet. Purchasing an infant automobile mirror to see your infant while you are in the car is a personal choice. There are styles that are safer than others and will be less likely to injure anyone in the car if an accident occurred. As previously mentioned, reading reviews on items you are looking to purchase is one of the best ways to get the average consumer's opinion; most infant automobile mirrors have mixed reviews. Some parents love them; others are disappointed in them.

You will want to look for the type of mirror that securely fastens to the back seat and will not be able to be jolted loose or knocked free by any bumps. Many styles of infant automobile mirrors that use safety pins to attach the mirror to the material of your car's back seat are considered to be quite safe, as it would be difficult to dislodge and undo the safety pins.

Infant automobile mirrors that use Velcro or are loosely strapped over the top of your car seat can become safety concerns, as they can easily be dislodged or unhooked and can become a projectile in your car.

Mobile mirrors that attach to the rear windshield of your car with a suction cup can fall still attached to broken glass or become a projectile in the event of an accident. As you look for the perfect, safe mirror to see your baby with in the car, look for plain styles. The fewer items attached to the mirror the less hazardous it will be. All the cute little hanging toys that are meant to entertain your baby can be just as dangerous as anything else flying through your car at high speeds. You will also want to look for a mirror that is covered in a soft material around the edges and corners; this way, if the mirror ever does become dislodged, there is less chance of injury, as the item will be padded at all edges.

Finding the right mirror for your car can be difficult; I did find one, and I have yet to find it again anywhere. The mirror that we used had large safety pins that held it securely to the back of the seat and was a plain rectangular mirror with soft edges in vibrant colored material; I was able to adjust the angle of the mirror with two belted straps. I believe our mirror was around only $15, and I am certain it was the Safety 1st brand.

After your car is secured you will want to move on to childproofing your home. Childproofing your home 100 percent is practically impossible. Every baby is different, developing at different speeds and getting interested in different things at different ages. Thankfully, there are a few things that all babies seem to do that can provide a guideline to get the major areas of childproofing covered.

Safety in Your Home

Your home will be the place your baby should be able to feel the most comfortable. This means that she needs to be able to move around in her environment without the worry of getting hurt every time she touches or grabs at something in her home. Your baby's environment needs to be a soft place where she can have adequate room to move once she is mobile and space to explore even when she is not mobile. Having a house made of china that is virtually untouchable will make your life much too stressful, and it will cause stress for your infant as well. Constantly giving her a "no" instead of encouragement to explore her world can have lasting effects. This does not mean you have to move out all your furniture and pad the walls; you can have some rooms that are made for baby and some that are not.

Quick TIP

Beware that even in the rooms where you will not be allowing your baby to roam free, there are still major childproofing areas that should be attended to.

Most childproofing for your home does not need to be done as soon as your infant comes home from the hospital. For the first four to five months of your baby's life, he will do little in the way of moving around the house unless he is in your arms. The main safety concerns for an infant under five months old will be making sure you are following safety rules yourself. These will mostly include things such as never leaving your baby unattended on the changing table or in the bath and other similar rules that I am sure you have read about in numerous parenting books. As far as your home is concerned, be sure that you have your outlets plugged, wires safely contained and away from your baby's reach, sharp objects stored out of baby's reach, cleaners stored safely on a shelf well out of your baby's reach or in locking cabinets, and gates protecting stairs or other walkways that you do not want your baby to access freely.

Outlets

Outlet plugs are easy to find and should be inserted in every outlet that is not in use in your home. These can be found in the safety and childproofing sections of nearly any baby superstore, as well as in the hardware or housewares section of most department stores. Usually, you can purchase outlet plugs in packages of ten or more. A package of ten outlet plugs will cost on average between $2 and $4. The more plugs in a package, the higher the price; this is not a large expense, and it may be a one-time expense. To avoid having to purchase more outlet plugs, always keep track of your outlet plugs. If you remove one to plug in the vacuum, be sure to replace it as soon as you are done.

Exploring the outlets in our home was one of our daughter's first fascinations in life; she was continually seeing her father and I plug in and unplug different household appliances, and naturally, she wanted to join in the fun as soon as she was able. I was happy I had decided to plug our outlets early, as she was not even six months old before I saw her attempting to stick all types of things near the outlets. They were all plugged, so there was no need to panic. I simply redirected her attention or, if she persisted, gave her a firm "no, no."

Wires and Electrical Cords

Wires are a concern when it comes to infants and barely mobile babies. It will seem to happen overnight; one day your baby will be diligently lying in the same place you put her throughout the entire day, and the next, you will notice she has rolled out of sight. The rolling stage of life is a fun one; usually starting between four and five months of age, your baby will realize that she can get from place to place by rolling around on the floor. It is not only fun for your baby to finally be able to move on her own, but it is fun to watch from a parent's point of view as your baby starts to explore her surroundings for the first time. The most important part of childproofing is to determine what in your house looks inviting. Take a moment to lie on your tummy or back on your floor and look around. This is what your baby is going to see. What looks like it might be fun to get into? Does anything resemble any of her toys or other things she might use on a daily basis? These are going to be the things that will most likely interest your baby.

Wires and cords may be at the top of this list; they are often a tangle of colors and shapes that your baby will find fascinating. There are several ways that you can childproof the areas of your house where wires or cords are present.

Quick TIP

In areas where only one cord is present, use wire pins or cord staples to secure the cord to the wall or floor so that your baby cannot pick it up or play with the slack that is common with loose wires and cords.

If there is too much slack or loose cord laying around, your baby can choke himself by getting it caught around his neck or follow it to the end where he will eventually want to know if it comes out of the wall and whether he can put it back in. Securing all cords and wires in your home is a must. This includes electrical cords, phone wires, cable cords, and electrical wiring. Stapling or tacking single cords and wires is a simple project that you will need only a hammer and some small staples for. Staples or wire tacks can be found in all home improvement stores and most department stores for $1 to $2 for a package of 30 or more. Using your hammer, gently trap the wire or cord against the wall, floor, or corner and tap the staple in so that it firmly holds the cord in place. You will want to repeat this process every foot or foot and a half so there is no loose wiring or slack in the cord.

If you have an area where a large amount of cords are present — this is most common behind the television or computer — you will need to find a way to keep all the electrical wires neat and tidy, as well as difficult for your baby to get to. Most often, these places are hard to get to already, as they may be behind a desk or entertainment center; however, keeping the cords organized and in a way that they cannot be accessed by little hands can be more difficult. The best solution to this is a Cord Control Kit. This is a kit that comes with a type of spiral or protective tubing that you can run your many various wires through. The cord control kits keep the cords straight, and organized and allow you to insert them and exit them through the spiral tubing wherever necessary so you can plug them in. One Step Ahead, a safety-conscious Web site, has the Just Right! Cord Control Kit, which you can find at **www.onestepahead.com** for $15.95 plus shipping and handling. This specific cord control kit comes with an eight-foot cord tube and color-coded labels for up to eight cords. The Just Right! Cord Control Kit has high ratings on this Web site as well as others and is an inexpensive way to keep your baby safe when it comes to electrical cords.

Sharp Objects

In the first five months of your baby's life, you should check your home for sharp objects that can cut or break through skin. Babies of all ages love to touch things, because it is one of their main methods of learning. Making sure that all sharp items are well out of your child's reach at all times will save you money at the emergency room, worry, and unneeded guilt. Being sure that all sharp items are stored out of your baby's reach will not only include the obvious, such as knives, scissors, and other cutting devices; also include anything

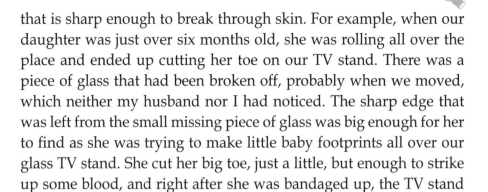

that is sharp enough to break through skin. For example, when our daughter was just over six months old, she was rolling all over the place and ended up cutting her toe on our TV stand. There was a piece of glass that had been broken off, probably when we moved, which neither my husband nor I had noticed. The sharp edge that was left from the small missing piece of glass was big enough for her to find as she was trying to make little baby footprints all over our glass TV stand. She cut her big toe, just a little, but enough to strike up some blood, and right after she was bandaged up, the TV stand was hauled out the door. Neither I nor my husband were aware of the broken area, but if we had gotten down on the floor to look around and see what looked like fun to play with, we likely would have seen it and been able to prevent the small cut.

Other sharp objects that should be put out of your baby's reach will include pictures with glass in them, staples, tacks, and any decorative items, such as candleholders made of glass or ceramic or that have barbs that hold the candle in place.

Quick TIP

Babies do not know what is appropriate to touch and not to touch, so storing many of your breakable items will not only preserve their form, it will also create a much safer environment for your baby.

There are some sharp things in your home that you might want to cushion — corners of coffee tables or similar things. This is a choice for you as a parent. Eventually, your child will have to learn that he cannot run into sharp corners without it hurting a bit, but if you want to cushion the blow for the first year, you can purchase edge guards and corner guards for most table-like surfaces. Corner guards are easy to find at most baby stores and department stores, and may cost $8 to $10 for a single set, which will include four guards. Edge guards are a bit more expensive, varying between $15 to $25 depending on the brand, size, and amount of cushioning you wish to purchase.

Corner and edge guards are not an item you must purchase, but if it makes you feel your baby will be safer, the saved stress might be worth the money.

Poisonous Products and Cleaners

Finally, you will want to be sure to move all cleaners and poisons to areas of your home that small children and babies cannot access. It is unlikely that your baby will have the ability to get into any type of cleaners in the first few months of her life; however, the risk is not worth the time you will save by not doing this. Moving cleaners and other poisons out of the areas your baby will eventually be able to access is a must. When babies start to move around, you do not get any warning about what they can and cannot do; no baby rolls over to the cabinet and then yells, "Hey Mom, look! I can open this cabinet full of bleach and dish soap." Most babies are silent explorers; they happily roll about until they find something that looks familiar or interesting and then proceed to play with it, which will often include putting it in their mouth. This is doubly likely to happen if your baby finds a cabinet full of cleaners or bottles that resemble baby bottles; many toilet cleaners come in a bottle that looks as though there is a nipple attached to it. Bottles and cleaners can be hazardous because many are poisonous, and the lids are choking hazards. Take the time to store these items on the top shelves or in locked cabinets.

Cabinet and Drawer Locks

Locking your cabinets is often a difficult and time consuming aspect of childproofing. This may not be a step that needs to be done until your baby is six to nine months old, especially if you have taken note to remove all poisons and cleaners from cabinets that are within your baby's reach. Installing childproof cabinet locks will protect your baby and your home in several different ways: safety, cleanliness, and injury. Safety and injury prevention will be the main reasons you will prefer to install childproof cabinet locks on certain cabinets. Not only do they keep your little one out of things that might be harmful, but they will also protect against little fingers getting caught in cabinet doors and drawers. Cleanliness is the last concern but might be important to you depending on what you keep in your cabinets; many people will keep their kitchen trash in the cabinet under the sink. This is a good place for it and a good place for a childproof lock so the trash does not end up all over the floor, on your baby, or in his mouth.

Childproof cabinet and drawer locks are often difficult to install. Depending on the type of wood your cabinets are made of, it can be difficult to screw the plastic pieces into place; lining up the parts can be difficult as well because of the angles you must put your body in to properly screw everything in place. Advice for this is not on the directions of the box; I know this because we made a vast effort to put in cabinet locks, but the wood our cabinets are made of was too strong for me. By the time my husband came home from work to help me, I was frustrated enough that I had moved everything that could possibly be harmful to the top shelf of the locking pantry, and that is where it has been ever since. So, speaking from experience, you do not have to lock your cabinets and drawers, but if you do not have a safe place to properly store everything, you should take the time to install childproof locks to those cabinets and drawers that must be locked.

 Cabinet and drawer locks come in several different styles, which include screw-mounted locks, adhesive locks, and sliding locks.

Of the three varieties, the adhesive locks and sliding locks are the easiest to install. Adhesive locks come with an adhesive tape on the back and can be easily mounted on cabinets and drawers. I was not aware of these when it was time to childproof our home. The adhesive locks work well and have good reviews from many parents; they stay in place and keep children out of cabinets and drawers you do not wish them to explore and can be found in many home safety departments of baby stores, online, and in a variety of department stores. The adhesive-style locks will cost you anywhere from $5 to $8 and usually come with one or two in a package.

Sliding locks for cabinets and drawers are again easy to install; there are two styles, one that is mounted with adhesive to the front of the drawer or cabinet and has an adjustable sliding strip of plastic that locks into place, while the second style fits directly over cabinet knobs and slides closed to hold the cabinet shut when it is not in use. The sliding style of cabinet lock is one that needs to be looked at closely; when purchasing, be sure to buy the style that will work for your cabinets. Most sliding locks say they can be opened with one hand, which, to a mother toting a baby is a must; however, test them out if you can, or consider whether you will be able to open them one-handed, regardless of what the description says. Most consumers are content with their sliding locks, with the exception that they are difficult to open one-handed. Most sliding locks come in packages of one or two and will cost between $4 and $6, depending on where you purchase them. Department stores and online vendors may have the best prices; baby superstores tend to cost a bit more when it comes to child safety items.

Screw-mounted locks are the most difficult to install but the easiest to find and offer the most protection, as they are permanent. A screw-mounted lock can come in several styles, the two most popular being the swivel locks and magnetic key locks. Swivel locks and spring-loaded locks are the more popular of the two; they are easy to open with one hand, difficult for young children to figure out, and may be hidden inside the cabinet or drawer, making your cabinet's appearance much nicer. The downside of screw-mounted swivel or spring-loaded locks is there are two pieces that need to line up correctly if the lock is to work properly. If you do not install them correctly, they might not work, and what you might think is a protected cabinet might not be. Depending on the type of wood your cabinets and drawers are made of, these can be easy or difficult to install.

Most screw-mounted locks come with a template that makes marking the inside of your cabinets and drawers much easier, but if your cabinets and drawers are composed of hard treated wood, screwing the small screws into place can be difficult and become a two-person job. Cabinet doors move as well as drawers, and applying too much pressure to secure the screws can be difficult on these moving parts. Because swivel and spring-loaded locks are installed on the inside of the cabinet or drawer, you are also working at odd angles to secure the locks. If you are handy with a power screwdriver or drill, installation of any screw-mounted lock will be much easier. Once you have the locks installed, they are virtually maintenance free and will last as long as you have a baby to protect. Swivel and spring-loaded locks can be found in all the same places as adhesive locks; baby stores will be the most expensive, and at online and department stores they will cost less. Average price for these styles of cabinet and drawer locks will range from $3 to $8, and they usually come in packages of two or four.

Magnetic key locks come in adhesive and screw-mounted styles with a magnetic key that allows you to open the cabinet or drawer. This style of lock is most often found in the screw-mounted style and is not good for drawers and cabinets you use often because every time you need to open the cabinet, you will need to have the magnetic key. They are good for seldom-used cabinets and if you are organized enough to remember where you have put the key after each use. This style of lock is good because there is no way for your child to open the cabinet or drawer unless she has the key and knows where to put it. Swivel locks or spring-loaded locks can often be figured out by most three- or four-year-olds, but magnetic key locks will work as long as your child does not have the key. Most magnetic key locks come in packages of two locks and one key; depending on where you find the right set of magnetic key locks for your style of cabinets and drawers, they will cost between $6 and $13.

Baby Gates

Baby gates can be a wonderful way to manipulate the areas of your home where your baby will spend most of her time, or they can simply be a waste of your time. Whether a baby gate will be useful for you will depend on your home and your style of living. Most homes with stairs should have at least one gate to keep your infant from accessing the stairs when you are not looking or are not in the same

area with your baby. Stairs are the major reason that you might need to have a baby gate in your home. No matter how careful you might think you will be, there will be a time when your baby will roll, crawl, or walk out of your sight and become curious about the stairs in your home. They look fun, at least to a child who has no idea what it feels like to fall down them. Many children will still want to play on or around the stairs, even after taking a tumble down them.

Securing a good-quality baby gate at the top or bottom of your stairs is a good idea. You will first want to consider where you would like the gate; there usually is not a need to have one at the top and bottom, just at the entrance you will be near the most. For example, if your stairs lead upstairs to the bedrooms, where you may not be for most of the day, you should consider putting the gate at the bottom of the stairs so your baby cannot access them unless you have taken him upstairs. If your stairs lead to a basement and you spend most of your time on the main floor of the house, you will want to consider installing your gate at the top of the stairs so your baby cannot fall down them. If you have a tri-level home and your basement stairs are not able to be closed off with a door, you might want to consider purchasing two baby gates so that both sets of stairs can be secured at all times. If you have a door that leads to either set of stairs, simply keeping the door shut except when you are accessing that part of your home will be a much more inexpensive way of making sure your little one does not take a tumble down the stairs.

Other uses for baby gates can be to block off rooms that you do not want your baby crawling or rolling into; again, if these rooms have a door, keep it shut, but if they do not, then a baby gate is a good idea, especially if the room is not childproofed or has items you do not want your baby playing with. My husband and I used baby gates to block our daughter in the main family and kitchen area, especially once she started to crawl; this was a good solution to let her have her freedom to explore while I did other things, like cook dinner or tend to chores that she did not want to be a part of.

Baby gates come in two main categories, mountable gates and tension gates. Mountable gates will be a more permanent solution to long-term areas, such as the tops of staircases.

Mountable gates will require that you mount them onto the walls, which means you need to find a stud to support the weight of the gate and secure it so it does not fall the first time your baby decides to pull himself up with the bars. Although mountable gates are more difficult to install than tension gates, the security of a gate that is safely mounted on the wall and cannot be wiggled loose will give you serenity later when your baby is a toddler and trying to dismantle the gate every chance he gets.

Tension gates, or pressure-mounted gates, will be easier to install and can be moved from doorway to doorway. A pressure-mounted gate will have sides that expand to fill most doorways and are adjusted to give a tight fit that will allow the gate to stay standing in the door even though it is not screwed into any of the walls. Most pressure-mounted gates now have release doors so you can come and go using only one hand and you do not have to remove the entire gate to move through the walkway it is protecting. We used our pressure-mounted gates all over the house for areas where no door was present or if I wanted our daughter to be able to see me but not be able to access certain rooms. Many times cleaning the bathroom, I used our pressure-mounted gate; I did not want our daughter near the cleaning supplies or touching the surfaces that had been sprayed with cleaners. If she could see me in the bathroom, she was content. Using a gate made us both happy; I could clean and do household chores, and she could see me while she explored the adjacent bedroom.

Baby gates can be found in a wide variety of prices, and you will be smart to shop and compare your needs with the price you are willing to pay. We went through about four baby gate styles before we found the right gate for our needs, and it happened to be one of the less-expensive styles of gate. Of course, the first three styles we purchased were the most expensive, and had we read the reviews and shopped a bit smarter, we could have saved nearly $150. Baby gates can be found from $20 and up; there is no need to spend more than $90 on a baby gate unless you have some specific needs to fulfill.

Quick TIP

Gates that cost more than $90 are often going to be long extension gates that are used to section off rooms with much larger-than-average doorways or wooden gates that will match the wood of your banisters or other décor.

Specialty gates should be carefully considered; if you believe you will need them for a long time, you might be wise to spend the greater amount of money, as the specialty gates are often constructed of more sturdy materials that are made to grow with your home over the years. Most parents purchasing gates with prices in excess of $90 are planning on having more than one child close together or are planning on leaving the gates up for more than three years.

If you are not planning that far ahead, or even if you are, there are some good gates that are much less expensive and will last well beyond the years you will need them. Most parents will need to have their safety gates up only for the first two to three years of their child's life, as once your baby has learned when and where he can go safely, the gates can be moved to the basement for storage if you are planning on a second baby.

Pressure-mounted gates are less expensive than hardware-mounted gates for two reasons: there is less hardware involved, and they are less expensive to make. Most pressure-mounted gates are good quality and will last for the two to three years you will need them most. They are easy to set up, take down, and move around the house for quick storage or new locations. Most pressure-mounted gates will not leave marks on your walls and will cost anywhere from $20 to $75, depending on the brand and style of gate that you prefer. Several options you will have in a pressure-mounted gate that you will want to consider are gates that pressure-mount semi-permanently with a swinging door within the gate, lift and lock gates, and soft versus hard gates. All these different styles of gates will work well in the right environments; the style you choose will need to be specific to fulfilling your personal needs. When purchasing your baby gate, answer these questions before making a decision:

- Will I need to access the gated area often, occasionally, or not at all?

- Do I need to be able to see through the gate?

- Will I want to remove the gate when I have guests in my home?

- Is there a stud in the wall adjacent to where I would like to place the gate?

Answering these questions will help you to select the right gate the first time around. If you are placing the baby gate in an area that needs to be accessed often, then you will want a gate that opens easily, possibly with one hand, and does not need to be removed entirely to access the gated area. If you will be accessing the gated area only seldom, or not at all, then a gate without a hinge will work well. Do you need to be able to see through the gate? Will your baby be playing on one side while you are on the other, or do you need to be able to see into the area that the gate will be blocking? If so, you will want a gate you can see through instead of a solid gate. If you would like to be able to easily remove the gate in high-traffic occasions or when you have guests at your home, you should consider a pressure-mounted gate because they are temporary and can be removed easily. Hardware-mounted gates are more permanent; they can be

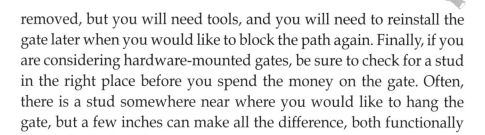

removed, but you will need tools, and you will need to reinstall the gate later when you would like to block the path again. Finally, if you are considering hardware-mounted gates, be sure to check for a stud in the right place before you spend the money on the gate. Often, there is a stud somewhere near where you would like to hang the gate, but a few inches can make all the difference, both functionally and in the look of the area.

After you have considered all these questions, you should shop around before purchasing your gate. Read reviews on gates you are interested in, and learn what other parents did or did not like about the product. Consumer reviews were a big help when we purchased our last gate — the one I found useful. There were mixed reviews, but the reviews helped me to decide whether the gate would be convenient in the area where I wanted to put it. This is important, because unlike a house plant that can be moved to different areas of the home to look nice, a baby gate will need to go in a specific place; therefore, you will want one that will serve you best in the area you are planning on installing it.

Baby Monitors.

Finally, many parents will want to purchase a baby monitor. Baby monitors are useful if you have a large home, are a heavy sleeper, or if your baby will be sleeping in an area where you will not be able to hear him throughout the entire home.

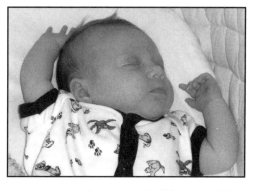

Baby monitors can alert you to the sounds your child is making through vision and noise amplification. There are video monitors and audio monitors, and the decision of which is going to be the best decision for you will depend on how you are as a parent. If you need to see what your baby is doing at all times of the day or night, a video monitor might be a good idea. Video monitors are expensive, ranging from $100 to $150, while an audio monitor will range from $20 to $90

Although no monitor might be necessary for some parents, if you feel you need one, an audio monitor will often suffice. It will let you know when your infant is awake and needs you for something or when she is just fussing or soothing herself back to sleep. Most moms and dads are thankful they purchased a baby monitor, and two of my favorite brands of monitors are the Safety 1st brand and the Sony brand. Both of these are reasonably priced — ranging from $30 to $40 — have good reviews, good reception, show a lighted display when baby is crying, and have an audio feed with an adjustable volume. Both of these brands usually come with dual receivers and are lightweight and easily attach to the top of your pants or a belt buckle, if you need to keep it with you.

Monitors can be a tricky item to purchase; most parents are swayed into purchasing the most expensive baby monitor they can find, but this does not mean you will never hear static or another baby in the neighborhood. Because of the way monitors work, this is likely on occasion with any monitor.

As with baby gates, you are going to make the best purchase based on your needs and reading other consumer reviews, which will help you decide what monitor will work best for you.

Case Study: Rachel Gromer

Rachel Gromer is a proud and busy mother of two young children, three-year-old Jade and one-year-old Ryan. Rachel is a mother by day and moonlights as a postpartum nurse taking care of new moms and infants.

When asked about her favorite baby- and parent-friendly items, she listed the Baby Bjorn, her breast pump, and her baby monitor. She was relieved to have peace of mind while her children slept. Having a baby monitor offers most parents a type of security without having to constantly check on their children in their beds. The baby monitor Rachel purchased and loves is a Safety 1st brand, has lasted two years, and will likely last through a few more. She feels her money was well spent, as her monitor cost only around $25.

Rachel has always been open to receiving hand-me-downs and purchasing gently used clothing and other baby gear and says that among the many borrowed or handed down items they received, clothing, crib, changing table, glider, and bike trailer were all very helpful and worked wonderfully for her and her children. When Rachel first began shopping for her new family, price was one of the most pressing concerns, but now that they are getting older and using items for longer, quality is becoming a top concern as well.

The most stressful time of the day for Rachel and her family has always been dinnertime; she dealt with this stressful time of the day by "mentally preparing myself. I would try to organize myself ahead of time and decrease other stresses, if possible."

When asked to share some advice with new parents, Rachel said, "Reading and playing are two of the most important things you can do with your children."

Emergency Readiness

No home is completely babyproof; all babies will find something to get into sooner or later that can be harmful or cause injury. Because of the exploratory nature of babies and children, it is a good idea to keep a list of important numbers and instructions at hand; we keep ours on the refrigerator.

When our daughter was young, she had an awful habit of choking on things. All babies love to put things in their mouths, and my husband and I had childproofed enough to remove most choking hazards from her reach. She was not putting things such as bottle caps or small toys in her mouth; she choked on food primarily. The first time this happened was when we were eating out with my in-laws, and even though both my husband and I had taken the infant CPR and choking classes, when it happened the first time, I was unprepared. By the time I realized that she was choking and worked out in my mind what I needed to do to help our daughter, my husband had already picked her up, flipped her over, and given her a good firm thump on the back, which dislodged the food and sent it flying to the floor. Had my husband not been there, I do not know how long it would have taken me to respond correctly. I would like to say it would have been only seconds later and all would have been fine, but I will never know that.

After this incident, we learned that our daughter was prone to choking on food, especially food that was more coarse than noodles or bread. There were many times when my husband and I both had to react quickly to our daughter's habit of choking, which made me consider that a plan for handling this should be easily accessible to both my husband and me, as well as to anyone who may be caring for our daughter at any time. After the first choking incident, I was alarmed at how panic had prevented me from performing a vital function of parenting — keeping our daughter safe from harm. I immediately posted on our refrigerator instructions on how to handle a choking infant, infant CPR, and emergency contact numbers, including 911, our cell phone numbers, pediatrician information, poison control hotline, insurance information, and a close neighbor's phone number. Throughout our daughter's three years, there have been numerous occasions I and others watching her have been thankful those numbers and instructions were so easily available.

I have had to urgently call poison control twice; both times our daughter was fine and it was a precautionary measure, but having the phone number in an easy-to-find place made the situation easier to handle while being worried that our daughter might have gotten into something she should not have. The first time, I found her chewing on a dryer sheet, which the operator at poison control looked up and advised me that the worst symptom she might develop would be a tummy ache. The second time, I accidentally gave her Children's Tylenol instead of Infants' Tylenol, which is not harmful but not advised. These are two incidents that happened by chance or accident, not because our house was not childproofed or we were being neglectful. They happened because unpredictable things just happen, and being as prepared as possible with information at hand was the best thing we could have done.

When it came time to put emergency information on our refrigerator, one alarming situation had already happened, so I would suggest doing this before you and your baby come home from delivery. You will likely want your doctor's number handy anyway so you can call him or her when you are nearing time to go to the hospital, so why not have all your emergency information written and posted as well? You could purchase charts and forms for this to hang on the refrigerator, but instead of spending the $10 to $20, you can just write it down and hang it up with an already available magnet, or print it out on your computer if you want it to look nice.

Quick **TIP**

Having your emergency information sheet will be helpful for you when you are home with your child as well as for others who may supervise or baby-sit in your home. You can also create copies; I kept one in my diaper bag as well.

Having a copy in the diaper bag meant that anytime a person was watching our daughter at their home, they would always have all the information they needed in an emergency situation.

A small note on leaving your baby with friends and family for babysitting is to be sure they have a safe home as well. No matter how much your friends and family might love your son or daughter, you as the parent need to be sure their home is safe. Many times, people do not realize what babies get into until they are consistently around them; you can help them by pointing these things out before leaving your child in a home that may have some safety concerns. You should be vigilant in checking all environments your baby will be living or playing in.

Again, I must stress that no home will be perfect; there will always be something out of place, dropped, or left lying around that a baby will want to take a closer look at, touch, or taste. Just knowing that you must be prepared and vigilant in an emergency situation will make you more comfortable, whether you realize it or not. You might never need to use a number from the information sheet on your refrigerator, or you might have a cabinet that your child never tried to get into that you locked anyway, and that is good. Childproofing is a precautionary step.

Chapter 7

The Nursery

The word nursery brings back so many memories, and most of them are fond. Finding out we were expecting our daughter brought so many plans to mind for the perfect nursery. In the first stages of dreaming about our daughter's nursery, there was never a price tag attached, but soon, that all changed. Focusing on the fond memories, however, it meant we were going to be able to pick out colors and decorations, as well as the perfect baby furniture. Creating your infant's nursery will often be a task that is close to your heart; your baby's nursery will be the room where she should feel at home, comfortable, and soothed. Your baby's room should be a place where she can see herself as well as her family and have a calm place to sleep, eat, and play. All these emotions and comforts can be provided within a reasonable price range; it just takes knowing what to look for and where to look for it all.

Paint

Painting your baby's room is going to be one of the least expensive ways to decorate it. Paint may cost only $5 to $12 a gallon, and most rooms can be painted with fewer than three gallons of paint. Painting your infant's nursery can be done several ways — you can paint a new solid color, split the room in half with one color on top and one on bottom, or create a fun setting with colorful characters, bugs, flowers, or any number of design patterns. Painting the decorations on to your little one's walls will provide two things. The first is that they will cost less. The second reason painting your baby's decorations is a idea is that it is completely personal and unique; granted, it takes a small amount of creative talent, but there are so many options of stencils and stickers that as long as you can trace, you can create unique and beautiful walls for less than $100. Most indoor paint is made to be safe, even in an enclosed area, and painting should not be a concern for Mom, but check with your doctor before you start.

Baby Furniture

Baby furniture will logically be the next step in your nursery after you have painted, if you choose to do so. Shopping for baby furniture can be fun, if you do not have to worry about a budget. Because most of us do need to take cost into consideration, it can also be stressful. Register for the nursery furniture — you might get lucky. If you are not that lucky, there is still a way to keep your baby furniture shopping affordable and low on the stress meter.

Quick TIP

The best way to start your furniture shopping expedition is at home. Take a good look the baby's room and measure it. There is no bigger waste of money and time than purchasing furniture that will not work for you or fit in your baby's room.

Visualize what you want the room to look like, where the furniture will go, and how much space will remain in the room after you have all the furniture. Next, you should consider what furniture items you will use. Will you use a dresser, changing table, crib, bassinet, bookshelf, or glider? These are the most commonly purchased items used in a nursery, but most rooms are not an adequate size to hold all these items. Having three large furniture items in your baby's room will likely fill the space but leave you enough room to comfortably move about.

Bassinets and Cribs

Deciding what is necessary for your baby will be the determining factor in purchasing furniture for the nursery. Most parents will without a doubt use a crib; bassinets are smaller and often used beside the bed in the parents' room.

If you cannot afford a crib, a bassinet is much more inexpensive and can be used for the first month or two after your baby is brought home.

After two months, most infants will have grown enough that a bassinet is no longer a comfortable or safe place for them to sleep. Bassinets can be used as long as your baby fits comfortably inside it or until your baby starts to sit or pull herself up along the sides of the bassinet. A comfortable, good-quality bassinet can be found at department stores with a wide baby selection, baby superstores, and at garage sales and secondhand stores.

New bassinets can run a large range in price, depending on the features you feel you must have. The truth of the matter is that even though there are bassinets that play music, vibrate, rock, zip shut, roll, and are elegantly decorated, a basic bassinet will provide as much comfortable sleeping time as any other. The price range for bassinets varies from $40 to $200. The lower range of prices may offer a place for your infant to sleep that is cozy and comfortable, as well as a lower basket to keep any supplies you might need throughout the night. The basic style of bassinet will offer the option of having casters at the floor for rolling, which can also be flipped out of the way to provide a rounded bottom for rocking your baby bedside.

I purchased one of the more basic styles of bassinets at a garage sale, and it worked wonderfully for our daughter. The bassinet I purchased offered a rocking or rolling bottom, which was used to rock our daughter while I lay in bed myself, breathable side walls through which I could also see her, a removable cloth canopy, bedding, and a basket below where I kept burp cloths and bottle supplies. We used our bassinet from the time our baby was two weeks old until she was six weeks old. The first two weeks, our infant slept downstairs while my husband and I stayed up in shifts, because during this time, our daughter was awake most of the night, adjusting from sleeping during the day in the womb and being up all night.

After her sleep schedule was a bit more like ours, the bassinet was placed near the side of the bed. When our daughter awoke for a feeding, I could easily reach over and pick her up to feed her without even having to get out of bed. This allowed me time to heal from my Cesarean section. We used our bassinet only long enough for me to be able to comfortably get in and out of bed to tend to our daughter, after which she was in her crib in her own room. Three weeks might not seem like a long time, but having our baby bedside while I healed made a world of difference to me and the amount of rest I was able to get in those first few weeks of our daughter's life. In hindsight, the $10 I spent at a garage sale for a bassinet that would have cost me around $70 new was money well spent.

Sooner or later, you will ultimately need a crib for your baby, unless you are planning on co-sleeping until he is big enough for a bed, which I would not suggest. Cribs can be expensive, and because it is unsafe to purchase used cribs, it is likely that you will need either to purchase one new or receive one on loan from someone you know well, such as a good friend or family member who has had a baby recently.

Quick TIP

Purchasing a used crib is considered a safety concern because many cribs are built with glues that can deteriorate after years of use and because some glues that were used in the past are no longer used because of harmful ingredients.

Besides the glues, reasons older and used cribs are not safe include spindles that can become loose or are spaced too far apart and faulty functioning due to age, wear, and tear. If you receive a crib from a good friend or family member that you trust, you should still make it a point to check the age of the crib, recall lists, and the spacing of the spindles used to create the sides of the crib to be sure all is safe and sound for your infant.

The crib you purchase will need to be sturdy enough to last nearly three years. Most children move from a crib to a toddler bed or twin bed between the ages of two and three years old. It is not difficult to find a crib that will last you this long, as they are made specifically for sleeping babies and young children. However, if you are planning on having a second or third child in the future, taking good care of your crib and purchasing one that will last will ultimately save you money. When looking at cribs, pay attention to several details. The first is price. Try to shop only in the price range you are comfortable with; this will keep you satisfied with your options, and if you do not know what you are missing out on, you will be less likely to overspend. The second detail you should look at is the functioning of the crib; be sure that you are purchasing a crib that is safe and easy for you to use. This will be helpful when getting your baby in and out of her crib, for your safety and hers.

Cribs come with two main ways of accessing your baby once the bottom of the crib is lowered. When your child is old enough to stand or sit up in his crib, you will need to lower the mattress so he cannot climb, crawl, or fall out of the crib; once the mattress is lowered, being able to  reach your child to lift her up can be difficult, especially if you are not a tall person. Some cribs have drop sides that lock into place, and when you need to, you can use a foot bar to drop the side of the crib down about a foot so you can better reach your baby. Other styles of cribs offer a hinged side that locks into place at each side; you pull the locks and the side folds down about six inches to a foot, depending on the style of crib.

The best way to determine which style will be best for you and your spouse will be to test the cribs that are set up in the store. Ask a sales person to help you lower the mattress to its lowest point and drop the side so you can practice leaning over to pick up "a baby" from the mattress. Our baby's crib was given to us as a gift, and although we loved it, the side of the crib did not move down enough for me to reach our baby after the mattress had been lowered. Granted, I am slightly less than five feet tall, but it is best to know that this is comfortable for you, no matter what your height. I eventually needed to purchase a stepstool to stand on to reach our daughter and safely pick her up. This was difficult, as there were times when picking up a squirming little girl while standing on a stepstool was much like tightrope walking.

Cribs include a wide range of prices, and again, it all depends on your budget and how fancy you want your baby's crib to be. Before you look at the price of various cribs, take into consideration that no matter what style or type of crib you get, it will ultimately look good in your baby's room. Cribs do not vary that much in looks, other than color, and once you see it in the room with the other pieces of furniture, you will likely love it just as much as you would one that might have cost much more. The cost of your crib will range from $170 and up through the thousands of dollars. Most cribs that cost $170 to $300 will have all the necessary function and style that most reasonable parents will need for their infant. The basic necessities in a crib will be covered by most four-in-one cribs. A four-in-one crib will convert from an infant crib to a toddler crib, to a toddler bed or toddler daybed, and finally, to a full-size bed. The final conversion to a full-size bed usually includes only the head- and footboard of the bed. Rails and mattresses will need to be purchased separately when the time comes.

Quick
TIP

Purchasing a four-in-one crib or a style that is similar will save you money in the long run, and they are at the lower end of the price range.

The crib that my husband and I received as a gift from family was not a crib that converts. We loved it, but if we had purchased our own crib, I would have purchased a four-in-one crib. The crib we had worked well. I am not sure what it cost, but as our daughter has grown, we have since purchased a toddler bed and will soon be purchasing a twin or full-size bed as well. The point is that if you are purchasing your own crib, purchasing one that can grow with your child will save you money as he or she grows. If you are receiving a crib as a gift, it is likely that the money you save by not having to purchase the crib in the first place will be as much as you will later spend on a toddler bed and finally a larger bed for your child. A crib as a gift is a wonderful thing; it will insure that you do not have to worry about the expense now, as there are still many other items you will likely want to purchase for your baby.

Along with a crib or bassinet, you will need to purchase sheets, a mattress for your crib, a mattress pad, and blankets. Blankets should not be purchased until after your shower. Of all the Case Studies I conducted for this book, and from talking with many parents over the years, blankets are one of the most popular items received at baby showers. You will likely need only a few blankets, as most children and babies find one or two that they fall in love with and will accept no substitute. Mattresses for cribs are affordable, ranging from $30 to $120. Although you are provided with a firmness choice, your baby will likely not care how firm or soft his mattress is. Because of suffocation concerns, baby mattresses are not made in extra soft, cushiony styles.

Purchasing a mid-grade or inexpensive mattress will not affect your baby's sleep habits. The mattress we used for our daughter was made long ago, and she slept just fine. I purchased it used at a garage sale and disinfected it with bleach water before she was born. The mattress was covered in a plastic material that can be easily washed, and this has been a lifesaver throughout the years. The first time our daughter was ill with a tummy virus, the idea that we could wash her mattress was wonderful. I would suggest looking for a mattress that can be cleaned with a washcloth and baby-safe disinfectant, as there will inevitably be a time when something yucky is all over your baby's bed. You will need only one mattress, and you will need to purchase it before you plan on using your baby's crib. If you plan on using your baby's crib as soon as he comes home from the hospital, you should purchase it before your baby is born. If you are planning on using a bassinet for a few weeks or months, you can get by with no mattress and just purchasing two or three sets of bassinet sheets until you and your baby are ready to use his crib. Bassinet sheets usually come in packages of one or two and cost between $8 and

$20, depending on the brand and how many sets of sheets you are purchasing in a package.

Case Study: Robyn Nieder

Robyn Nieder is a new mom with a handsome little four-month-old boy named Brayden. One of Robyn's biggest struggles in shopping for baby items arose when the time came to purchase bedding.

She questioned mattresses and mattress pads. "Was there really much difference in mattress quality, mattress pads, cover, waterproof, absorbency…? There were so many choices — how many choices do you actually need?" Another problem that Robyn faced at the store was a lack of knowledgeable help to give her direction in this decision.

On the other hand, Robyn and her husband did enjoy shopping at Babies "R" Us. "It was nice to have all things in one location, with some help from staff in selecting brands."

Robyn and her husband did not do much price-comparison except for in the area of car seats. Part of this was due to the fact that they had developed a budget and knew how much they were able to spend on the things they needed for their baby. They found their budget very useful. When shopping for baby items, Robyn stated that the safety of the product was first on their list of importance before purchasing an item, and price was the second factor taken into consideration.

Robyn admits that the most useful item another parent has given to her has been the Baby Wise series of books, and she would pass them along to other moms in the future as great resources. She has also learned that patience is one of the most valuable things to have as a mother. The only thing she would change about the infancy of her son is that she would have sought help with breast-feeding issues sooner.

Have mattress pads as well, especially as your baby grows, and they will cost between $8 and $35. A mattress pad will not only protect your baby's mattress from stains and wetness, but it can also add a bit of cushion to the more firm mattresses. The best part about a mattress pad is that if your baby becomes ill and her diaper does not withstand the effects of an upset tummy, or worse, she is vomiting, changing your sick baby's bed linens and removing the mattress pad after a mess will make for a quick and easy cleanup in the middle of the night, as far as the crib is concerned. Our mattress pad was also helpful in the summer months, because, with a plastic-covered mattress, our daughter was warmer in her crib when the sun was out and therefore perspired more during the summer months. The extra-absorbent cloth mattress pad helped our daughter to sleep more comfortably in the hottest summer months and absorbed any perspiration so she was not waking up from being too hot.

Linens for your baby's crib are necessary too. Before you start using your crib, you should plan to have two to three sets of linens on hand. Changing your baby's crib linens will need only to be done every few weeks, unless he is prone to spitting up or vomiting while he is sleeping. Having more than one set of sheets for the crib will make it easier to change your baby's crib quickly and still have it available for when he is ready for bed at various times throughout the day and night.

Crib linens are reasonably priced from $10 to $25 and can be found cheaper at secondhand shops and thrift stores. There is no need to purchase expensive bedding for your baby, as she will not care about what her bed looks like.

If you purchase a crib set for decorating purposes, it will often come with one set of sheets, leaving you only the expense of purchasing one or two extra sets.

Changing Tables

The second most commonly purchased piece of furniture for baby nurseries is a changing table. Although a changing table is not an absolutely necessary item — after all, you can change your baby anywhere — it is nice to have. Furnishing your baby's room with a changing table will mean that not only do you have the convenience of changing your infant in a comfortable standing position during the day, but in the middle of the night, you will have an area that is comfortable, convenient, and safe for changing your baby. Most changing tables will offer adequate space to store all the items you will need for changing your little one.

The most common style of changing table will have a top changing area with a small containment ledge and two shelves below for storage. The shelves below will provide adequate room for wipes, diapers, baby powder, diaper cream, diaper warmer, and many other supplies. There are other styles of changing tables that will offer drawers, smaller shelves, and cubby holes to store all the items you will wish to keep on your changing table. You can also find changing table and dresser combinations. Most of these furniture pieces will not have the containment ledge at the top of the changing area, but since this ledge is not meant to hold your baby in place without you present, it is not a necessary piece to have. All these styles of changing tables can easily be found in the price range of $80 to $250. There are more expensive styles and brands of changing tables, but there is only so much that can be offered in a table to change your infant on. I would recommend keeping to the lower end of the price scale, as this is an item of convenience and most will get the job done just fine, no matter what the price. Changing tables can also be found used at garage sales and secondhand shops or thrift stores, where the price will often be much better.

Case Study: Nicole Fowler

Nicole Fowler is a patient and kind mom who has four amazing children ages one, two, three, and five. Being the proud mother of three boys, Thomas, William, and Evan, and one girl, Sophie, has made Nicole a very busy mom.

She not only deals with her own life's good and bad days, but also spends much of her time volunteering for her Mothers of Preschoolers (MOPS) group and helping other mothers with advice and a sympathetic ear for all types of crazy kid and mom moments.

Nicole listed some of her favorite items as the Baby Bjorn, her double stroller, a wagon, and zoo passes. All of these items help Nicole keep her kids entertained and close to her while out and about. While it might seem to some new moms that wagons and zoo passes are for the older child only, they both are very good for entertaining any children who can sit up and support their own weight. What child says no to a fun ride or seeing new and exciting animals?

Nicole also shared the item she struggled most with before purchasing — a changing table. She debated the cost of the changing table and how much space it would take up in the nursery. Nicole did purchase a secondhand changing table, which she uses frequently and is happy with. Purchasing the changing table secondhand brought the price of the changing table down, which made the purchase easier on their finances and a much more comfortable buy.

Nicole admitted that she and her husband did not have a budget specifically created for their family until their fourth child was born. Nicole wishes they had developed one sooner.

When asked to think of the most valuable piece of knowledge Nicole has learned since becoming a parent, she shared a touching statement with me. "No one can truly know your personal or family struggles, so it is important to never compare your child, situation, or life to that of another."

For our daughter, we purchased a dresser/changing table combination. It worked well. I was able to keep clothing in the three bottom drawers of the dresser, and in the top drawer, I kept all the items I needed for tending to our daughter's diaper changes and other convenient items. Now that she is past the age of requiring diaper changes, the top of the dresser is filled with pictures and other decorations that she loves to see in her room, and the best part is, I do not have an extra piece of furniture sitting in our basement wondering if we will use it again and what to do with it until then. Our changing table/dresser combination was purchased at a garage sale for $20, and I stained it to match the rest of the nursery furniture, so in total, it may have cost around $25 and two hours of time to stain it properly.

The changing table can be used for a variety of different things as your baby grows as well. During his infancy, the changing table can be used for changing your baby day and night; it will keep diaper stains off your carpet and can be fitted with a changing pad and cover so you will be able to easily wash away any stains or soils.

Most babies will become too big to be changed on a changing table by the time they are two years old. I have many friends and acquaintances who have children over the age of two and still use their changing tables for storing items they use in their child's room or as bookshelves for the many books and toys their children have accumulated over the years.

Changing pads for changing tables or dresser-combination furniture will provide your baby a safe and comfortable place to lie while you change her diaper. Most changing pads that are made for changing tables are shaped to help hold your baby in the center while providing a place to change her comfortably for you both. Purchasing a changing pad for your changing table or dresser is simple, as most changing tables provide a similar amount of room for changing your infant.

The only caution is to be sure the changing pad you have selected will fit securely to the top of your changing table or dresser. Often, changing pads made for this purpose will be equipped with a strap and buckle to help hold them in place while your baby is on them. If you will be using a dresser top for a changing table, be sure the dresser top is wide enough to hold a changing pad so your infant is comfortable while you are changing her diaper.

Purchasing your changing table or dresser combination at the same time as the changing pad you will place on top can be convenient, as most stores will have a model of the furniture item displayed and you can take the changing pad you want to the model to see if the size is correct. You will also want to purchase one or two changing pad covers; you can usually find these in white or pastel colors that will match most baby rooms. A changing pad may cost between $15 and $30 or less if you can find it used at a secondhand store or garage sale. Covers for most changing pads can be purchased separately in packages of one or two and will cost from $8 to $15, depending on the design, style, pattern, and brand name you choose. When purchasing a changing pad cover, look for the style that comes similar to a fitted sheet. These are easy to put on and take off your changing pad and offer quick, one-handed removal when needed.

Rocking Chairs, Gliders, and Ottomans

The third and final furniture item you might want to consider for your baby's nursery will be a rocking chair or glider and ottoman. These can be expensive. The first thing you will want to do is to assess whether you believe you will spend time rocking your baby in a rocking chair or glider. Some babies prefer to be rocked, and some do not like it. There is no harm in waiting to purchase this item until after your baby has arrived and you can determine whether he likes to be gently rocked to sleep, while he is eating, or to soothe and calm him. It can be hard to wait to purchase such an item, but once you look at the cost, you might be convinced to wait until you are more acquainted with your baby. If you cannot wait, one way to predict whether your baby will be a rocker or not is to watch yourself. Do you often spend time swaying side to side or back and forth while you are carrying your baby in your womb? If not, your baby might still like to be rocked, but you may not be certain. If you do spend a good amount of time "rocking" your baby in your tummy, chances are that she will enjoy being rocked during different times of the day.

After you have decided whether you would like to purchase a rocking chair or glider and ottoman, you need to decide which is right for you. Gliders and ottomans are the most popular rocking items, but they are much more expensive than old-style rocking chairs. They are more comfortable and easier to function while holding or feeding a baby. Because the ottoman and glider can rock together, it takes little effort to move the chair back and forth, and they are often covered in thick, plush cushioning that makes you comfortable while sitting in the chair. Being that you might often be rocking your baby in the early morning hours or throughout the night, easy might be what you need. Rocking chairs are easy to use but can be difficult when you are trying to breast-feed your child while rocking her.

Gliders and ottomans can be found sold together or separately. Check that the ottoman you want comes included in the price of the glider, just to be sure. Glider and ottoman sets may start out priced around $130 and can range into the upper hundreds, depending on what you are looking for. The thing about looking for a glider and ottoman is they all do the same thing; there are not a hundred different options to make the job of choosing any more complicated than it needs to be. The only options that you have to look at are the color of the fabric and wood, whether you find the glider comfortable, and whether the ottoman is included. Some gliders also have the option of reclining; these will often be more expensive, but if it is important to you, then you should test one out to see whether you think you will use that option.

Many used gliders, ottomans, and rocking chairs can be found in the classified section of your newspaper, at thrift stores, and at secondhand baby stores or garage sales much cheaper. The glider and ottoman we purchased was not the most elegant or beautiful chair, but it served its purpose well — it provided me comfort in feeding our daughter and gave me a way to rock her to sleep during rough nights when she was fitful and restless. We purchased our glider from a couple who had placed an ad in the classified section of my husband's company newsletter, and it cost us $35. It was well worth it, and I am planning on re-covering it to match the room for our second child when the time comes. Gliders can be a wonderful way to rock your baby to sleep, enjoy one another's company, or make you more comfortable while feeding your baby. Affording one can be made easy, even if you are on a tight budget. If you can afford to purchase a new glider and ottoman or rocking chair, buy one that is reasonably priced. You can save the additional money to spend on something much more fun and exciting, like decorating your baby's room.

Decorating and Final Touches

Decorating your baby's nursery is a process that touches the hearts of most moms and many dads. Decorating your baby's nursery is also a process that touches the bank account repeatedly if you go overboard. The key to decorating your baby's room is to keep it simple. Your baby will not even be able to see many of the decorations for the first few weeks of his life, and going overboard with many colors and wall decorations can become overstimulating for many infants once they can see all around the room. Painting can save you money in many ways, but there are many parents who feel they are not artistic enough to paint a room that will be worthy of their baby's admiration.

If you decide that painting alone is not the way to go for decorating your baby's room, there are other ways around the costly art of decorating the room of your dreams for your baby. The key to decorating your baby's room on a well-maintained budget is to be patient. As you choose the things you would like to put in your baby's room, save for them and purchase only what your budget allows. You have nearly ten months to complete this work of art.

Starting small in decorating any room is a wise idea. First, picture what you want your baby's room to look like. Do you want bright or pastel? What color of furniture have you picked out for your infant's room, and what will complement that furniture to bring the room together in a comfortable and cozy space? Starting small and picturing what you want for your baby can be tough, but this will save you the costly mistake of over-purchasing things you do not have room for. Once you know what furniture you will be getting and how much room it will take, you can start to plan what type of decorations you would like to get for your baby's room. Of the many ways to decorate, there are a few things that are favorites among parents these days, including rugs, curtains, pictures or framed art, lettering, small lamps, borders, wall stickers, and mobiles. Many of these favorite decorating items are practical and can be used as your baby grows.

Rugs, Big or Small

Rugs are a way to protect your baby's carpet or flooring while adding a bit of pizzazz to your infant's room. Rugs these days can be as cute and vibrant as you want and can come in all different sizes to cover different-sized areas of floor. The only problem with rugs is that unless you can find a sale or find them used but in good condition, they can be expensive. They will be useful in the future as your child grows into a toddler, and even beyond, as long as you purchase a rug that is not too "baby themed" for an older child to enjoy having. A rug might be worth the cost. It will protect hardwood floors and carpeting throughout the years, but finding the funds to purchase one can be difficult. Depending on the size of rug you are looking to purchase, the cost will vary. Small area rugs that work well in front of the crib or changing table will have a price range of $15 to $50. Larger rugs that will cover a good amount of space and ultimately be used for floor protection and decoration, will range in cost from $120 to $400. Purchasing a rug for your baby's nursery is not a must, but if you can afford one and have the need to protect or hide the floor in this room, it can be a good buy. The key to finding a good price on the rug of your dreams is to shop around, wait for sales, look at online auctions, and be patient so you do not overspend.

Curtains and other Window Treatments

Curtains or window treatments of some variety will add to your baby's room in two ways — they will decorate almost an entire wall and they will add color, characters, festivity, or calm to the room, depending on the style of window coverings you choose.

 Heavier curtains or blackout window covers can also be helpful when your baby is napping or if she goes to bed before nightfall, as most babies do.

Blackout shades or window coverings will help to keep your baby's room dark and cool in the summer and warm in the winter because they will block out sun and hold in heat. The price of window treatments for your infant's room will vary, depending on the type of window treatment you choose. Blackout shades can be found in many different places, including many baby superstores, online, and in specialty stores for window coverings. Where you decide to purchase blackout shades will cause the price to vary; they can be found priced anywhere from $19 up into the hundreds of dollars. When shopping for a blackout shade or any other window treatment, you will need to know the measurements of the windows you are planning to cover.

Curtains for your infant's room are another option and can be used in conjunction with blackout shades or with sheer panels if you would like to let the sunlight into your baby's room. Most babies do not need complete darkness to sleep, so a blackout shade is not necessary; it is simply a preference of some parents. Others will prefer blinds and curtains or sheer panels. It is important to have some type of window covering, not only to add to the decoration of your baby's room, but also to provide privacy if you are planning on feeding your baby in her room.

Curtains, blinds, and window panels will all vary in cost. Most of these items can be found from around $20 and up, depending on where you shop. Shopping for window treatments online can help you to find the lowest prices before going to individual stores. If you prefer to shop in person, baby superstores and department stores with a wide variety of nursery décor will have designs and styles that will be complementary to a baby's room, but they might not have the best prices. The curtains I purchased for our daughter's room are wonderful; they are thick and heavy, cover the entire widow with sheer panels beneath to let the light in when she is not sleeping, and are appropriate for a young or older child's room, with lavender and pink pinstripes. I found the curtains on sale at Pottery Barn Kids, and they cost me $68. The sheer panels from Wal-Mart were a total of $12, and the floor length on both of them add decoration to the entire west wall of her room.

Photos, Pictures, and Framed Art

Decorating the walls of your precious baby's room can be done with family photographs, framed pictures that fit the theme you have set, or with framed artwork. Family photographs are the most inexpensive way to decorate various wall spaces in your baby's room. Many families have photo printers from which they can print their own photographs, or you can easily order them for about $.12 up to $1.75 from many online vendors or from your local department store. Printing family photos and framing them in inexpensive frames will not only add sincere and touching décor to your infant's room, it will also help him begin to recognize the people who will be near him most.

If you decide to frame your own photographs or any other type of wall hanging, purchase frames at discount stores or secondhand stores; these may cost between $.25 and $3. Frames from garage sales, secondhand stores, and discount stores may be in good condition. Another reason to search for good deals on frames at thrift stores or discount stores, like Big Lots, is that you can purchase frames for the cheaper price and then redesign them to fit the style of your baby's room. Many baby rooms are full of pastel colors or basic bold colors; adding a simple coat of paint to an inexpensive frame can bring out the accent colors of the room and make it more personal.

You can purchase a small bottle of wood paint and discount frames often for much less than the designer frames found in every baby magazine and advertisement you see. Purchasing plain frames from discount stores will also often be cheaper than your local department store. Paint the frames any color you like and add family photos, maternity pictures, or other artwork or pictures you have purchased or collected to decorate your baby's nursery with.

Decorating our daughter's room was a fun and exciting process, but it had to be done with a budget in mind; we could not afford to spend endless amounts of money at designer stores. The three most wonderful decorating tips I used for decorating our daughter's room were used frames, art sales at discount stores, and creating simple flower ensembles from craft store sales. The first and most inexpensive decorating tip I used was to purchase used frames from thrift stores or garage sales, in which I inserted maternity photos of my husband and me together after painting the frames to match the lavender color scheme of our daughter's room. The second tip I used was to purchase matted pictures that we wanted displayed as part of the décor in our daughter's room. There are many craft stores such as Hobby Lobby and Michaels that will have 50- to 75-percent-off sales on these items. They may be found in the framing area of the store, and if you purchase only the matted pictures and used frames you have found at secondhand stores and garage sales, you can spend a minimal amount of money.

We hung a total of 12 pictures and photographs in the nursery, and it cost under $100. This includes the price of professional maternity photography, which was $58. The third tip I used was purchasing flowers and vines on sale at craft stores as well. I took the vines and inserted flowers that matched our décor to create a feminine look that hangs above our daughter's windows and closets; this cost us less than $25 and is one of the most beautiful focal points of the room. Flowers might not be the best for a baby boy's room, but you can do the same with greenery and pine cones or fern branches.

Lettering and Names

One of the most popular ways to take up a large amount of wall space in your infant's nursery is to add lettering or her name to an empty space. This style of decorating may effortlessly join any decorating theme or style, and letters can be found in many different fonts and styles. Adding a set of the ABCs or your baby's name to the wall will not only add a playful touch to the room, it can take up as much space as you desire. Also, having those letters ever present will make your baby more aware of them at an early age. Finding the right style of lettering for your baby's room will be quickly accomplished by using the Internet and doing a search for "decorative lettering."

There are many Web sites that have a variety of different types of lettering styles, and choosing what will best accommodate your décor will be a matter of finding the right letters at the right price. Lettering is not as inexpensive as the other methods of decorating listed in this chapter, but for the amount of wall you can cover, the price is less than you might spend purchasing decorations at baby stores or department stores. The average cost of plain block or script lettering that is 12 inches in height will be $12 to $18 per letter; this will include the letter and a ribbon or hooked back for easy installation or hanging.

The room my husband and I decorated for our daughter included a large wall where we hung the letters of her name. The letters are 12 inches tall, from 6 to 12 inches wide, and take up nearly 10 feet of wall space. Not only are the letters decorative and hung with wonderful accenting pink ribbons, but they were recognized by our daughter as soon as she could focus across the room. The bright ribbons drew her eye, and she began recognizing her letters at an early age. At only two and a half years old she could spell her name for anyone who asked. I do not think this is because our daughter is a genius; I believe she memorized the sequence of letters on her wall, and because we have told her that is her name, she put these two pieces of information together. I do believe this has fostered an interest in learning in the areas of alphabet, spelling, and writing. Everything you do can make a difference in your child's life and introducing educational materials (even if it is only seeing the letters) is always a priority on your list of things to do as a parent.

Finishing Touches

Finally, in decorating your baby's new room, you can add some finishing touches that will be useful items but also add to the look of the nursery. Small lamps, mobiles, borders or wall stickers, and a hamper will all be either useful or inexpensive and add some dimension to the nursery.

Small lamps will be useful, especially for late-night feedings and diaper changes. They light the room minimally so you do not shock your baby into wakefulness but will provide enough light to get whatever job you need to, as quickly as possible.

Lamps for your baby's nursery can be found in many different styles, designs, shapes, and sizes. Smaller lamps may be best, as they will provide a small amount of light, and most baby departments of stores and lighting or décor departments of baby superstores will carry a wide variety to choose from. Most decorative baby lamps will cost between $20 and $30. This will be an item that you will be able to use for years, and you can adjust the brightness of the light simply by changing the bulb. Of course, do not exceed the recommendation for wattage, but you can use less wattage for a dimmer-lighted area. Most lamps in baby motif are sold separately from the large bedding ensembles you can purchase for the crib, giving you a wide selection to choose from, even if you choose not to purchase an expensive crib bedding set.

Another item that is often sold separately from the large crib bedding ensembles is the baby mobile. This means that again, you will have a nearly endless selection without having to purchase an entire bedding set for your baby's crib. Choosing a mobile to match your baby's room should not

be difficult, as there are all shapes, sizes, and colors of fun characters and designs to choose from. A baby mobile is not a must-have, but it does entertain most babies long enough for you to slip in a quick shower as your baby watches the colorful patterns or characters move to the music. Mobiles will provide something for your baby to look at while he is trying to put himself to sleep and can keep him entertained after he has woken up if he has no immediate needs to be met.

Most crib mobiles bought brand new will cost between $35 and $60. If you are hesitant to spend such a large amount of money on twirling, singing animals, look for a crib mobile at secondhand baby shops or garage sales. You can also find mobiles that are wall mounted for $10 to $20 new, and although they are not as luxurious looking, your baby will not care, as long as it is fun to look at and has some nice, soft music for falling asleep if you decide to use it at bed and nap times. A wall-mounted mobile will work for your baby's crib, as long as it is positioned next to a wall; most cribs are, but if you have arranged your baby's nursery otherwise, a crib-attached mobile will be a better fit.

Wall stickers and borders may be an addition to room décor that you will add right after painting your baby's nursery. However, if you have your room "complete" or your budget is not allowing you to add much more, you can always return to this inexpensive way to add to each wall of your room easily. Applying a border or wall stickers is virtually pain free, and the price is close to painless as well.

Borders for your infant's walls can be found in your local department store, baby superstore, and sometimes in secondhand stores if they were purchased and never used. Applying a border to your walls is as simple as cutting the length of border you need, marking the wall so it is attached straight, and then gluing the border up with the adhesive back or with water, much like wallpaper. There is little mess, and we hung our daughter's border in less than two hours. The border we used added a whole new look to the room and is still cherished by our daughter today at three years old. You can purchase borders, which will run the length of each wall in your baby's nursery, for under $30. This is a way to split the room in half, add some color, or just add a splash of character to a room that might not have turned out exactly as you pictured.

Wall stickers are even easier to apply to your walls than borders; they are also cheaper and can be removed from the walls and taken with you if you move or decide that you no longer want them as part of the room's decorations.

Wall stickers can also be hung on each wall or on specific walls that you choose; they give you a bit more flexibility with how the room is decorated while still providing the addition of playful, colorful, and fun characters or designs. A wall sticker is just that, a large sticker that comes with an adhesive back that you place on the wall where ever you like. If you want to move it, you simply take it down, move it, and re-stick it in a new spot, giving you a wide variety of decorating options. Wall stickers cost less than borders and can be found in just as many designs, characters, and styles. Most department stores carry a good variety of wall stickers that are appropriate for infant nurseries. You can also find a wide selection of wall stickers online by doing a simple search, finding unused packages of stickers in online auctions, or at secondhand stores. An average package of wall stickers will come with four to eight large stickers or ten to 20 smaller stickers, and prices can range from $12 to $40.

Finally, we come to the hamper. Hampers that are made for infant nurseries or young children's rooms now are decorative and can add to the look of your baby's room. Not only will a hamper be useful for the rest of your child's life, it will help you to keep the dirty clothes in one place and give you easy transport when getting them to the laundry room. Hampers are offered in all sorts of different styles, from folding to plastic, and can feature a simple and elegant look or be covered with princesses or cars. Most hampers found in baby superstores or department stores are reasonably priced, between $10 and $25.

Once you have made some decisions about what you would like to have in your infant's room and what you and your baby can live without, you should be able to decorate her room for under $300; this does not include furniture, of course. If you were to shop high-end decorating stores, it could cost you nearly $2,000 to decorate with the same styles and designs as revealed in this final part of the chapter. Keep in mind your budget and your vision as you shop for decorations and remember that finding a good deal on items that can be altered, painted, re-covered, or rearranged will be beneficial in the long run as your baby grows and begins to know what he likes or dislikes. Before long, you will likely have a opinionated toddler, and having decorations that you can switch up to make his or her room exciting without spending excess money will be fun and inexpensive.

Chapter 8

Items that Can Break the Bank

Having a baby means that there will be some expensive items that you might need to buy. Some of the baby items in this section will be absolutely necessary, while others are just convenient to have as your infant grows and her needs change throughout the first year of her life. The items in this chapter that you will surely want to have will include an appropriate vehicle, highchair, and stroller. You will also want to be sure to have a good infant car seat and attaching carrier, but because you have read about what to look for and how to purchase these items in Chapter 2, we will not discuss them here. Items that might be optional for some parents might not seem

optional for others. Some of the items that can be expensive that can be optional include portable playpens or Pack 'n Plays, bouncy seats, jumpers, swings, and walkers.

Some of these items you might already have, especially a vehicle. You might want to upgrade to be more appropriate for the uses you will have for it in the near future, or you might not need to worry about it, as the vehicles you already have might suffice. Some of this will depend on your budget and what you can afford versus what you want. Every baby does need a car seat if you have a car, but not every baby needs to have a bouncy seat, walker, or portable playpen.

An Appropriate Vehicle

When a couple finds out that they are expecting a child, the last thing to cross their mind might be the mode of transportation they are using. Most vehicles work for kids; there are only a select few families that must consider changing the vehicle they are currently driving. However, if you are in that select few and the thought of having a different type of vehicle does not cross your mind, it can cause problems once your baby is born. The vehicles that might not be appropriate for a new family can include those that will seat only one or two people, such as sports cars or motorcycles. Other vehicles that you might want to consider trading in for something more appropriate are those that are mechanically unsafe, that you might not be able to fix, or that will not be comfortable in accommodating the entire family. If this is the case and you believe it wise to investigate the options of a different vehicle, shop for a vehicle that costs less than the current one you own, has the accommodations you desire as a family, and will provide as inexpensive long-term use as possible.

Some of the options you might look for in a new vehicle if you determine you need one include low gas mileage, enough room for the family you are planning on having, comfort getting in and out, ease for both parents to drive, and safe for children.

When my husband and I discovered our little one was on the way, we owned a 1994 Ford Escort with mechanical problems and a 2004 Jeep Rubicon. Not one of these cars was, in our opinion, suitable for our family. My husband was worried about the mother of his child driving a car that was bound to spontaneously combust at any moment, and I was not about to be bumped and jostled all the way to the hospital while in labor in a topless Jeep. At the time, our budget would allow for only one car payment, and because the Ford Escort was paid in full and the Jeep had a expensive monthly payment, we made the decision to keep the Escort and trade in the Jeep Rubicon. This was a painful decision for my husband, as it was his favorite car he had ever owned, but it was the responsible thing to do. We traded in our Jeep and purchased a car that was suitable for our upcoming family. After our daughter was born and our "new" used car was paid off, we donated the Escort to charity and were lucky to have a car handed down from my generous in-laws. We now have two good, family-friendly cars that have been completely paid off. If you shop wisely and purchase a used car with a payment that fits comfortably into your budget, you will likely be able to pay your car off ahead of time and relieve your family of one more monthly bill.

Highchairs

Having a highchair for your baby may not seem like an item you will need at this point in time, but when your baby becomes old enough to start eating foods other than breast milk or formula and you see what a mess feeding can be, you will likely change your mind. Feeding your baby food with a spoon will be fun, challenging, and messy. Having a highchair that will help your baby to stay in an upright position, semi-contain the mess, and be easy to clean will be a lifesaver. Most babies are already sitting on their own by the time they are ready to eat baby food, but because all babies develop and learn in their own time, some are not sitting steady by this time and need additional support. The last thing you want is your carrot-covered baby rolling away all over your carpet while you are trying to feed him.

Highchairs can be expensive, and the price ranges will vary considerably. Most highchairs will cost about $130, but the range in prices varies from $30 up to $210. This price may offer you a sturdy highchair, made to grow with your baby in all the stages of young feeding. The options you will find in most highchairs that come with a similar price tag are a feeding tray, soft cushioned plastic or cloth-covered seat, safety harness, and adjustable seat.

The best features you will want to look for in a highchair will include a feeding tray; some highchairs have a removable food tray, which makes cleanup much easier, as it can usually be safely washed in the dishwasher or easily washed by hand in your kitchen sink.

Whether you decide to purchase a highchair with a plastic- or cloth-covered seat will be a personal preference. Most cloth-covered seats look much nicer and might seem to be more comfortable for your baby, but a plastic-covered cushioned seat is just as comfortable and is much easier to clean — and it will get dirty. The smooth plastic wipes down quickly and easily, and there is no hassle of removing the seat cover to wash it in the laundry or try to remove tough stains.

The highchair you purchase must have a safety harness. This is not only to protect your baby as an infant from falling out, but also when she is older and decides to attempt climbing out while your back is turned for a second. Not only is purchasing a highchair with a safety harness necessary, but you must remember to use it no matter how unhappy your baby might be about it. Finding a highchair with a

safety harness is not difficult, as nearly all them come equipped with a three-point or five-point harness. Finally, you will want to look for a highchair with an adjustable seat. You will want a highchair to adjust in height so it can be moved to fit whatever height your table is, or for many other instances when you will want to change the height at which your baby is sitting. You will also want to purchase a highchair with an adjustable back or lean to the seat. This will be most necessary for babies who cannot support themselves fully in the upright sitting position or are prone to exploring what is on the other side of the arm of their highchairs. Having the ability to adjust the back of your baby's highchair will help you keep her settled where she needs to be to learn how to sit comfortably and eat her food.

After exploring all these options and deciding what features you believe will be the most helpful for you in feeding your baby, you will want to start to narrow down your choices at the store. The Baby Trend Safari Baby's Highchair is one of the best buys with all the features that are listed above. This $80 highchair comes with two removable feeding trays, adjusts with six different settings for height and four different recline settings, a five-point safety harness, and a removable washable seat pad. Other features that make this Baby Trend highchair a good purchase include the fold-away design, which makes the seat easy to store when you are not using it, and it is set on locking casters, making it easy to move about your kitchen whether baby is in it or not. Other highchairs you might want to look at will include the Graco Contempo™ Highchair and the Chicco Polly Highchair. Both of these highchairs have all the same features as the Baby Trend, plus some extras; the price is a bit higher, ranging from $90 to $110.

No matter what type of highchair you choose, be sure it has a safety harness and will accommodate your baby and your kitchen space before purchasing. Most highchairs are returnable if they are still in the original packaging, but returning an unwanted highchair in an opened box can be difficult and frustrating.

Strollers

Finding the right stroller or strollers for your life style will be a key in convenience for you and your family. Without the right strollers for your hobbies or day-to-day life, you might find yourself not doing the things that you love and find that you regret not looking into all the possibilities for mobility with an infant. Even as your baby grows beyond the years of infancy, you will continue to use your strollers daily. One day your baby will become mobile through crawling and walking, but just because your little one can walk does not mean that she will be able to keep up with your pace where ever your daily travels may take you.

There are many different types of strollers that will serve different purposes in your life. The things you and your family enjoy doing will determine what types of strollers you need as well as how many.

Quick TIP

There are five main categories of strollers that you will have to choose from — lightweight strollers, standard strollers, convertible travel system strollers, double and triple strollers, and all-terrain or jogging strollers.

Some parents might feel they will need only one or two types of strollers. Others will find throughout their lives as parents they will need three or even four different types of strollers. When deciding what types of strollers you will need for your life style and your baby, you will first need to know what features each type of stroller will offer.

Lightweight strollers are a must-have for most moms and dads. They are inexpensive, weigh less than 15 pounds, and are compact for travel. Most lightweight strollers will cost between $20 and $40, depending on the brand and quality of stroller you choose. This does not mean that a $20 lightweight stroller will not be an adequate match for the amount of use you will get from it. Because lightweight strollers are made for travel and day-to-day living, most are of good quality and will last you a long time. Lightweight strollers are made primarily for babies that can support their own weight in a sitting position, as the seat may be made of a soft and less supportive material with no padding. The other reason lightweight strollers are for babies beyond the stages of infancy is that there is no option for recline on a lightweight stroller; the baby can sleep in the stroller, but he will be in an upright sitting position. One of the most convenient aspects of a lightweight stroller is that it will fit into most overhead compartments on airplanes and fit into your trunk compactly enough for you to also bring home groceries or other shopping items.

Finding the right lightweight stroller for you is not hard, as long as you are shopping for a baby that is past the stages of infancy. The only extra options you will have to choose from are the appearance of the stroller, a retractable sunshade, and a detachable bag for personal affects or things you would like to carry with you. Other than these few additions, a lightweight stroller, which is often referred to as an umbrella stroller, will come with the bare necessities — a place for your child to sit and a safety harness to keep him in place.

Standard strollers are the next size up from a lightweight stroller. They are slightly larger and do not fold down as compactly for travel or storage. Most standard strollers will weigh between 18 and 25 pounds and may offer a cup holder for you and your baby, a small tray for your baby, a supportive back and a seat that reclines slightly, an adjustable handle, and an undercarriage basket for storing your purse, diaper bag, or other things you might be carrying with you  at any given point in time. The advantages of having a standard stroller are that they are more sturdy, better quality, and have good-quality safety belts or harnesses and washable seat padding. Most also have easy-open and -close mechanisms and locking wheel brakes and will often last you through a number of children. Standard-sized strollers are still compact enough to store in most vehicle trunks while still having enough room to store a number of items that you might need to fit in your trunk as well. They are also small enough to carry on a plane, but you will need to hand them over to the flight crew for the duration of your flight and pick them up after you have landed as you exit the plane. A standard stroller is more expensive but might be worth the extra money if your primary need of a stroller does not include a much travel on airplanes, as they are not as easily stored as lightweight strollers.

The price of a standard stroller can range from $50 to $500 depending on the style, brand name, and features you are looking for to accommodate your life style. The Graco Metrolite series and Combi City Savvy series are the two most popular brands and styles of standard strollers among many parents. They are priced in the median and lower ranges of the price range of standard strollers. Both the Graco Metrolite series and Combi City Savvy series look great, offer all the features that are most important overall to busy parents, and come from well-known baby manufacturing name brands. The Graco Metrolite strollers will cost from $170 to $200, and the Combi City Savvy stroller series will range in cost from $50 to $110.

Depending on your needs, one of these brands might be better for you than the other. The Combi City Savvy series is smaller and more compact than the Graco Metrolite series but also offers less in the way of options for comfort in travel, around town or abroad. If you are a traveling family that has a need for more than a lightweight stroller has to offer but would still prefer the convenience of a smaller stroller, the Combi strollers might be a good option to explore. If storage

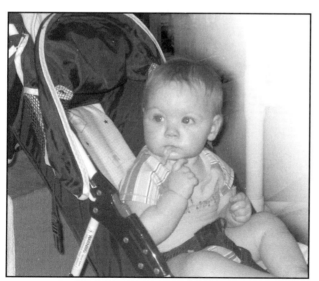

space is less of a need than comfort for you, then the Graco Metrolite series might be a better choice; again, this is a buying decision that must be made with your needs and life style kept in mind.

Case Study: Emily Gary

Emily Gary, mother of two wonderful boys now three and five years old in Littleton, Colorado, used her Graco Metrolite stroller and car seat carrier daily and listed them as two of the most user-friendly items she experienced using during her time of mothering two young boys and still uses them for her three-year-old.

The items were not only used on a daily basis, but they were durable, quality items that have lasted through two rough-and-tumble boys. When asked to elaborate on her uses of these items Emily said, "We used the carrier daily. Sometimes the baby slept in the carrier if he was sick, during which times we would put the carrier in his nursery. The stroller was used daily for walks and trips to stores and was extremely useful while making travels through the airport."

Emily admits that they struggled with the purchase of the Graco Metrolite Travel System, purchased at approximately $150. Emily said, "We wanted a lightweight stroller that was compact but also offered enough usable features, such as cup holders and an under-carriage basket so we could travel in comfort no matter where we were." This stroller set has lasted for five years and is still being used because of the amount of storage the stroller has that is a big help in daily outings.

Emily also shared items that she purchased that she felt were unnecessary. These included a crib bumper ($80) and a video monitor ($100+). Both of these were rarely used, and she felt the money would have been better spent elsewhere. When shopping, Emily and her husband first considered quality and safety. At times, brand name was a consideration, but only when the brand name proved to be a better quality than the lower-priced competitors.

When asked to share what she has learned as a mother, she said, "Everything is a phase and it is always changing, and do not spend too much time wishing for one stage to end and the next to begin, because the days go by so fast. They are not babies for long."

Even larger than the standard stroller are convertible travel system strollers; these are often sold in sets with a car seat carrier, base, and stroller that the carrier will fit into. You purchase them separately, but the sets fit together to offer the ultimate comfort in daily travel. Once your baby has outgrown the infant carrier, the stroller can be used without the infant carrier, giving the stroller a longer life to accommodate you and your baby. Travel system strollers come with a wide variety of luxuries and are often one of the most popular strollers for parents with infants and a large quantity of items to carry along with them when leaving home with their infants. A convertible travel system stroller set is a deluxe version of the standard stroller; however, some can be larger and heavier than standard strollers.

The main advantages of a travel system are the convenience of moving your baby from the car to the stroller without disturbing him, which is especially helpful when your baby has fallen asleep in the car.

Also helpful is the ability to fully cover your baby while he sleeps in the convertible travel system stroller so he is not disturbed by light, passing people, or noise. For an infant, this can be monumental, especially for accomplishing daily tasks while your infant sleeps. Travel system strollers are often more expensive than standard strollers, ranging in price from $250 to $400. Keep in mind the pricing for most travel systems will include the infant carrier, car seat base and stroller; each can be purchased separately or together for the above listed price ranges.

The price of a convertible travel system is quite reasonable once you factor in that you are purchasing all the components necessary to equip your car with a child safety seat as well as a stroller that accommodates the car seat and carrier. Some of the most popular brands again will include the Combi and Graco convertible travel systems, but less popular brands will work just as well. The decision must be based on the features of the item and what you feel you will most likely need as new parents.

Double and triple strollers are not needed if you are expecting one baby, unless you are sure you are going to continue with your family additions shortly after your first child is born. This would mean that  you would have a large stroller for the first child, though. A double or triple stroller is necessary for your first baby only if you have discovered that your "first baby" will be "babies." These strollers are for siblings close in age, twins, or triplets. If you are expecting twins or triplets (or more), you will likely want to consider a double or triple stroller. Some options to investigate before purchasing any double stroller will be to test some out. Side by side, double strollers can often be wide and cumbersome to parents, as they often do not fit as easily through some stores or establishments as a tandem double stroller. Tandem double strollers place one child in front of the other, and although they are easier to fit through tight spaces, they will inevitably cause an argument in the future about who will sit in the front. Most double or triple strollers are priced from $100 to $800, depending on the style of stroller you need and the amount of available seating room.

All-terrain or jogging strollers fill an entirely separate set of stroller needs. These types of strollers are for parents who have a hobby of running, jogging, walking off trail, or other exercise on a regular basis. A standard lightweight or convertible travel system stroller can be used for leisurely walks on solid surfaces, but an all-terrain or jogging stroller will better suit those more adventurous parents who are planning on keeping with their love of the outdoors after their infant is born. Most strollers are fine for walking, but the advantages that an all-terrain stroller will offer to parents and baby are large wheels for smoother rides, suspension, and lightweight design. There are disadvantages and reasons that this may not be the best choice to have as your only stroller, which include that they are not designed for infants with no head or body support, and they are often large and long. These are not strollers that fold down to fit in compact spaces; many do not fold down and are not able to travel with you easily on airplanes or other modes of transportation. However, the cons will not outweigh the advantages for those parents who are avid outdoor explorers or who love to exercise and want to continue to do so after their baby is born.

Finally, when shopping for the right stroller or strollers for you and your family, you can save money by shopping in secondhand stores or at garage sales. If your budget warrants that secondhand is the best option for you or sometimes the only option, there are specific points to remember while looking for a used stroller. First, if you are considering a travel system, purchasing the stroller used is fine, but the base and infant carrier should be purchased new, as it is important to your baby's safety to know that his car seat has never been in an accident that might have damaged it. Whether you can see the damage or not, car accidents can make any car seat unsafe.

Quick TIP

When looking at strollers in secondhand stores or at garage sales, be sure to thoroughly inspect the entire stroller for any safety concerns. Check to see that all the wheels are working appropriately and safely, safety harnesses and seat belts are secure and undamaged, and that the frame is sturdy. Check all surfaces and the frame of the stroller for cracks, splits, punctures, or any other sort of damage.

A stroller is an item that you will likely use daily, and purchasing a safe and sturdy stroller is important; purchasing them used is not a problem as long as you inspect the stroller closely and test it out. Another note to take when making a used stroller purchase is to check *Consumer Reports* for recalls on the brand and model of stroller you are purchasing; if the stroller has been recalled for any reason, do not purchase it. You can check *Consumer Reports* for recalls on all types of items by visiting **www.consumerreports.org**.

While expecting our daughter, my husband and I looked at many different convertible travel systems and strollers. Finally, we decided that looking for a used stroller was going to be the best option for our family, and we ended up receiving an entire convertible travel system from a friend who found one free at a church donation center. Before our daughter was born, we checked all the components to be sure they had not been recalled and also looked up the identification number on the car seat to check that it had not been involved in any automobile accidents. At the time, my husband and I thought that we had covered all the appropriate bases to be sure our daughter's travel system was safe, and it served us well for the year we used it. However, being a more educated mother and father now tells us that we should have purchased the infant carrier and car seat base new. There are many accidents every year that are not reported, and there is often no way to tell whether a used infant carrier and car seat base were ever involved in an accident. Everything we used seemed to be safe, and although we had no issues with the car seat base or carrier, our next child will be riding in a new one or one that we receive as a hand-me-down from a close friend or family member.

Portable Playards

Portable playards, otherwise known as Pack 'n Plays or portable playpens, are an expensive item that some parents use on a daily basis and others end up leaving in a closet for years without ever using. So how do you determine whether you will use a portable playard? There are several questions that you can ask yourself that will help you make a decision about this expensive item.

- Do you have an appropriate place to put your baby in your main living area for diaper changes, restricted play, and naps?

- Do you often go out in the evenings when your child would need a place to sleep while you are visiting with friends?

- Will you often have a babysitter sit at their home where there is not a crib or other appropriate place for your child to nap or sleep?

- Do you have an appropriate place to keep your baby out of harm's way while you do a task that might require your full attention for any amount of time?

If you do not have an appropriate place for your child to spend a small amount of restricted playtime while your attention might be elsewhere, a place to change him, or for him to sleep during the day other than his room, you might find a portable playard useful. If you are parents who intend to enjoy spending time out, with our without your child, and need to accommodate sleeping arrangements at grandparents', friends' or babysitters' homes, you also might find a portable playard useful. Portable playards are a resource for you and your baby if you believe you will use one. We received a Graco Pack 'n Play for our baby shower, and we used it every day of our daughter's life for the first nine months. After that, and still today, we use our Pack 'n Play for many different reasons and plan on using it for our second child as well. It has been worth every penny that my best friends spent on it for us as a gift.

The main convenience of a portable playard is that it is just that; portable. You can use it in many different situations for your baby to sleep in and play in. Most also come with a changing table that can easily be removed as well. Our Pack 'n Play has traveled to many different states and has been used in homes of friends, of family, hotel rooms, and even in a hotel bathroom. We also use it when friends come to visit with younger toddlers and babies for a convenient place for their children to sleep if we would like to visit past the early hour of the 7:30 or 8 p.m. bedtime of most young children.

Portable playards can be purchased new or used, depending on your preferences and budget. Purchasing a portable playard used is not a concern, as long as you check to see that it functions correctly, is easy to set up and take down, and comes with all the necessary pieces. When purchasing a used playard, you might not find all the options that new ones come with, but at a price of $30 to $100, you might be able to forfeit some of the fancy features to save a little money. Options in portable playards have grown so much over the years that now there are an almost endless variety of features  you can choose from. Be careful not to get carried away, as the more features your portable playard comes with, the higher the price will climb. Some of the many features that portable playards can come with are changing tables, mobiles, adjustable floors, music, vibrating mattresses, diaper holders, and natural colors that will fit into the décor of most living areas of your home. The main features that will make your portable playard the most useful will be an adjustable floor, easy assembly and breakdown, ease of storage, a changing table, and a place for diaper storage if you are going to use it in a common area for changing diapers.

The price of most new portable playards varies from $60 to $200; the average price with the most fun for your money will be around $130. Most playards at the $130 price will offer most of the functions that you would prefer your playard to have. Our Graco Pack 'n Play was $120 and spent the greater part of nine months in our family room where we changed our daughter, let her nap when she fell asleep in our arms, and put her when I needed to have a few minutes to myself, answer the door, take an important call without the sounds of a baby in the background, and many other instances. After the Pack 'n Play was no longer a daily used item, it was stored easily in a closet and used nearly every weekend for our daughter or a visiting friend's baby for naps or bedtime. Traveling with the Pack 'n Play was easy and convenient, as it travels just like any other piece of luggage and could be used in hotel rooms or friends' homes. It was also once put in our hotel bathroom so my husband and I could stay up in our room watching television after 6:30 in the evening when our daughter needed to go to bed. Use your own judgment as to whether a playard will be useful for you; ask friends, and be sure to test out used ones before purchasing them to be sure all is easy to operate and in working order.

Bouncers, Jumpers, and ExerSaucers

Bouncers are a way to keep your infant in one spot but still entertain him. They are smaller than playards and can be used in smaller areas, securely set up off the floor away from other children or pets, and travel well no matter where you might be going. Most bouncers are easy to assemble and take apart for quick storage and easy travel. Most young babies will enjoy them, as they are soft and comfortable. Most have fun toys to look at and play with as well as vibrate when turned on or rock when your baby bounces around in the seat. A bouncer will not only give your baby a place to play, sit, and sleep, but the movements will also help to strengthen his muscles for sitting by himself, crawling, and walking.

There are plenty of styles, designs, and brands to choose from, all with different features and accessories for your baby to play with. The easiest way to choose a bouncer for your baby is to determine how much you would like to spend, and stick to that decision. You will have a wide variety of price ranges to choose from, as bouncers can cost anywhere from $25 up to $130. The less-expensive bouncers may offer a spring-loaded back that moves when your baby moves, a safety harness, and a detachable mobile for your baby to look at and play with. As you climb higher in the price range, you will find bouncers with vibration options, music, rocking or swinging motions, and some are more cushioned and plush than those on the less-expensive end of the price range.

We bought a bouncer for our daughter at a garage sale and also received one as a gift. The one we received as a gift was nicer than the one we purchased, as it vibrated and played music. It was also more padded in the sitting area and had more toys to play with and look at. However, it did not seem to matter to our daughter. She preferred the $2 bouncer we bought from the garage sale. This was a simple bouncer with a spring-loaded back and one set of removable toys. Our daughter enjoyed this item until she was about a year old, and then it was stored in the basement and is patiently waiting for another baby to sit in it. In my opinion, one year of use for $2 was a terrific deal, especially when I could buckle her safely into her bouncer seat set on the counter where she could watch contentedly while I made dinner and talked to her.

Most babies will enjoy a bouncer; some do not, and so it is wise not to go crazy when purchasing bouncers and similar items. When you continuously buy the most expensive item you can find for your baby, you are not giving him the "best." You might be spending a good deal of money on items that your child might never use or might dislike so much that you are not able to use them when the time comes. Some of this money would be much better used for college savings, items you will need, or even a nice evening out for you and your spouse alone. This sounds trivial now, but once you have a full-time baby on your hands, a night out alone is all too often a rare treat.

Jumpers are the graduated bouncer in my opinion. Jumpers are for babies that are old enough to support themselves and are working hard on strengthening their legs for walking. Some babies love jumpers; others hate them. It just depends on your baby's personality and what she likes and dislikes. We bought our daughter a jumper from a neighbor's garage sale. I looked it up and knew it would have cost nearly $85; we paid $10 for it, and it was still in the packaging. Their daughter hated it, and unfortunately, so did our daughter. However, I gave it to my best friend for her son to use, and he practically lived in the contraption. A jumper is like a swing that you either hang from a doorway, or it comes pre-hung on a metal or plastic frame much like a baby

swing. The seat of the jumper is suspended with stretchy material that allows your baby to jump or bounce from the floor until his little heart is content. Jumpers are another way to keep your baby safely entertained while you tend to matters in the same room or one nearby. When your baby is safely strapped into the jumper he cannot escape, and you will know where he is and what he is doing with only a glance up to see his smiling face.

Depending on what style of jumper you are interested in purchasing, the cost will vary. Jumpers that are hung by you from a doorway are often less expensive, ranging from $20 to $40, but if you are not tall enough to reach the top of your doorways, these will be more of a nuisance than it is often worth. This is because when your baby is not playing in his jumper you will likely want to remove it from the doorway so you are not constantly running into it, having to push it out of the way, or just because your home will look tidier without a jumper hanging from every doorway. Floor jumpers that are suspended on an A-frame are a bit more expensive, ranging from $60 to $110, but they are easy to move from room to room and you do not need a doorway to hang them. You simply set them on the floor in the room where your baby will have enough room to bounce himself around for a bit.

Quick **TIP**
Jumpers are not easy to pack and take on vacations with you, and they are primarily an item you will use in your own home for entertaining and exercising your baby.

Most floor jumpers, which can include Evenflo ExerSaucers, are large and bulky and do not store well. If you are weary that your baby might not like a jumper that is suspended, an ExerSaucer is a alternative. ExerSaucers will allow your baby to bounce and jump as well as offer her a wide variety of toys to play with as she sits or stands in the ExerSaucer. Although our daughter hated any type of jumpers, she loved her ExerSaucer. Today, at three years old,

our daughter still is terrified of swinging, and in my opinion, this is why she did not like jumpers; being suspended in mid-air is simply not in her comfort zone.

An ExerSaucer or stationary entertainer is a round, table-like toy with a seat in the center. Most have the option of using legs or the concave design that lets the ExerSaucer totter from side to side a bit. ExerSaucers not only entertain babies who are strong enough to support their own weight, but they are also for core muscle strengthening, balance, and strengthening leg muscles. In my opinion, an ExerSaucer is the best toy out of all the jumpers and swings for older babies, but that is mainly because our daughter loved hers so much. ExerSaucers are priced competitively with free-standing jumpers, ranging from $40 to $130; the more money you spend, the more toys will be attached to the top of the ExerSaucer table. Most ExerSaucers have three to four adjustments for height and have a removable washable seat pad. ExerSaucers are just like bouncers and jumpers in that they are nice items to find at secondhand shops and garage sales. Most of these expensive but fun items for your baby are gently used, and purchasing one secondhand is fine, as long as you check to see that it is in good condition. Our ExerSaucer was purchased at a garage sale. Although it would have cost nearly $100 new, we paid only $10 for it, and it was just like new when we bought it.

Check out **www.craigslist.org**. This Web site allows you to choose your location, and you can find many gently used baby items here. It is especially good for larger items.

Case Study: Lauren Ferencko

Lauren Ferencko, a mother of one, in Seattle, Washington, found that there were many useful items that were not only helpful to her as a mother, but to her son's entertainment and playtime during the pre-walking stages of life.

When asked about the most parent- and infant-friendly items she used, she listed her Evenflo ExerSaucer®, Fisher-Price® bouncy chair, and Evenflo® playard. "All of these items were great for keeping my son occupied and safe before he could walk. They were also easy to set up and move around." All of these items Lauren and her husband received as gifts from friends and family members, and all of the items were generally used on a daily basis.

Other items that Lauren and her family enjoyed were her Boppy® pillow, which made it much more comfortable to nurse her son for long periods of time, and the Gymini play mat, which was great for entertaining her son while he was less than a year old. "The Gymini kept my son occupied and amused for about 30 minutes a day when he was under a year."

Lauren and her family spent most of their time shopping at Target and Babies "R" Us because she feels the stores are easy to navigate, the products are good quality, and the prices are reasonable. While many of the items that Lauren and her family purchased were new, the used and secondhand items she purchased or received included clothing, toys, a crib, a stroller, and a changing table. When shopping for any items for their son, Lauren said the most attention was paid to safety, quality, and price of the items.

When Lauren was asked to pass on a piece of advice and what she has learned as a parent, she said, "Even when they can not talk, children have ways of communicating their needs and wants. It is important to slow down and be receptive to the way they express their feelings and desires. Trust your instincts when it comes to your child and make time each day to have a quiet moment with them."

Swings and Walkers.

Swings and walkers are again optional items that your baby might love or hate, depending on his preferences. Swings are a way to keep many babies soothed and sleeping through hectic times of the day. Because your baby is enjoying a gentle rocking motion in your womb right now every time you move, many babies are comfortable in swings from the day they are born until they are too big to fit in the swing seat. Three years ago, the question was what type of swing should we buy; at least that is what my husband and I struggled with at 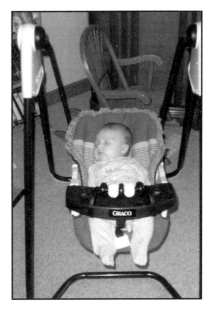 the baby store. We bought the wrong one; thankfully we bought it at a garage sale for $5 instead of from the baby superstore for $105. Now most infant swings are made so that you do not need to choose from a front-swinging swing or a side-to-side swinging swing. We purchased a swing that moved back and forth, thinking that this was going to be the preferred way to swing.

Our daughter, as always, had a mind of her own and was terrified of the swing that moved from front to back and loved the swings that swung side to side. The thing about this decision now is that it no longer exists, given the right swing. Many swings have a rotating arm that will allow the swing to swing either way. We discovered what our daughter liked in the way of swinging because she enjoyed being cradled in one of our laps while we rocked our legs from side-to-side. Once we learned that she enjoyed this motion, we borrowed a side-to-side swing from our friends, and it was a dream come true. There were many nights when our daughter would sleep lazily in her swing while we ate dinner in peace and quiet.

The most difficult part of purchasing a swing for your infant is making the decision about whether he will like to swing. Many parents are smart to wait and make this purchase after they have delivered their baby. Once you have met your baby in person, you will start to get a feel for what she likes; does she enjoy the swinging or rocking motion in your arms or while sitting in your lap? If not, then maybe a bouncer will be a more appropriate place for your baby to relax, as most babies do not mind sitting in a bouncy seat. Swings will come with a variety of different options. Some offer the choice of swinging motions; will have toys or mirrors suspended above the seat; play music; vibrate; and some even have lights that will keep your baby in awe while she gently rocks back and forth. As with many other items, the more bells and whistles the swing has, the more the price will often be. Most swings fall into the price range of $50 to $160. The average price for a dual swinging swing is $110 and is likely to be used daily by babies that enjoy them for the first year of life.

Walkers are less popular than they were many years ago, but if they are used safely and under the right supervision, a walker is still a way for your baby to exercise, practice walking and balance, and learn how to maneuver his body in the upright position. Walkers should be used only under close

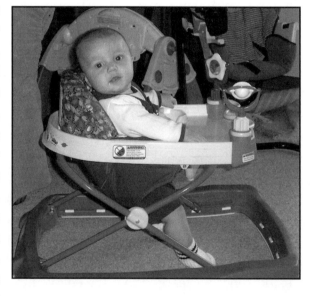

supervision and never in an area where stairs can be accessed. Aside from that, a walker is a fun way for your baby to start to explore his environment in the upright position and build up confidence.

Most walkers will come with four wheels and are in a rounded square shape. They will have a tray for holding toys, snacks, or whatever else you might give your baby while she trolls around your home. Many walkers also come equipped with a good amount of toys for your baby to play with attached to the tray top, making times of rest from walking fun too. Most walkers are more reasonably priced than many of the stationary entertainers and usually fall into a range of $25 to $100, depending on style and features you want your baby's walker to have.

Quick TIP

A walker is most appropriate for babies that are in the process of learning to pull themselves up and taking their first wobbly steps. This usually happens around nine months to a year old, but you can start your baby early to help in strengthening her legs and improving her balance.

We purchased a $4 walker from a garage sale; however, our daughter enjoyed her ExerSaucer so much that the walker never even made it out of the basement.

After looking at all these expensive items, deciding what you need and do not need and deciding what to purchase new or used, you may feel overwhelmed. Take a few days to let this all process. Your baby can live without all these things; they are simply nice to have if you can afford them or want to have them. If you cannot afford them or choose not to purchase them, your baby will never know the difference, and she will love you just as much. Always remember to check for good deals at discount stores, secondhand stores, and garage sales before paying full price at the local baby superstore. These types of items can be expensive, and looking for deals might take some time, but it will pay off in the end. Finally, remember that even if you can work many of these expensive items into your budget, you do not need to have them all. If you decide that your baby will enjoy a stationary entertainer, you likely will not need to purchase a jumper or walker.

Every baby is different. What may be "necessary equipment" for one might not interest your baby.

Chapter 9

Fun Stuff and Playtime

By the time you have reached this chapter, you should be feeling a bit more confident about what you need and desire to have for your infant, as well as what you can afford to provide him with. We have made it through how to create your budget, feeding and diapering, clothing, what to expect for your baby shower and registering, health and safety, decorating, and large items that can be costly, and now it is time to have some fun with your little one. In this chapter, we will reveal not only toys, books, videos, and music that will entertain and aid in the learning processes of your baby, we will also dive into a few fun and educational items for Mom and Dad.

Toys for Babies Less than One Year Old

All babies need to be entertained eventually. Most babies will not require much in the way of entertainment in the first two to three months; it takes a few weeks for your baby to even be able to focus his eyes on toys well enough to figure them out. For the first three months of your infant's life, you will need only a few fun toys that he will enjoy. These will often include a few colorful, exploratory toys with mirrors, a variety of different materials, and all types of textures, shapes, and soft, pliable parts that do not disconnect from the toy. The main toys you will purchase for your baby at first will be rattles or similar toys that make a noise when your baby touches, shakes, or moves them.

Some favorite toys for ages 0 to 12 months old that I have found through research and experience with our daughter include the Baby Counting Pal. This colorful caterpillar is affordable, costing around $17, depending on where you purchase it. The colors are bright and vibrant, and it plays different types of music and animal noises and even has a setting for counting. Our daughter loved this toy from the time she was three months old and throughout the first year of her life. When I was pregnant, my husband used to make the caterpillar play music and set it on my belly. Sometimes our daughter would kick when he did this. This is an interactive toy that your baby can learn to use in time. Other toys include the Giggle Ball, which can be bought for less than $13; the Gund Tinkle, Crinkle, Rattle, and Squeak Worm for less than $10; the Fisher-Price Waterfall Soother for $30; and the Me-in-the-Mirror Toy for less than $13. All these toys offer a wide variety of learning experiences and educational influence for babies less than one year old. They are also toys that will grow with your children.

Another type of toy you will want to consider purchasing for your infant is a play mat. These are toys for all types of play. The main purpose of a play mat is to eventually use it for tummy time, although there are many things for your baby to see while he lies on his back as well. All babies need to spend an adequate amount of time on their tummies, which helps them to strengthen their necks and backs so they will have the ability to support their own head. Most babies do not enjoy playing or lying on their tummies. A play mat will not only make the experience more fun for your baby with bright colors and things to look at, touch, and explore. Some babies will have so much fun they will forget that they are even on their tummies.

Infant play mats can be expensive, but they do not need to be. Your baby will never know or care whether you purchased her a $20 play mat or a $100 play mat. Some popular infant play mats include the Sassy Lilly Pad Lagoon Activity Pad for $60 and the Fisher-Price Ocean Wonders Kick and Crawl play mat, which can be found for $30. The Sassy Lilly Pad Lagoon Activity Pad is a play mat for babies that need a good deal to keep them entertained. This play mat has many overhead hanging toys as well as a fun and exciting floor pad. The Sassy Lilly Pad Lagoon Activity Pad is a bit on the pricey side, but the extra dollars are well spent if your baby bores easily with activity pads with only three or four toys.

Our daughter absolutely loved the Fisher-Price Ocean Wonders Kick & Crawl™ play mat. It entertained her through many stages of life. Before she was ready for tummy time, she could lie on her back while she kicked and hit the six colorful fish that hung above her and rewarded her with music when she moved the middle one. When she was ready to be on her tummy, there were wonderful colors and a bubble window to look through, and when she was ready to crawl, the play mat was converted into a tunnel with a fun bubble window and "swimming" fish at each end of the tunnel. Our daughter has just turned three years old, and she and her friends still use the tunnel version of the Ocean Wonders play mat as an entrance and exit to the many playhouses and forts they build together.

Case Study: Erin Jagels

Erin Jagels is a proud mother of three, ages 18, 14, and two years old. She is a wonderful mom who spends her days at home with her children as well as working from home in the fields of public relations, development, and marketing.

Erin participated in a Case Study to share with you some of the favorite items she and her two-year-old son have enjoyed together. One of Erin's most-loved items she purchased for her son is the Ocean Wonders play gym; it entertains her son and leaves her a bit of quiet time to do odds and ends with her job as well as a small amount of time to herself.

"The Ocean Wonders play gym was wonderful for playtime, fun time, motor skill development, and since my little guy needed tummy time and really did not enjoy it, it had a tummy-time-focused layout. This helped him to spend some time on his tummy without crying. Also, the play mat converted to a tunnel for crawl play too."

One of the reasons that Erin loved the Ocean Wonders play gym so much is the ability of this toy to grow with her child's needs. Erin suggests, "As often as possible, try to buy items that develop, change, and adapt to babies as they grow. This way, the item is useful and fun for longer."

Other items that Erin received as gifts for her third child included a book on baby sleeping habits, <u>Healthy Sleep Habits, Happy Child</u>, and a baby ExerSaucer. Both of these items she found to be very helpful throughout the first year with her youngest son.

When asked what advice she wished she had before becoming a mother, Erin offered these pearls. "A little dirt, even if it is consumed from a Cheerio off the floor, will not hurt. Do not overbuy, but get the basics and then see what fits your life and parenting style as your baby is growing up and developing."

Other play mats include Gymini play mats, which range from $35 to $70, Baby Einstein play mats, which range from $50 to $75, and Boppy play mats, priced at an inexpensive $25. Gymini and Baby Einstein play mats offer a good amount of toys for infants who have a wide range of curiosity and do not get overstimulated too quickly. Boppy play mats are good as they feature a miniature Boppy pillow to help your baby stay elevated, giving more freedom to look around, grab, and strengthen tummy, neck, and back muscles. The Boppy play mats have fewer toys and feature none overhead because they are made primarily for tummy play.

If a play mat does not fit into your budget, wait to purchase one until you are sure your child needs that extra entertainment while spending some time by herself on the floor. Some babies will find plenty to look at, touch, and play with simply by rolling around and exploring as much as their bodies will let them.

Books, Music, and Videos

Books, music, and videos are some of the main entertainment options that will add to and enrich the young life of your infant. Of course, you will want to exercise restraint in the amount of television you allow any child to watch, but there are DVDs and age-appropriate shows that foster the points of learning, even at two to three months old.

Quick TIP

Reading books is the best thing that you can do for your child; no matter how old your baby is, you should read to him or her for 15 minutes a day.

Not only will reading enrich and add to the strong bond you want to build with your child, but reading to your child daily will help in many other areas of cognitive development, especially in the first year of life.

From the time your baby is born, he is developing cognitively. Cognitive development includes several learning processes — memory, language, thinking, and reasoning. Reading to your infant will help him begin to sharpen his cognitive skills by learning to recognize the sound of your voice and to focus his eyes on you or the book as you capture his attention with an age-appropriate book. The more you read to your baby in infancy and throughout the rest of his life, the more he will grasp language development skills and recognize sounds.

So what should you be reading to your baby? In the young months of infancy, you can read many different books to your child. He or she will have no preference in the beginning; just that you are holding and reading a story will add to the baby's day, your bonding as a family, and the learning processes. Some books that many infants love and will last throughout the first few years of your child's life include *Goodnight Moon; Are You My Mother?; Brown Bear, Brown Bear, What Do You See?; The Very Hungry*  *Caterpillar; Where's Baby's Belly Button?; Dear Zoo;* and *Elmo's Big Lift-and-Look Book.* All these titles offer pictures for your baby to look at and easy, fun reading for you both to share for years to come. Some of the best places to purchase books for children are discount stores and secondhand stores. Discount stores, such as Ross or Big Lots, will have good books that are brand-new for much more reasonable prices than book chain stores or even your local department store.

You can often find books for more than 50 percent less than cover price at discount stores. Although secondhand stores might have good prices on books, you will want to check to see that they are in good condition so that your child will be able to follow a story if he is old enough to understand what you are reading and that the pages are in good condition so he can look at the pictures.

Quick TIP

Check out **www.frugalreader.com**. This is a free site that allows you to exchange all types of books with other members, paying only for postage to ship the books.

Of course, if you want to get the best deal for your money, you should pull out your library card. Checking out books from the library is free, and you can often renew your return dates online now, making overdue fees much more avoidable than they used to be. Using the library to find out what books your son or daughter loves can save you money, and once you find a book that your baby just will not let go of, then purchase it from a store so you will have your own copy at home. Scholastic book clubs are also a way to get amazing deals on good books for children of any age. If you know an educator or an educational program that has access to Scholastic book orders, check them out; the books they offer are educational at all levels of reading, and they are affordable.

As a family, we read every night before bed and often off and on throughout the day; our daughter also often will take it on herself as she has gotten older to simply sit down with a book by herself. She does this because she was made familiar with books early in life; she learned how to turn the pages and make up the story as she learned to say various different words. Exposing your child to the pictures and words will pique their curiosity about how a book works, what the pictures are about, and what the letters are for. Read to your child as often as you can, even if you think he is not listening.

Case Study: Kimberly Wiser

Tots in Motion
7539 E. Stroh Rd., Parker, CO 80134
www.totsinmotion.com • k.wiser@hotmail.com
Ph: 303-204-3705
Kimberly Wiser, Instructor, Teacher, Author,
Educational Consultant

Kim Wiser is a fantastic teacher and mom who has enjoyed a full and wonderful career as well as her two children, who are now seven and nine years old. Even though her children are a bit older than most of those featured in our Case Studies, Kim has a wealth of knowledge that comes from her expertise in the area of child development.

As a mother, Kim found that one of her favorite items for her children was Baby's First Picture Book, which is a soft-material book of "pages" that provides a slot for parents to insert photographs. Any picture book will be wonderful for your children, but Kim remarks, "My children loved looking at the family photos, and they were able to chew and drool on this particular book without damaging it." The photo book, like many others, is available for approximately $6 and will give your children a long-lasting look at the photos you want them to see over and over again.

Kim believes that it is imperative that you read and learn with your child as they grow from the time of birth to beyond the days when they can read themselves. When asked for one valuable piece of information to share with new parents, Kim provided these wonderful thoughts.

"Things you can do that are interactive with your baby that will stimulate discussion and language-building are some of the best things you can do with your child. Read, sing, and move with your infant. Their brains are little sponges, and they learn through rhyme, rhythm, and repetition. Take more time to enjoy each day."

There are many different ways to teach your children to use their minds; reading books to your child, and with them as they get older, is one of the best ways to develop many different cognitive and language skills.

Quick TIP

Music and nursery rhymes are another way to develop and entertain your baby. Music will not only help your baby with language development, it will also help later in life with mathematics.

Most babies enjoy music; when our daughter was an infant, she loved to listen to all types of music. She loved her Baby Bach and Baby Mozart CDs as well as some of the music that I preferred to listen to. In the car, when she was between six months and one year old, she would immediately quiet down if a Green Day song came on the radio; do not ask me why — she just seemed to enjoy the music. Even today at three years old, she spends a large part of her day singing along with various toys, movies, and books.

Our daughter's first introduction to music was the day she came home from the hospital. A friend gave us a CD of womb and heartbeat sounds. This type of soundtrack can be womb and heartbeats alone or set to music and is supposed to help your baby adjust to life outside the womb. Often, these CDs are used to assist in lulling your baby to sleep and getting her set on the "this is daytime, when you are supposed to be awake, and this is nighttime when you are supposed to sleep" schedule. For the last nine months, your baby has been hearing these sounds continuously, and once she is born, these comforting sounds simply disappear. I never once considered that this would become my favorite CD for the first three weeks of my baby's life and beyond. The sounds on the CD helped our daughter to fall into a peaceful sleep for as long as possible while she adjusted to life in the world. Even after she became more alert during the days and sleepy in the nights and evenings, we still used the CD as background music to help her get to sleep. I think I would have lost my mind if I had not had that CD. It was so relaxing; even if we were stressed to the point of thinking that sleep would be impossible, there were many nights I fell asleep to it on the couch along with my baby.

Music is easy to find for your child, and it may be inexpensive. Most baby music or lullaby CDs cost less than $12. Some favorite music selections include classical music, heartbeat and womb tracks, lullabies, nursery rhymes, and other child's favorites. We use our CDs for dancing time in the evenings, in the car, and in our daughter's room during playtimes. No matter when, where, or how you incorporate music into your baby's life, it will enrich his or her mind, imagination, and motivation to learn new things. One of the most heartwarming things I have seen is the pride in our daughter's eyes when she has mastered the lyrics to a song she has been listening to since her birth; it is touching and adds not only to your child's life but to yours as well.

Television or DVDs are another item that you may want to have on hand for your child's first year of development. A small amount of DVDs and children's programming is not going to harm your child. Although too much television is not healthy for any person, letting your infant watch 15 to 20 minutes of an age-appropriate television show or DVD every few days or twice a week can enrich and expose your baby to things you might not otherwise be able to provide. It will also allow you to have a small but often needed break occasionally. Letting your infant watch a show that is made for her developmental age is not inappropriate. However, you must be sure not to abuse the amount of time you allow your child, of any age, to watch DVDs and television.

As a baby, our daughter was allowed to watch Brainy Baby DVDs and Baby Einstein DVDs. In my opinion, these types of shows added to our daughter's day and development and gave Mom and Dad a few minutes to talk, prepare dinner, or even take a deep breath without having to attend to something. Most of these shows are 30 to 60 minutes long, but we often did not let the entire DVD play. In most cases, 15 to 20 minutes every other day was plenty of time for our daughter to have some educational entertainment. As our daughter got a bit older, she was allowed to watch an entire DVD once or twice a week but never more than an hour in a day. Yes, I will be the first to admit that on off-days, there was a full hour of television entertainment; this is not going to send your infant into a downward spiral throughout the rest of his life. Mom and Dad need time too, and if you cannot get time while your child is sleeping, you can at least capture a few minutes of connection while an age-appropriate show is entertaining your baby.

Baby Einstein and Brainy Baby DVDs are good. They are all labeled with the age groups that will best benefit and take interest in the concepts being displayed across the screen. They most often are composed to classical music, have fun characters with bright colors, and have large enough objects for infants and babies in the age groups suggested to focus on. Some are offered in different languages. Although she may not be speaking French at two months old, the experience can be enriching for everyone in the family.

At one point or another, everyone who is a parent was a new parent, and there are many things that I did not think of (as well as many other parents in the world). For example, I do not know a second language, nor did I have time to learn one with an infant in the house. Some of the DVDs that our daughter was allowed to watch from infancy to now when she is three years old are those shows that provide and teach a second language. At three years old, our daughter knows more Spanish than I have ever known in my life. I do now too, thanks to Dora and Boots, among many other shows she is allowed to watch. There are shows and inappropriate things on television that you will want to avoid, and leaving the television on all day is not the answer to any parenting dilemma. However, choosing carefully what you want your child to be exposed to in today's world will start with television at a young age and continue for the rest of your lives. Make decisions that you and your significant other are comfortable with and that fit into your life style and beliefs.

Scrapbooks and Baby Books

Memories of your baby, the first days after he is born, and even the first years of his life will inevitably fade in your mind as time goes by. You will not think so now or when you first bring your amazing new little infant home, but the memories will fade faster than you think. When you register, at some point in your pregnancy, or shortly after your baby is born, be sure to find some book, photo album, scrapbook, or memory capsule to store mementos. This can be whatever style you choose and may be a fun item for parents to pick out together. Most baby stores will have the best variety and selection in these types of items. Department stores with well-stocked baby sections will also have a fair selection. Look around and find a book or capsule that will entice you to fill in the blanks. You might not get to it right away, and do not stress yourself out about filling in every detail as it happens. Just have it on hand to jot things in when you have some time and want to recall those precious memories into a lasting piece of history.

One of the best gifts I received as an expecting mom was a small book called *A Mothers Journal*. Contrary to popular belief, not all writers love to journal. I rarely take the time to journal my own experiences and thoughts. However, I did use my mother's journal. I did not use it every day, and I often use it only when something touching, monumental, or downright hilarious happens, but sitting down and reading through the moments I have captured makes me use it even more. Some entries bring me to tears, and others make me giggle uncontrollably. I have a record of the important things I have learned, laughed about, and loved from my work as a mother and from our daughter's life. It is the best read I have ever known.

Chapter 10

Enjoying Baby and Budget Together

You have made it to the last chapter. You have learned about all the important decisions you need to make when it comes to purchasing various items for your baby. Now you need to jump back to something we visited in the first few chapters. Do not let the amount of items and products you need and want cause undue stress in your life. All loving parents want to provide the best for their children. Often, parents get too concerned with or caught up in the need to purchase everything they see that their baby might like. Babies are people, and their needs are basic. We all want many different things, but if you focus on what you need, there is not much to it. You need a place to live, food to eat, and clothing to keep you warm; other than that, you could survive without a Lexus, a nicely decorated home, or even your microwave.

> **Quick TIP**
>
> Babies are the same in material needs — they simply need shelter, food, and clothing. Other things that they need that should be provided free of charge will of course include unconditional love, guidance, and to be surrounded with caring and trustworthy people.

Because it is so easy to begin to focus only on the financial aspect of having a baby, it is a good idea to stop and reflect often throughout your pregnancy and shopping frenzies about what having a baby means to you as a mom, dad, and human. Take time each day to stop thinking about all the things you still do not have, need to get, and are worried you will not find at the best price, and then remember what having your child means to you. I used to do this often. Before our daughter was born, I loved to take a little time each day and sit in her then-unfinished nursery and dream about what I envisioned our lives to be after she would come into this world. This was a good way for me to relax. In the beginning, there were only four walls with some new paint on them, but it was still nice to sit and daydream in what would someday be her room. Now that we have a spunky little three-year-old on our hands, the days of idle daydreaming about what could be are all but over. I am lucky to have enough energy to crawl up the stairs at night and get into bed, much less use my imagination much.

Learning to keep your budget in the back of your mind and your baby in the front of your mind will help you practice the art of enjoying your new baby while sticking with your budget. When you walk into a store that will have 50 things you want to purchase for your new little one, this is when you should focus on the stress of keeping a budget while expecting a baby. It is hard enough to keep track of any budget and much more difficult when you have added stress and a gang of crazy pregnancy hormones racing through your bloodstream.

When you bring your baby home, you might not have everything you wanted to have, and it might not be in the order you want it to be in. If this is the case, remember that you are not alone. Many babies come at unexpected times — and some come at unexpected places — but just the fact that you have a healthy, happy baby will be the most important thing in your life at that moment. If you are one of the many parents whose child makes an entrance before you are fully prepared, focus on the basic needs of your infant first, and then, instead of focusing on what you do not have or maybe cannot afford at that moment, try to think about what you might be able to do to better the situation without purchasing expensive items. Many of the Case Studies in this book have some good tips for saving some money, but this one in particular gives some good ideas for the bigger picture and items that are extra stressful on your budget.

Case Study: Karri Haugsness

Belle's and Beau's Academy
6150 S. Tower Rd., Aurora, CO 80015
www.bellesandbeausacademy.com
Ph: 303-693-6715 • Fax: 303-693-3171
Karri Haugsness, Director of Child Care

Karri Haugsness is an experienced, kind, and loving mother of two children, ages three years old and four months old. In her experience, both as a mother and a child care giver, she has learned a great deal, from money-saving tips for some of the more expensive items you might need to purchase, to sound advice that any new parents will be grateful to have in the back of their minds.

Money-saving tips that Karrie provided included how to keep your budget under control in the long run for more than one child and how to save big on those items that you will need or want, whether you plan to have one child or five.

"Do not buy gender-specific big items — car seat, Pack 'n Play, stroller, highchair — especially if you think you may have another child. All of the pink stuff is cuter than the neutral colors, but buying it all again the second time is really expensive." Karri experienced this gender-specific problem with her glider, yet prevailed with a great idea that can be applied to other types of furniture and products you might already have for your infant. "I had my very expensive glider re-covered by a friend instead of buying a new one. It went from pink plaid to red. It saved so much money and worked great for both a girl and a boy room."

When asked to share a few pieces of advice every parent should have, Karri offered these thoughts, "Learn how to swaddle your newborn baby. Learn it at the hospital; it will make the first weeks at home so much better."

Keep in mind, "when he is really tired and fighting sleep, it is frustrating, but hang in there. If you put in a few extra minutes, you are going to get a really nice nap for him and maybe for you too."

Finding ways to accentuate pieces you already have or can find at lower prices but might not be the ideal color, style, or wood type is easy to overcome with a little time and creativity. Our daughter's dresser was given to us; it was the wrong color of wood, so I spent two hours outside staining it. Our daughter's glider did not match her purple and lavender room; it was green, so I hung some greenery above her windows and closets, and it tied the glider in well for the first year we needed it in her room. Our daughter's room colors were based around the paint we picked, a crib set that was on sale, and the crib that was given to us. Everything else in the room was eventually painted or stained, or items were added to the décor to tie in the colors of pieces we could not adjust. Her room in the end was a color scheme of purple, lavender, white, and green. These were not the colors I had in mind at first, but her nursery became an original and beautiful place for her to sleep, play, and relax.

Many of these Case Studies will be good reminders to you that your main points of struggle in becoming a parent will be far from what you can and cannot provide for your baby materially. It is essential for your happiness as a family to focus on care, love, and time with your new baby. Your baby  will never remember whether she had the "best" rattle or most expensive playard; how much you loved her, the time you spent with her, and the ways you show your love will be played out over and over again throughout your child's life in the ways that she shows her love for you.

Works Cited

Fields, Denise and Alan. 2007. *Baby Bargains.* Boulder, CO: Windsor Peak Press.

Gordon, Sandra. 2007. *Consumer Reports: Best Baby Products.* Yonkers, NY: Consumers Union of United States, Inc.

Johnson, Tricia. 2005. *Baby Cents: How to Financially Plan for a Baby.* Irving, TX: Gowberry Group LLC.

Web Sites

All the Daze You Spend with Children. 2002. November 14, 2007. **www. allthedaze.com**

Consumer Reports. 2007. Consumers Union of U.S. Inc. October 22 – November 14, 2007. **www.consumerreports.org**

Scholastic. 2007. Scholastic, Inc. November 13, 2007. **www.scholastic. com**

Appendix

Money-Saving References

Throughout this book, I have given you guidance to help financially prepare for your new baby. In this section, I have listed more than 400 sources for baby items. They are grouped according to categories and will be useful in comparison-shopping, safety and finding just what you are looking for. Note: Most Web sites should come up without the www; if they do not, try adding it to the beginning of the addresses presented here when typing one into your browser.

Product Manufacturers

Baby Trend
Ph: 800-328-7363 • 909-773-0018
1567 South Campus Avenue
Ontario, CA 91761
babytrend.com

Chicco
Ph: 877-4-CHICCO
1835 Freedom Road
Lancaster, PA 17601
chiccousa.com
info@chiccousa.com

Dorel Juvenile Group
Ph: 800-457-5276 • 812-372-0141
2525 State Street
Columbus, IN 47201-7494
djgusa.com

Evenflo
Ph: 800-233-5921
1801 Commerce Drive
Piqua, OH 45356
evenflo.com
parentlink@evenflo.com

Fisher-Price
Ph: 800-828-4000 • 716-687-3000
fisher-price.com

Graco Children's Products Inc.
Ph: 800-345-4109 (U.S.)
Ph: 800-667-8184 (Canada)
150 Oaklands Boulevard
Exton, PA 19341
gracobaby.com

Peg Perego
Ph: 800-225-1558 • 260-482-8191
3625 Independence Drive
Fort Wayne, IN 46808
perego.com

Safety 1st
Ph: 800-544-1108 • 781-364-3100
PO Box 2609
Columbus, IN 47202-2609
safety1st.com

Clothing & Apparel

Baby Gap
Ph: 800-427-7895
100 Gap Online Drive
Grove City, OH 43123-8605

babygap.com
custserv@gap.com

Baby Lulu
babylulu.com
info@babylulu.com

Bobux Shoes
Ph: 800-315-3039
bobuxusa.com
customerservice@bobuxusa.com

Carter's
Ph: 888-782-9548 • 770-961-8722
carters.com
contactus@carters.com

Children's Place
Ph: 877-PLACE USA
915 Secaucus Road
Secaucus, NJ 07094
childrensplace.com

Children's Wear
Ph: 800-242-5437 • 276-670-2192
3607 Mayland Court
Richmond, VA 23233-1453
cwdkids.com

Disney Store
Ph: 800-3280368 • 800-328-0368
disneystore.com

Flap Happy
Ph: 800-234-3527 • 310-453-3527
2330 Michigan Avenue
Santa Monica, CA 90404
flaphappy.com
custsvc@flaphappy.com

Flapdoodles
212-643-0801
112 West 34th Street, Ste 1000
New York, NY 10120
flapdoodles.com
info@flapdoodles.com

Funtasia! Too
Ph: 214-634-7770
4747 Irving Blvd., Ste 230 Dallas,
TX 75247
funtasiatoo.com
funtasiatoo@sbcglobal.net

Gymboree
Ph: 877-449-6932
gymboree.com
customer_service@gymboree.com

H & M
Ph: 212-564-9922
47 West 34th Street, 3rd floor
New York, NY 10001
hm.com

Hanna Andersson
Ph: 800-222-0544
hannaandersson.com

Hedgehog
Ph: 703-973-5311
3024 Hunt Road
Oakton, VA 22124
hedgehogusa.com
sarah@hedgehogusa.com

Jake and Me
Ph: 970-396-6364
PO Box 337504
Greeley, CO 80633
jakeandme.com
nancy@jakeandme.com

Janie and Jack
Ph: 877-449-8800 • 707-678-1315
janieandjack.com

JCPenny
Ph: 800-222-6161
PO Box 8178
Manchester, CT 06040-1463
jcpenny.com

Lands' End
Ph: 800-963-4816
1 Lands' End Lane
Dodgeville, WI 53595
landsend.com

Little Lubbaloo
Ph: 949-395-8036
29 Winfield Drive
Ladera Ranch, CA 92694
littlelubbaloo.com
info@littlelubbaloo.com

Little Me
Ph: 877-545-2229
PO Box 308
Budd Lake, NJ 07828
littleme.com

LL Bean
Ph: 800-552-5437 (kids' dept.)
llbean.com

Lullabye Baby
Ph: 888-588-7267 • 318-483-1857
1501 A Wimbeldon Drive
Alexandria, LA 71301
Lullabyebaby.com
sales@dorightservices.com

Mini Boden
Ph: 866-206-9508
3580 NW 56th Street
Fort Lauderdale, FL 33309
miniboden.com

Mommy-to-Be & Lil' Me
Ph: 303-649-2229
7600 E. Park Meadows Drive
Lone Tree, CO 80124
Mommy2b-lilme@comcast.net

MulberriBush/Tumbleweed Too
mulberribush.com
debra_krebs@mulberribush.com

Once Upon a Child
Ph: 614-791-0000
ouac.com
ouac-corporate-operations@ouac.com

OshKosh B'Gosh
Ph: 800-692-4674 • 920-231-8800
oshkoshbgosh.com
consumerbgosh@carters.com

Patagonia Kids
Ph: 800-638-6464
PO Box 32050
Reno, NV 89523-2050
patagonia.com

Patsy Aiken
Ph: 919-872-8789
4812 Hargrove Road
Raleigh, NC 27616
patsyaiken.com
chezami@patsyaiken.com

Pingorama
pingorama.com
bethany@bzbdesigner.com

Preemie.com
Ph: 651-636-5005
1682 Roxanna Lane
New Brighton, MN 55112
preemie.com

Retro Baby
Ph: 954-607-2124
Retrobaby.com

Robeez Shoes
Ph: 604-435-9011 • 800-929-2649
7979 Enterprise Street
Burnaby, British Columbia
Canada V5A 1V5
robeez.com
info@robeez.co.uk

Scootees/Baby Abby
Ph: 800-972-7357 • 303-733-5376
5151 Franklin Street
Denver, CO 80216
babyabby.com
info@babyabby.com

Sierra Trading Post
Ph: 800-713-4534
5025 Campstool Road
Cheyenne, WY 82007-1898
sierratradingpost.com

Sprockets/Mervyn's
Ph: 800-637-8967
22301 Foothill Blvd.
MS 2115 Hayward, CA 94541
mervyns.com

Suddenly Mommies
Ph: 317-441-5313
3676 East State Road 234
Greenfield, IN 46140
suddenlymommies.com
inquire@suddenlymommies.
com

Sweet Potatoes/Spudz
Ph: 800-634-2584
2390 Fourth Street
Berkeley, CA 94710
sweetpotatoesinc.com
sweetpotatoes@
sweetpotatoesinc.com

Talbots Kids
800-992-9010 • 781-740-8888
One Talbots Drive
Hingham, MA 02043
talbots.com
customer.service@talbots.com

Target
Ph: 800-591-3869 (online info)
Ph: 800-440-0680 (store info)
target.com

Tiny Treasures Baby.com
Ph: 888-570-2229 • 520-836-5575
1664 East Florence Blvd, Ste 4
PMB 128
Casa Grande, AZ 85222
tinytreasuresbaby.com
customerservice@
tinytreasuresbaby.com

Wal-Mart
Ph: 800-925-6278
702 SW 8th Street
Bentonville, AR 72716
walmart.com

Wes & Willy
wesandwilly.com

Zutano
zutano.com
zutano@zutano.com

Decorating & Bedding

Amy Coe
Ph: 203-227-9900
151 Post Road East
Westport, CT 06880
amycoe.com

Baby Guess
ccipinc.com

Baby Supermarket
Ph: 866-977-4006 • 601-362-7203
4754 I-55 North
Jackson, MS 39211
babysupermarket.com
support@babysupermarket.com

Bananafish
Ph: 800-899-8689 • 818-727-1645
8845 Shirley Avenue
Northridge, CA 91324
bananafishinc.com
info@bananafish.com

Basic Comfort
Ph: 800-456-8687 • 303-778-7535
5151 Franklin Street
Denver, CO 80216
basiccomfort.com
inquiry@basiccomfort.com

Beautiful Baby
Ph: 903-295-2229
2807 West Marshall Avenue
Longview, TX 75604
bbaby.com

Bilk Re-Stik Stickers
Ph: 866-262-2545
PO Box 1663
Venice, CA 90294
whatisblik.com

Brandee Danielle
Ph: 800-720-5656 • 714-957-1240
brandeedanielle.com
sales@brandeedanielle.com

California Kids
Ph: 800-548-5214 • 650-637-9054
935 Washington Street
San Carlos, CA 94070
calkids.com
info@calkids.com

Carter's
Ph: 888-782-9548
carters.com
contactus@carters.com

Celebrations
Ph: 310-279-3779 • 310-279-6107
baby-celebrations.com
pam@baby-celebrations.com

Clouds and Stars
Ph: 866-325-6837 • 720-929-1099
7144 East Ohio Drive
Denver, CO 80224
cloudsandstars.com
info@cloudsandstars.com

CoCaLo
Ph: 714-434-7200
2920 Red Hill Avenue
Costa Mesa, CA 92626
cocalo.com
info@cocalo.com

The Company Store
Ph: 800-323-8000
companykids.com
custserv@thecompanystore.com

Cotton Tale
Ph: 800-628-2621 • 714-435-9558
11175 Condor Avenue
Fountain Valley, CA 92708
cottontaledesigns.com
jazmin@cottontaledesigns.com

Country Lane
Ph: 800-769-5961 • 724-538-8391
PO Box 240
Callery, PA 16024

countrylane.com
sales@countrylane.com

Creative Images Artwork
Ph: 800-784-5415
PO Box 1269
St. Augustine, FL 32095-1269
crimages.com
info@crimages.com

Dwell
Ph: 212-219-9343
155 6th Avenue 7th Floor
New York City, NY 10013
dwellshop.com
sales@dwellstudio.com

Eddie Bauer
Ph: 800-625-7935
PO Box 7001
Groveport, OH 43125
eddiebauer.com

Fleece Baby
Ph: 866-353-2916 • 206-984-1319
fleecebaby.com

Garnet Hill
Ph: 800-870-3513
231 Main Street

Franconia, NH 03580
garnethill.com

Gerber
Ph: 800-443-7237
445 State Street
Fremont, MI 49413-0001
gerber.com

Glenna Jean
Ph: 800-446-6018 • 804-861-0687
glennajean.com
customerservice@glennajean.com

Graham Kracker
Ph: 800-489-2820
404 Andrews Hwy
Midland, TX 79701
grahamkracker.com
gkbedding@aol.com

Hoohobbers
Ph: 800-533-1505 • 773-342-0004
hoohobbers.com
sales@hoohobbers.com

The Interior Alternative
Ph: 413-743-1986

Kiddopotamus
800-772-8339 • 913-851-2987
7360 West 161st Street
Stilwell, KS 66085
kiddopotamus.com
contact@kiddopotamus.com

Kids Line
Ph: 310-660-0110
kidslineinc.com

Kimberly Grant
Ph: 714-546-4411
711 West Walnut Street
Compton, CA 90220
kimberlygrant.com

Lambs & Ivy
Ph: 800-345-2627 • 310-322-3800
2040-2042 E Maple Avenue
El Segundo, CA 90245-5008
lambsivy.com
customerservice@lambsivy.com

Land of Nod
Ph: 800-933-9904
2177 Shermer Road
Northbrook, IL 60062
landofnod.com
customerservice@landofnod.com

Lands' End
Ph: 800-963-4816
1 Lands' End Lane
Dodgeville, WI 53595
landsend.com

Maddie Boo
Ph: 281-298-9798
26009 Budde Road, Ste A-100
Woodlands, TX 77380
maddieboobedding.com

Martha Stewart
Ph: 866-562-7848
kmart.com
help@customerservice.kmart.com

Michaels Arts, Crafts & More...
Ph: 800-642-4235
8000 Bent Branch Drive
Irving, TX 75063
michaels.com

Mr. Bobbles Blankets
Ph: 204-401-5595
mrbobblesblankets.com
renee@mrbobblesblankets.com

My Baby Sam
Ph: 904-247-7834
1882 Mealy Street South, Ste 2
Atlantic Beach, FL 32233
mybabysam.com

Nava's Design
Ph: 818-988-9050
16742 Stagg Street, Unit 106
Van Nuys, CA 91406
navasdesigns.com

Nojo
Ph: 800-854-8760 • 310-763-8100
nojo.com

Overstock
overstock.com

Patchkraft
Ph: 800-866-2229 • 201-833-2201
patchkraft.com
patchkraft@aol.com

Pine Creek
Ph: 503-266-6275
PO Box 14
Aurora, OR 97002
pinecreekbedding.com
pinecreekbedding@canby.com

Pottery Barn Kids
Ph: 800-993-4923
potterybarnkids.com

Quiltex
212-594-2205
quiltex.com

Sleeping Partners
Ph: 212-254-1515
24 East 23rd Street 4th floor
New York, NY 10010
sleepingpartners.com
info@sleepingpartners.com

Springs
Ph: 888-926-7888 • 803-547-1500
PO Box 70
Fort Mill, SC 29716
springs.com

Stay Put Safety Sheet
Ph: 781-551-9836
5 Kings Way
Norwood, MA 02062
babysheets.com
info@babysheets.com

Sumersault
Ph: 800-232-3006 • 201-768-7890
PO Box 269
Scarsdale, NY 10583
sumersault.com

Sweet Kyla
Ph: 800-265-2229 • 519-895-0250
330 Trillium Drive
Kitchener, Ontario
Canada N2E 2K6
sweetkyla.com
info@sweetkyla.com

Sweet Pea
Ph: 626-578-0866

Trend Lab Baby
Ph: 866-873-6352 • 952-890-6700
3190 West County Road 42
Burnsville, MN 55337
trend-lab.com
sales@trend-lab.com

Wall Nutz
Ph: 877-360-3325 • 503-884-6089
12675 NW Cornell Road, Ste B
Portland, OR 97229-5886
wallnutz.com
jodi@wallnutz.com

Wallies
Ph: 800-255-2762
PO Box 3100
Manhattan, KS 66505-3100
wallies.com
info@wallies.com

WallPops!
Ph: 781-963-4800
67 Pacella Park Drive
Randolph, MA 02368
wall-pops.com

Wendy Bellissimo
Ph: 818-348-3682
wendybellissimo.com

Diapers & Related Items

All Together Diaper
Ph: 877-215-9004 • 801-566-7579
131 West 7065 South
Midvale, UT 84047
clothdiaper.com
customerservice@clothdiaper.com

Amy Michelle
Ph: 303-279-0690
2215 Ford Street
Golden, CO 80401
amymichellebags.com

Baby Because
Ph: 866-734-2634
babybecause.com
customerservice@babybecause.
com

Baby Bunz
Ph: 800-676-4559 • 360-354-1320
PO Box 113
Lynden, WA 98264
babybunz.com
info@babybunz.com

Baby J • babyj.com

Baby Lane
Ph: 888-387-0019
thebabylane.com

Baby Works
Ph: 800-422-2910 • 503-224-4696
2537A NW Upshur Street
Portland, OR 97210
babyworks.com

Barefoot Baby
Ph: 800-735-2082
500 Welsh Lane
Granville, OH 43023
Barefootbaby.com
cservice@barefootbaby.com

Bumkins
Ph: 866-286-5467 • 480-481-3618
7802 E Gray Road, Ste 500
Scottsdale, AZ 85260
bumkins.com

Chester Handbags
Ph: 310-446-8084
chesterhandbags.com
info@chesterstyle.com

Costco
Ph: 800-774-2678
PO Box 34331
Seattle, WA 98124
costco.com

CVS Pharmacy
Ph: 888-607-4287
1 CVS Drive
Woonsocket, RI 02895
cvspharmacy.com
customercare@cvs.com

DEX Products
Ph: 800-546-1996 • 707-748-4199
602-A Stone Road
Benicia, CA 94510
dexproducts.com
mail@dexproducts.com

Diaper Site
Ph: 888-254-8433
diapersite.com

Diapers 4 Less
Ph: 800-270-1816 • 763-478-2984
8401 73rd Avenue North #77
Brooklyn Park, MN 55428
diapers4less.com
sales@diapers-4-less.com

Ella
Ph: 706-891-1430
ella-bags.com
ella@ella-bags.com

Fleurville
Ph: 866-510-8967 • 415-482-8510
637 Lindaro Street, Ste 201
San Rafael, CA 94901
fleurville.com
info@fleurville.com

Haiku Diaper Bags
Ph: 510-654-1001
haikubags.com
e.info@haikubags.com

Happy Hieny's
Ph: 619-258-6867
1529 North Cuyamaca Street
El Cajon, CA 92020
happyheinys.com
linda@happyheinys.com

Holly Aiken
Ph: 919-833-8770
521 West North Street
Raleigh, NC 27603
hollyaiken.com
info@hollyaiken.com

Huggies
Ph: 888-525-8388
PO Box 2020
Neenah, WI 54957-2020
huggies.com

I'm Still Me
Ph: 203-426-8133
85 Hill Road
Redding, CT 06896
imstillme.com

Jardine Diapers
jardinediapers.com

Kate Spade
Ph: 866-999-5283
katespade.com

Kelly's Closet
Ph: 207-583-2764
PO Box 203
Waterford, ME 04088
kellyscloset.com

Kushies
Ph: 800-841-5330 • 905-643-9118
555 Barton Street
Stoney Creek, Ontario
Canada L8E 5S1
kushies.com

Luvs
luvs.com

Mother-Ease
Ph: 800-416-1475 • 905-988-5188
6391 Walmore Road
Niagara Falls, NY 14304
motherease.com

Oi Oi
Ph: 877-905-3800
PO Box 335
Malvern Victoria 3144
Australia
oioi.com.au
info@oioibabybags.com

One Cool Chick
onecoolchick.com
mail@onecoolchick.com

Pampers
Ph: 800-726-7377
pampers.com

Reese Li
Ph: 800-735-8228 • 703-313-8898
5810 Kingstowne Center Drive
Ste 120-185
Alexandria, VA 22315
reeseli.com
info@reeseli.com

Sam's Club
Ph: 888-746-7726
608 Southwest 8th Street
Bentonville, AR 72716
samsclub.com

Seventh Generation
Ph: 800-456-1191 • 802-658-3773
60 Lake Street
Burlington, VA 05401-5218
seventhgeneration.com

Skip Hop
Ph: 877-4-SKIPHOP • 212-868-9850
146 West 29th Street 8th Floor
New York, NY 10001
skiphop.com
info@skiphop.com

Sugar Plum Babies
monkeytoediapers.com/
sugarplumbaby
susan@sugarplumbaby.com

Timbuk2
Ph: 800-865-2513
333 Alabama Street
San Francisco, CA 94110
timbuk2.com
customerservice@timbuk2.com

Tumi
Ph: 800-299-8864
tumi.com

Tushies
Ph: 800-344-6379 • 715-833-1409
tushies.com
tushies123@aol.com

Vera Bradley
Ph: 888-855-8372
2208 Production Road
Fort Wayne, IN 46808
verabradley.com

For Mommies

2 Chix
Ph: 877-896-2449
11835 W. Olympic Blvd., Ste 715 E
Los Angeles, CA 90064
2chix.com
customerservice@2chix.com

Ann Taylor Loft
Ph: 800-342-5266
100 Ann Taylor Drive
PO Box 571650
Taylorsville, UT 84157-1650
anntaylor.com

Baby Becoming Maternity
Ph: 888-666-6810 • 401-658-0688
PO Box 2
Manville, RI 02838
babybecoming.com
info@babybecoming.com

Baby Center
Ph: 866-710-2229
163 Freelon Street
San Francisco, CA 94107
babycenter.com

BeBe Sounds
Ph: 212-736-6760
15 West 36th Street 6th Floor
New York, NY 10018
bebesounds.com
info@unisar.com

Bella Band
Ph: 415-409-2900
2220 Fillmore Street, Ste 2
San Francisco, CA 94115
bellaband.com

Bella Blu Maternity
Ph: 866-406-4135 • 405-285-9003
323 South Blackwelder Avenue
Edmond, OK 73034
bellablumaternity.com
customerservice@
bellablumaternity.com

Birth and Baby
Ph: 888-398-7987 • 509-677-5177
PO Box 280
316 North I Street
Lind, WA 99341
birthandbaby.com
pj@birthandbaby.com

Bravado Bras
Ph: 800-590-7802 • 416-466-8652
41 Hollinger Road
Toronto, Ontario
Canada M4B 3G4
bravadodesigns.com
customerservice@
bravadodesigns.com

Danish Wool Breast Pads
Ph: 802-878-6089
PO Box 124
Westford, VT 05494
danishwool.com

Decent Exposures
Ph: 800-524-4949 • 206-364-4540
12554 Lake City Way NE
Seattle, WA 98125
decentexposures.com
info@decentexposures.com

**Destination Maternity
Superstore**
Ph: 800-466-6223
456 North 5th Street
Philadelphia, PA 19123
destinationmaternity.com
ci@destinationmaternity.com

Due Maternity
Ph: 866-746-7383
duematernity.com
info@duematernity.com

Elizabeth Lee
Ph: 435-353-4344
PO Box 10
Neola, UT 84053
elizabethlee.com

eMommie.com
Ph: 623-670-6439
17633 West Golden Eye Avenue
Goodyear, AZ 85338

emommie.com
emommie@cox.net

Estyle
Ph: 877-378-9537
estyle.com
custcare@babystyle.com

Eva Lillian
Ph: 800-556-9720 • 866-882-3922
116 Winifred Avenue
Lansing, MI 48917
evalillian.com
service@evalillian.com

Expressiva
Ph: 877-933-9773
2221 Faulkner Road
Atlanta, GA 30324
expressiva.com
customercare@expressiva.com

Fashion Bug
PO Box 26916
Tucson, AZ 85775-6916
fashionbug.com

Fat Wallet
fatwallet.com

Fit Maternity
Ph: 888-961-9100 • 530-313-5138
5122 Lake Shastina Drive
Weed, CA 96094
fitmaternity.com
info@fitmaternity.com

Imaternity
Ph: 800-466-6223
456 North 5th Street
Philadelphia, PA 19123
Imaternity.com

Isabella Oliver
Ph: 866-614-9387
Isabellaoliver.com
theteam@isabellaoliver.com

Jake and Me Clothing Co
970-396-6364
PO Box 337504
Greeley, CO 80633
jakeandme.com
nancy@jakeandme.com

JCPenny
Ph: 800-322-1189
PO Box 8178
Manchester, CT 06040-1463
jcpenny.com

Lily Padz
lilypadz.com
feedback@lilypadz.com

Majamas
PO Box 948
Oak Park, IL 60303-0948
majamas.com
info@majamas.com

Maternity 4 Less
Ph: 800-304-6403 • 518-439-8330
maternity4less.com
orders@maternity4less.com

Maternity Mall
Ph: 800-466-6223
456 North 5th Street
Philadelphia, PA 19123
maternitymall.com
ci@maternitymall.com

McCall Patterns
Ph: 800-782-0323
PO Box 3755
Manhatten, KS 66505
mccallpattern.com
consumerservice@mccallpattern.com

Mimi Maternity
Ph: 877-646-4666
456 North 5th Street
Philadelphia, PA 19123
mimimaternity.com

Mobicam
Ph: 877-662-4462 • 818-771-1620
7635 San Fernando Road, Ste A
Burbank, CA 91505
getmobi.com
info@getmobi.com

Mom Shop
Ph: 800-854-1213 • 503-345-9238
PO Box 41
Kelso, WA 98626
momshop.com
customerservice@momshop.com

Mommy Gear
Ph: 888-624-4327 • 724-238-9633
107 South St. Clair
Ligonier, PA 15658
mommygear.com
higgins@mommygear.com

Motherhood
Ph: 800-466-6223
456 North 5th Street
Philadelphia, PA 19123
maternitymall.com

Motherwear
Ph: 800-950-2500
320 Riverside Drive, Ste C
Florence, MA 01062
motherwear.com
customerservice@motherwear.com

Mums N Bumps
Ph: +44-1964-623321
68 St. Martins Road
Thorngumbald
East Riding of Yorkshire
HU12 9PL
United Kingdom
mumsnbumps.co.uk
enquiries@mumsnbumps.co.uk

Naissance Maternity
Ph: 888-802-1133 • 773-862-1133
1647 North Damen Avenue
Chicago, IL 60647
naissancematernity.com
info@bellydancematernity.com

Old Navy
Ph: 800-653-6289
oldnavy.com
custserv@oldnavy.com

One Hanes Place
Ph: 800-671-5056 • 800-671-1674
PO Box 748
Rural Hall, NC 27098-0748
onehanesplace.com

One Hot Mama
Ph: 818-980-9802
4804 Laurel Canyon Blvd., #369
Valley Village, CA 91607
onehotmama.com
help@onehotmama.com

Pea in the Pod
Ph: 877-273-2763 • 215-625-3843
456 North 5th Street
Philadelphia, PA 19123
apeainthepod.com

Philips Baby Monitors
Ph: 877-744-5477
consumer.philips.com

Plus Maternity
Ph: 888-44-PICKLES
plusmaternity.com
cat@plusmaternity.com

Prenatal Cradle
Ph: 800-607-3572
PO Box 443
Hamburg, MI 48139-0443
prenatalcradle.com
prenatal@prenatalcradle.com

Simplicity Patterns
simplicity.com

Soothies
Ph: 800-944-4006
9823 Pacific Heights Blvd., Ste H
San Diego, CA 92121
soothies.com
info@soothies.com

Summer Infant Products
1275 Park East Drive
Woonsocket, RI 02895
summerinfant.com Thyme

Maternity
250 Sauve West
Montreal, Quebec
Canada H3L 1Z2
thymematernity.com
customers@thymematernity.com

Twinkle Little Star
Ph: 902-659-2331
2476 Trans Canada Highway
Flat River, Prince Edward Island
Canada C0A 1B0
twinklelittlestar.com
kimberly@twinklelittlestar.com

Wears the Baby
Ph: 800-527-8985
wearsthebaby.com
katie@wearsthebaby.com

WIC Information
www.fns.usda.gov/wic

Furniture

Amby Baby Bed
Ph: 866-519-2229 • 952-974-5100
6600 City West Parkway, Ste 205
Minneapolis, MN 55344
ambybaby.com

Amish Furniture Makers
Ph: 217-268-4504
401 E County 200 North
Arcola, IL 61910
simplyamish.com

Angel Line
Ph: 800-889-8158 • 856-678-6300
88 Industrial Park Road
Pennsville, NJ 08070
angelline.com
crib@angelline.com

AP Industries
800-463-0145 • 418-728-2145
346 St. Joseph Blvd.
Laurier-Station, Quebec
Canada G0S 1N0
apindustries.com
info@apindustries.com

Babies R Us
Ph: 888-222-9787
babiesrus.com

Baby Appleseed
babyappleseed.com
customerservice@
babyappleseed.com

Baby Boudoir
Ph: 800-272-2293 • 508-998-2166

Baby Bunk
800-697-8944
babybunk.com
ilene@babybunk.com

Baby Catalog America
Ph: 800-752-9736 • 203-931-7760
738 Washington Avenue
West Haven, CT 06516
babycatalog.com

Baby Depot
Ph: 800-444-2628
coat.com

Baby Direct
Ph: 800-346-0395
15841 Pines Blvd. #394
Pembroke Pines, FL 33027-1220
babydirect.com
customerservice@babydirect.com

Baby Furniture Outlet
Ph: 800-613-9280 • 519-649-2590
270 Adelaide Street South
London, Ontario • Canada N5Z 3L1
babyfurnitureoutlet.com

Baby Furniture Plus
Ph: 256-825-3080
288 Blue Creek Circle
Dadeville, AL 36853-5800
babyfurnitureplus.com

Baby Furniture Warehouse
Ph: 781-843-5353
128 Market Place
One General Way
Reading, MA 01867
babyfurniturewarehouse.com
info@babyfurniturewarehouse.com

Baby News
Ph: 925-245-1370
6909 Las Positas Road
Livermore, CA 94551
babynewsstores.com
info@stanforddistributing.com

Baby Style
Ph: 877-378-9537
babystyle.com
custcare@babystyle.com

Baby's Dream
Ph: 800-835-2742 • 912-649-4404
babysdream.com

Bassett
Ph: 877-525-7070 • 276-629-6000
3525 Fairystone Park Hwy
PO Box 626
Bassett, VA 24055
bassettfurniture.com
juvenile@bassettfurniture.com

Bellini
Ph: 800-332-2229 • 212-517-9233
1305 Second Avenue
New York, NY 10021
bellini.com
bellini165@aol.com

Berg
Ph: 908-354-5252
bergfurniture.com

Best Chair
bestchair.com

Bonavita
Ph: 888-266-2848 • 609-409-2495
257 Prospect Plains Road
Cranbury, NJ 08512
bonvita-cribs.com
info@lajobi.com

Boon
Ph: 888-376-4763
7404 West Detroit Street, Ste 100
Chandler, AZ 85226
booninc.com
info@booninc.com

Bratt Décor
Ph: 888-242-7288 • 410-464-9400
PO Box 20808
Baltimore, MD 21209
brattdecor.com
info@brattdecor.com

Brooks
Ph: 800-427-6657 • 423-626-1111

Buy Buy Baby
Ph: 516-507-3417 • 877-328-9222
895 East Gate Blvd.
Garden City, NY 11530
buybuybaby.com
info@buybuybaby.com

Calla Chair
callachair.com

Camelot Furniture
714-283-4194

Capretti Home
1500 Weston Road, Ste 220
Weston, FL 33326
caprettihome.com
mail@caprettihome.com

Cara Mia
Ph: 877-728-0342 • 905-361-1970
3455 Wolfedale Road
Mississauga, Ontario
Canada L5C 1V8
caramiafurniture.com
info@caramiafurniture.com

Child Craft
Ph: 800-631-5652 • 812-883-3111
PO Box 3239
Lancaster, PA 17604
childcraftind.com
service@childcrafteducation.com

Consumer Product Safety Commission
Ph: 800-638-2772 • 301-504-7923
4330 East West Highway
Bethesda, MD 20814
cpsc.gov

Corsican Kids
Ph: 800-421-6247 • 323-587-3101
1933 South Broadway, Ste #1230
Los Angeles, CA 90007
corsican.com

Crib N Carriage
Ph: 865-691-8565
7933 Ray Mears Blvd.
Knoxville, TN 37919
cribncarriage.com
sales@cribncarriage.com

CSN Baby
Ph: 800- 675-4041 • 617-532-6118
800 Boylston Street, Ste 1600
Boston, MA 02199
csnbaby.com
service@csnbaby.com

Decorate Today
Ph: 800-575-8016 • 734-266-3900
31557 Schoolcraft Road
Livonia, MI 48150-1847
decoratetoday.com

Eco Baby
Ph: 800-596-7450
7550 Miramar Road, Ste #220
San Diego, CA 92126
ecobaby.com
dottie@ecobaby.com

Ethan Allen
Ph: 888-324-3571
PO Box 1966
Danbury, CT 06813-1966
Ethanallen.com

Evenflo
Ph: 800-233-5921
1801 Commerce Drive
Piqua, OH 45356
www.evenflo.com
parentlink@evenflo.com

Fun Rugs
Ph: 877-745-4400
PO Box 10866
Costa Mesa, CA 92627
funrugs.com
info@laruginc.com

Graco Children's Products Inc.
Ph: 800-345-4109 (US)
Ph: 800-667-8184 (Canada)
150 Oaklands Boulevard
Exton, PA 19341
gracobaby.com

Great Beginnings
Ph: 800-886-9077 • 301-417-9702
18501 North Frederick Avenue
Gaithersburg, MD 20879
childrensfurniture.com

Hoot Judkins
Ph: 650-952-5600
1400 El Camino Real
Millbrae CA
hootjudkins.com
info@hootjudkins.com

IKEA
Ph: 610-834-0180
ikea.com

Kiddie Kastle
Ph: 502-499-9667

Moonlight Slumber
Ph: 847-289-0101
18 North State Street
Elgin, IL 60123
moonlightslumber.com
tiffiani@moonlightslumber.com

Natura World
Ph: 888-628-8723 • 519-620-0510
181 Pinebush Road
Cambridge, Ontario
Canada N1R 7H8
naturaworld.com

NaturePedic
Ph: 800-917-3342 • 216-297-9666
4614 Prospect Avenue
Cleveland, OH 44103
naturepedic.com

Net Kids Wear
netkidswear.com

Newport Cottage
Ph: 951-549-0590
4111 Buchanan Avenue
Riverside, CA 92503
newportcottages.com
info@newportcottages.com

NINFRA
Ph: 225-927-0719
8312 Jefferson Highway Ste #2
Baton Rouge, LA 70809
ninfra.com
info@ninfra.com

Nursery Smart
Ph: 626-333-1919
nurserysmart.com

Oeuf
Ph: 800-691-8810
323 6th Street, Ste #4
Brooklyn, NY 11215
oeufnyc.com
help@oeufnyc.com

Pali
Ph: 877-725-4772
1525 Hymus
Dorval, Quebec
Canada H9P 1J5
www.paliItaly.com
customerservice@pali-design.com

Pottery Barn Kids
Ph: 800-993-4923
potterybarnkids.com

Ragazzi
Ph: 604-448-3317
ragazzi.com
info@ragazzi.com

Relics
Ph: 877-477-8585 • 612-371-0861
2123 C Broadway Street NE
Minneapolis, MN 55413
relicsfurniture.com
relicsff@msn.com

Rochelle
Ph: 800-223-6047
PO Box 649
Ludington, MI 49431
rochellefurniture.com
customerservice@
rochellefurniture.com

Rocking Chair Outlet
Ph: 800-613-9280 • 519-649-2590
270 Adelaide Street South
London ON N5Z 3L1
rockingchairoutlet.com

Rocking Chairs 100%
Ph: 800-476-2537
rocking-chairs.com
matt@rocking-chairs.com

Room & Board
Ph: 800-301-9720
4600 Olson Memorial Hwy
Minneapolis, MN 55422
roomandboard.com
shop@roomandboard.com

RT Furniture
Ph: 877-826-6800
1186 N. Industrial Park Drive
Orem, UT 84057
rtfurnitureusa.com
info@rtfurniture.com

Rugs USA
Ph: 800-982-7210 • 516-248-2220
106 E Jericho Turnpike
Mineola, NY 11501
rugsusa.com
info@rugsusa.com

Safety 1st
Ph: 800-544-1108 • 781-364-3100
PO Box 2609
Columbus, IN 47202-2609
safety1st.com

Sauder
Ph: 800-523-3987
sauder.com
info@sauder.com

Sears
Ph: 800-549-4505
3333 Beverly Road Hoffman
Estates, IL 60179
sears.com

Simmons
Ph: 877-399-9379
simmonsjp.com
customerservice@sjfdec.com

Simplicity
Ph: 800-858-8323
501 South 9th Street
Reading, PA 19602
simplicityforchildren.com
customerservice@simplicityfor
children.com

Sorrell
Ph: 201-531-1919
46 Whelan Road
East Rutherford, NJ 07073
sorellefurniture.com

Stanley
Ph: 276-627-2540
stanleyfurniture.com

Stokke
Ph: 877-978-6553
1100 Cobb Place Blvd., Ste 100
Kennesaw, GA 30144
stokkeusa.com
info-usa@stokke.com

Stork Craft
Ph: 877-274-0277 • 604-274-5121
7433 Nelson Road
Richmond, British Columbia
Canada V6W 1G3
storkcraft.com

USA Baby
Ph: 800-323-4108
793 Springer Drive
Lombard, IL 60148
usababy.com

Westwood Design
Ph: 908-719-4707
635 N. Billy Mitchell Road, Ste B
Salt Lake City, UT 84116
westwoodbaby.com
support@westwoodbaby.com

Young America
Ph: 276-627-2540
stanleyfurniture.com

In the Bathroom

Babies R Us
888-222-9787
babiesrus.com

Container Store
Ph: 888-266-8246
containerstore.com

DEX Products
Ph: 800-546-1996 • 707-748-4199
602-A Stone Road
Benicia, CA 94510
dexproducts.com
mail@dexproducts.com

Hand Made Just 4 You
Ph: 502-426-3542
6905 Chippenham Road
Louisville, KY 40222
paulaspremuimproducts.com
support@handmadejust4you.
com

Infantino
Ph: 800-365-8182 • 858-457-9797
4920 Carroll Canyon Rd., Ste 200
San Diego, CA 92121
infantino.com
customersupport@infantino.com

Kel-Gar
Ph: 800-388-1848 • 972-250-3838
PO Box 796934
Dallas, TX 75379
kelgar.com
info@kelgar.com

Lullabye Baby
Ph: 888-588-7267 • 318-483-1857
1501 A Wimbeldon Drive
Alexandria, LA 71301
Lullabyebaby.com
sales@dorightservices.com

Playtex Baby
Ph: 888-310-4290
PO Box 701
Allendale, NJ 07401-1600
playtexbaby.com

Primo
Ph: 973-926-5900
149 Shaw Avenue
Irvington, NJ 07111
primobaby.com
info@primobaby.com

Secure Baby
Ph: 877-271-8438 • 317-758-9375
securebaby.com
info@securebaby.com

Target
Ph: 800-591-3869 (online info)
Ph: 800-440-0680 (store info)
target.com

Wal-Mart
Ph: 800-925-6278
702 SW 8th Street
Bentonville, AR 72716
walmart.com

Music & Movies

Babies R Us
Ph: 888-222-9787
babiesrus.com

Baby Einstein
Ph: 800-793-1454 • 818-553-3900
babyeinstein.com
customerservice@babyeinstein.
com

Barnes & Nobles
barnesandnoble.com

Brainy Baby
Ph: 678-762-1100
460 Brogdon Road, Ste 400
Suwanee, GA 30024
brainybaby.com

Lovely Baby CD
Ph: 877-695-2229 • 516-409-5433
PO Box 1374
Bellmore, NY 11710-0992
lovelybabycd.com
info@lovelybabycd.com

Rockabye Baby!
rockabyebabymusic.com

Sleep Lullabies
6219 Whittondale Drive
Tallahassee, FL 32312
sleeplullabies.com
sales@sleeplullabies.com

Target
Ph: 800-591-3869 (online info)
Ph: 800-440-0680 (store info)
target.com

Wal-Mart
Ph: 800-925-6278
702 SW 8th Street
Bentonville, AR 72716
walmart.com

Nursing

Affordable Medela Pumps
Ph: 877-463-3352
1 Sherwood Drive
Shalimar, FL 32579
affordable-medela-pumps.com
sales@affordable-breast-feeding-supplies.com

Ameda Egnell
Ph: 888-740-8999
2000 Hollister Drive
Libertyville, IL 60048
hollister.com

Avent
Ph: 800-542-8368
aventamerica.com

Bosom Buddies
Ph: 888-860-0041 • 720-482-0109
8331-c South Willow Street
Lone Tree, CO 80124
bosombuddies.com

Breast Friend
breast-friends.org
info@breast-friends.org

Breast-feeding Resources
Ph: 215-886-2433
117 North Easton Road
Glenside, PA 19038
breast-feedingresourcecenter.org

DEX Products
Ph: 800-546-1996 • 707-748-4199
602-A Stone Road
Benicia, CA 94510
dexproducts.com
mail@dexproducts.com

Int'l Lactation Consultants Associations
Ph: 703-560-7330
7245 Arlington Blvd., Ste 200
Falls Church, VA 22042-3217
iblce.org
iblce@iblce.org

La Leche League
Ph: 800-525-3243
lalecheleague.org

Medela
Ph: 800-435-8316
medela.com

Mother's Milk
Ph: 877-892-4932
mothersmilkbreast-feeding. com

Nursing Mother's Council
nursingmothers.org

Nutrition & Feeding

Baby's Only Organic
Ph: 800-259-9774
10645 North Tatum Blvd.
Ste 200-424
Phoenix, AZ 85028
babyorganic.com

Beech-Nut
Ph: 800-233-2468
beechnut.com

Bottle Burper
Ph: 800-699-2877

BreastBottle
Ph: 888-768-4459
2248 Park Boulevard
Palo Alto, CA 94306
breastbottle.com

DEX Products
Ph: 800-546-1996 • 707-748-4199
602-A Stone Road
Benicia, CA 94510
dexproducts.com
mail@dexproducts.com

Earth's Best
Ph: 800-434-4246
4600 Sleepytime Drive
Boulder, CO 80301
earthsbest.com

Enfamil
Ph: 800-222-9123
enfamil.com
enfamilresourcecenter@enfamil.
com

Gerber
Ph: 800-443-7237
445 State Street
Fremont, MI 49413-0001
gerber.com

Healthy Times
healthytimes.com
htbaby@healthytimes.com

Mother's Milk Mate
Ph: 800-499-3506 • 312-492-7860
PO Box 59953
Chicago, IL 60659-0953
mothersmilkmate.com
support@mothersmilkmate.com

Munchkin
Ph: 800-344-2229 • 818-893-5000
16689 Schoenborn Street
North Hills, CA 91343
munchkininc.com
cserv@munchkin.com

Nature's Goodness
Ph: 800-872-2229
PO Box 763
Hersham, PA 19044
naturesgoodness.com

Playtex Baby
Ph: 888-310-4290
PO Box 701
Allendale, NJ 07401-1600
playtexbaby.com

Similac
800-227-5767
similac.com

Super Baby Food Book
superbabyfood.com

WIC Information
fns.usda.gov/wic

On the Go Gear

Aprica
Ph: 877-827-7422
125 Orchard Drive
Boonsboro, MD 21713
apricausa.com
aprica@gesacinc.com

Baby Bijorn
Ph: 886-424-0200
5700 Lombardo Center Drive
Rock Run North, Ste 202
Cleveland, OH 44131
babybjorn.com
info@babyswede.com

Baby Jogger
Ph: 800-241-1848
8575 Magellan Parkway, Ste 1000
Richmond, VA 23227
babyjogger.com
customerservice@babyjogger.com

Baby Planet
Ph: 877-790-3113 • 630-790-3113
800 Roosevelt Road
Building B, Ste 311
Glen Ellyn, IL 60137
baby-planet.com

Baby Trekke
Ph: 800-665-3957
28 North Avenue
Flin Flon, Manitoba
Canada R8A 0T2
babytrekker.com
judy@babytrekker.com

BeBeLove USA
bebeloveusa.com

BOB Strollers
Ph: 800-893-2447 • 208-375-5171
5475 Gage Street
Boise, ID 83706
bobgear.com

Britax
Ph: 888-427-4829
13501 South Ridge Drive
Charlotte, NC 28273
britaxusa.com

BumbleRide
Ph: 800-530-3930
PO Box 7851
San Diego, CA 92167
bumbleride.com
info@bumbleride.com

Burley
Ph: 800-311-5294 • 541-687-1644
4020 Stewart Road
Eugene, OR 97402
burley.com
burley@burley.com

Chariot
Ph: 403-640-0822
#105 - 5760 9th Street SE
Calgary, Alberta
Canada T2H 1Z9
chariotcarriers.com
ask-us@charriotcarriers.com

Chicco
Ph: 877-4-CHICCO
1835 Freedom Road
Lancaster, PA 17601
chiccousa.com
info@chiccousa.com

Compass
Ph: 888-899-2229
PO Box 429
Kings Mills OH 45034-9981
compassbaby.com

Cuddle Karrier
Ph: 877-283-3535
1928 Wildflower Drive
Pickering, Ontario
Canada L1V 7A7
cuddlekarrier.com
customerservice@cuddlekarrier.
com

DEX Products
Ph: 800-546-1996 • 707-748-4199
602-A Stone Road
Benicia, CA 94510
dexproducts.com
mail@dexproducts.com

Dreamer Design
Ph: 800-278-9626
PO Box 369
Selah, WA 98942
dreamerdesign.net
customerservice@
dreamerdesign.net

Ergo
Ph: 888-416-4888 • 808-572-6983
1215 Pi'iholo Road
Makawao, HI 96768
ergobabycarrier.com
info@ergobabycarrier.com

GoGo Babyz
Ph: 888-686-2552
7011 Realm Drive, Ste A5
San Jose, CA 95119
gogobabyz.com
info@gogobabyz.com

Graco Children's Products Inc.
Ph: 800-345-4109 (U.S.)
Ph: 800-667-8184 (Canada)
150 Oaklands Boulevard
Exton, PA 19341
gracobaby.com

Hip Hammock
Ph: 208-343-0016
1220 North Manville Street
Boise, ID 83706
hiphammock.com
swanke@hiphammock.com

Infantino
Ph: 800-365-8182 • 858-457-9797
4920 Carroll Canyon Rd., Ste 200
San Diego, CA 92121
infantino.com
customersupport@infantino.com

Inglesina
inglesina.com

J. Mason
Ph: 800-242-1922 • 818-768-8688
10671 Lanark Street
Sun Valley, CA 91352
jmason.com
customerservice@jmason.com

Jané
Ph: 415-824-1237
PO Box 410007
San Francisco, CA 94141-0007
janeusa.com
info@janeusa.com

Joovy
Ph: 877-456-5049
2919 Canton Street
Dallas, TX 75226
joovy.com
customerservice@joovy.com

Kangaroo Korner
2974 Rice Street
Little Canada, MN 55113
kangarookorner.com
info@kangarookorner.com

Kel-Gar
Ph: 800-388-1848 • 972-250-3838
PO Box 796934
Dallas, TX 75379
kelgar.com
info@kelgar.com

Kelty
Ph: 800-423-2320
6235 Lookout Road
Boulder, CO 80301
kelty.com

Kool Stop
Ph: 800-586-3332 • 503-636-4673
1061 South Cypress Street
La Habra, CA 90632
koolstop.com

Maclaren
Ph: 877-442-4622
4 Testa Place
South Norwalk, CT 06854
maclarenbaby.com
info@maclarenbaby.com

MacraLite Strollers
euro-baby.com
info@euro-baby.com

MaxiMom
4coolkids.com
support@4coolkids.com

Maya Wrap
Ph: 888-629-2972
mayawrap.com

Mia Moda
Ph: 866-642-6632
miamodainc.com

Motobecane
motobecane.com
info@motobecane.com

Mountain Buggy
866-524-8805
208 Commerce Drive Ste 3
Fort Collins, CO 80524
mountainbuggy.com
support@mountainbuggyusa.com

Mutsy
Ph: 973-691-5200
500 International Drive, Ste 120
Mt. Olive, NJ 07828
mutsy.com

Over the Shoulder Baby Holder
Ph: 800-637-9426
babyholder.com
info@littlesmooches.com

Phil & Ted Most
102 - 112 Daniell Street
Wellington, New Zealand
philandteds.com

Playtex Baby
Ph: 888-310-4290
PO Box 701
Allendale, NJ 07401-1600
playtexbaby.com

Quinny
800-951-4113
quinny.com
consumer@quinny-us.com

Rock Star Baby/ Esprit
877-428-2545
gtbaby.com
info@gtbaby.com

Sherpa Mountain
Ph: 800-321-3423 • 604-872-2506
145 West Broadway
Vancouver, British Columbia
Canada V5Y 1P4
sherpa-mtn.com
service@sherpa-mtn.com

Silver Cross
Ph: 877-422-1802
silvercrossamerica.com
customerservice@
silvercrossamerica.com

SnazzySeat
Ph: 213-291-9740 • 213-291-7548
snazzybaby.com
info@snazzybaby.com

Stokke
Ph: 877-978-6553
1100 Cobb Place Blvd., Ste 100
Kennesaw GA 30144
stokkeusa.com
info-usa@stokke.com

Tike Tech
Ph: 800-296-4602
35 Continental Drive
Wayne, NJ 07470
xtechoutdoors.com
info@tiketech.com

Tough Traveler
Ph: 800-468-6844
1012 State Street
Schenectady, NY 12307
toughtraveler.com
service@toughtraveler.com

Traveling Tikes
Ph: 877-698-4537 • 310-234-9551
travelingtikes.com
sales@travelingtikes.com

UPPABaby
Ph: 800-760-2060
371 Liberty Street, Ste 308
Rockland, MA 02370
uppababy.com

Valco
Ph: 800-610-7850
valcobaby.com
info@valcobaby.com

Walking Rock Farm
walkingrockfarm.com
info@walkingrockfarm.com

Water Tot
watertot.com
sales@watertot.com

ZoloWear
Ph: 888-285-0044 • 512-912-0044
321 West Ben White Blvd., Ste
101
Austin, TX 78704
zolowear.com

Zooper
Ph: 888-742-9899 • 503-352-0939
10140 SW Allen Blvd., Ste E
Beaverton, OR 97005
zooper.com
info@zooper.com

Registries

Babies R Us
Ph: 888-222-9787
babiesrus.com

Baby Style
Ph: 877-378-9537
babystyle.com
custcare@babystyle.com

Felicite Registries
felicite.com

JCPenny
Ph: 800-322-1189 • 800-222-6161
jcpenny.com

Mama's Earth
Ph: 800-620-7388
mamasearth.com
gina@mamasearth.com

My Registry
PO Box 1646
Fort Lee, NJ 07024
myregistry.com

Pottery Barn Kids
Ph: 800-993-4923
potterybarnkids.com

The Right Start
Ph: 888-548-8531
therightstart.com
customerservice@rightstart.com

Sears
Ph: 800-549-4505
3333 Beverly Road
Hoffman Estates, IL 60179
sears.com

Target
Ph: 800-591-3869 (online info)
Ph: 800-440-0680 (store info)
target.com

Wal-Mart
Ph: 800-925-6278
702 SW 8th Street
Bentonville, AR 72716
walmart.com

Safety & Childproofing

American Academy of Pediatrics
Ph: 847-434-4000
141 Northwest Point Blvd.
Elk Grove Village, IL 60007-1098
aap.org

Auto Safety Hot line
Ph: 800-424-9393

Babies R Us
Ph: 888-222-9787
babiesrus.com

Car Seat Data
carseatdata.org

National Highway Traffic Safety Administration
Ph: 888-327-4236
1200 New Jersey Avenue SE
West Building
Washington, DC 20590
www.nhtsa.dot.gov

National Safe Kids Campaign
Ph: 202-662-0600
1301 Pennsylvania Avenue NW
Ste 1000
Washington, DC 20004
safekids.org
info@safekids.org

Orbit
37330 Cedar Boulevard Ste J
Newark, CA 94560
orbitbaby.com
info@orbitbaby.com

Playtex Baby
Ph: 888-310-4290
PO Box 701
Allendale, NJ 07401-1600
playtexbaby.com

Recaro
Ph: 284-364-3818
4120 Luella Lane
Auburn Hills, MI 48326
Recaro.com
info@recarousa.com

SafeGuard
Ph: 800586-7839
18881 US 31 North
Westfield, IN 46074
safeguardseat.com

Safety Alerts
safetyalerts.com

Safety Belt Safe USA
PO Box 553
Altadena, CA 91003
carseat.org

Secure Baby
Ph: 877-271-8438 • 317-758-9375
securebaby.com
info@securebaby.com

Target
Ph: 800-591-3869 (online info)
Ph: 800-440-0680 (store info)
target.com

Wal-Mart
Ph: 800-925-6278
702 SW 8th Street
Bentonville, AR 72716
walmart.com

Toys & Books

Babies R Us
Ph: 888-222-9787
babiesrus.com

Baby Einstein
Ph: 800-793-1454 • 818-553-3900
babyeinstien.com
customerservice@babyeinstein.com

Baby Style
Ph: 877-378-9537
babystyle.com
custcare@babystyle.com

Discovery
Ph: 800-889-9950
PO Box 788
Florence, KY 41022-0788
discovery.com

Infantino
Ph: 800-365-8182 • 858-457-9797
4920 Carroll Canyon Rd., Ste 200
San Diego, CA 92121
infantino.com
customersupport@infantino.com

Lullabye Baby
Ph: 888-588-7267 • 318-483-1857
1501 A Wimbeldon Drive
Alexandria, LA 71301
Lullabyebaby.com
sales@dorightservices.com

Mary Meyer
Ph: 800-451-4387
1 Teddy Bear Lane PO Box 275
Townshend, VT 05353
marymeyer.com
info@marymeyer.com

Tiny Love
Ph: 888-TINY-LOVE
Ph: 714-898-0807
12622 Monarch Street
Garden Grove, CA 92841
tinylove.com
customerservice@mayagroup.com

Toys R Us
toysrus.com

Wal-Mart
800-925-6278
702 SW 8th Street
Bentonville, AR 72716
walmart.com

Web Sites for Gently Used Baby Items

www.babyloot.com

Baby Loot allows members to post used baby items with photos, descriptions, and price.

www.babyoutfitter.com

Babyoutfitter.com is a full-service, exclusively upscale children's resale shopping destination with more than 1,000 items daily. It offers new and gently used baby clothing and other items from blankets and bibs to shoes and accessories as well as children's videos, toys, and books, most under $10.

www.craigslist.org

Local classifieds and forums for 450 cities worldwide, community moderated, and largely free.

www.ebay.com

Possibly the world's largest auction site. You can find almost anything here.

www.Freecycle.org

Freecycle.org is a national movement of community bulletin boards who are committed to the concept of "one man's junk."

www.gently-used.com

Gently-used.com is a simple-to-use site for buying and selling used maternity and baby items, including toys, clothes, strollers, baby furniture, electronics, highchairs, and playpens. It's like being the first visitor at all the best garage sales and flea markets at once.

www.nikkiraes.com

Nikki Rae's sells new and gently used baby clothes and cool children's clothes your kids want to wear.

www.stylishstork.com

Online resale clothing shop specializing in gently used baby clothes, used children's clothing, and used maternity clothes at wholesale prices. Quality brand-name clothing includes designer names such as Gymboree, Gap, OshKosh B'Gosh, Old Navy, Carters, Motherhood, and In Due Time.

www.rascalsresale.com

Specializing in name-brand baby clothes and children's clothes at discount prices.

www.taketwomaternity.com

Your one-stop mommy shop featuring stylish hip maternity, designer diaper bags, unique crib bedding, Moses baskets, and baby shower gifts. It also sells gently used baby clothes.

www.zwaggle.com

Zwaggle is an online community for parents to share with other parents. Using a points-based sharing system, parents spend less money, time, and resources providing for their children. Zwaggle provides members with a trusted place to give away used goods that are no longer needed and receive value from their used goods via the points system, to obtain other items.

Index

The End

A

accessories 18

adhesive locks 146

air purifier 126

allergies 83

automobile 24

Aveeno 91

Avent 46, 75, 79

B

Babies "R" Us 57, 79, 99

Babybear Shop 91

Baby Bjorn 101, 155, 170

Baby Einstein 220

baby food 60, 68, 78, 81, 83, 188

baby gates 61, 148

baby monitors 153

baby shades 136

baby shower 49, 55, 63

babysitting 158

Baby Trend 190

baby wipes 45, 93

bacteria 80

bassinet 26, 60, 161

bathing 117

bathtubs 117

bedding 181

Belle's and Beau's 71

bibs 84, 85

blankets 61

books 215

Booty Budder Recipe 92

Boppy pillow 26, 215

borders 181

bottles 40, 60, 69, 74, 95

bottle warmers 77

Boudreaux's 91

bouncer 61, 202

Brainy Baby 220

brand names 27, 39, 58

breast-feeding 38, 68, 128

breast milk 127

breast pump 39, 60, 71

budget 17, 20, 31, 51, 63, 90, 184, 211

burp 128

burp cloths 84

Burt's Bees 120

C

cabinets 145

cable 23

cables 141

carriers 100

car seat 24, 29, 49, 60, 195, 226

Cartwright, Jill 83

cash flow 19, 26

CDs 33

cell phone 23

cereal 60, 68

changing pad 95, 172

changing table 60, 161, 169, 170

childproofing 138, 145, 158

choking 156

clean 115

cleaners 144

cloth diapers 35, 42, 88

clothing 18, 46, 52, 60, 104

colds 130

colic 39, 46, 76, 127

college 32

comfort 107

Consumer Reports 51

convertible carrier cover 132

convertible travel system
  strollers 195

cords 141

corner guards 143

coupons 42, 45, 74

CPR 157

crawling 149

credit card 28

crib 29, 60, 161, 163

curtains 175

D

decorating 175, 180

delivery 30

dental hygiene 129

Desitin 91

DEX 78

diaper bag 61, 95, 158

diaper buying strategy 45

Diaper Champ 99

Diaper Genie 99

diaper pail 61, 98

Diaper rash ointment 91

diapers 35, 42, 44, 52, 53, 58, 60,
  68, 88

Dorman, Amy 65

double strollers 196

drawer locks 145

Dreft 112

dresser 161

dresses 105

E

Earth's Best 82

eBay 41, 105

edge guards 143

emergencies 157

Enfamil 40, 95

Evenflo 49, 51, 75

Evenflo ExerSaucers 204

expenses 22

F

feeding 60

Ferencko, Lauren 206

fever reducers 125

finances 18

first-aid kit 122

Fisher-Price 213

formula 39, 52, 58, 60, 69, 70, 73, 84, 95, 127

four-in-one crib 165

Fowler, Nicole 170

free 19, 95

furniture 60, 160, 171

G

garage sales 29, 85, 162, 197

Gary, Emily 194

gas 127

gas mileage 24, 187

gates 148

Gerber 75, 82

germs 130

glider 172

Graco 49, 190

Gripe Water 128

Gromer, Rachel 155

H

hamper 60, 184

hat 105, 111

Haugsness, Karri 226

healthcare 30

health insurance 30

highchair 187, 226

Hindman, Ashleigh 71

holiday clothing 105

home loan 24

hooded baby towels 119

Huggies 94

humidifier 61, 126

I

immune system 131

income 20, 22

infant car seat 136

infant mirrors 137

Infant Motrin 125

Infant Tylenol Drops 125

installing car seats 49

insurance 30

Internet service 23

J

Jagels, Erin 214

JCPenney 57

jogging strollers 196

jumper 61, 203

K

Kindell, Lori 102

L

labor 30

La Leche League 72

lamps 181

late payments 29

laundry 43, 47, 85, 86, 104

library 217

living costs 21

locks 145

lotion 116

M

maternity clothes 29

mattress 166

mattress pads 168

Medela 71

microwave 78

mirrors 138

mobile 19, 181, 182

Mommy-to-Be & Lil Me

Boutique 65

monitor 61, 153

monthly budget 25

mortgage 24

Motallebi, Armita 129

mountable gates 150

Munchkin Healthflow 76

music 215

mutual funds 33

Mylicon 128

N

nail clippers 116

name-brand clothing 107

Nieder, Robyn 167

nipple ointment 39

nipples 40, 60, 74

NUK 86

nursery 19, 159, 174

O

Ocean Wonders play gym 214

onesies 47, 60, 105, 109

online auction 41

organic 91

organization 52

outlet 140

Oxyclean 113

P

Pacifiers 58

pacifiers 68, 86

Pack 'n Play 198, 226

Padden, Monica 46

paint 160

painting 174

Pampers 94

pants 47, 60, 105

phone 23

photo album 222

plants 144

play mat 212

playpens 58, 60, 198

Playtex 75

poison control 157

poisons 144

Portable playards 198

Pottery Barn Kids 57, 177

price 62

Prince Lionheart 78

purchasing in bulk 94

Q

quality 51

R

rash cream 58

Rath, Bryn 35

recalls 50, 101

registry 56

registry cards 57

rocking chair 172

Roth IRA 33

rugs 175

S

safe transportation 24

safety 50, 135, 139, 163

Safety 1st 49, 137

safety harness 189

savings 21, 25

savings accounts 33

Your New Baby: Insider Secrets to Save Thousands on All Your Baby's Needs

scalp brush 116, 120

schedule 26

scrapbook 222

screw-mounted locks 146

secondhand 18, 29, 85

secondhand store 105, 197

Section 529 Plans 33

shades 136, 176

shampoo 116

sharp objects 143

shelves 60

shirts 47, 60, 105

shopping 37

shopping cart cover 132

Similac 40, 46

Skelton, Julie 26

sleep 70, 162

sleepers 47, 60, 105

sleep gown 110

sliding locks 146

sling 61, 101

Snuggly 103

soap 116

socks 47, 60, 105, 109

spending habits 23

stain remover 112

stairs 149

Stauth, Aimee 51

sterilizers 77

sterilizing 87

stress 19

stroller 60, 170, 190, 226

swaddle 111

swing 207

T

Target 57, 99

teething 133

television 220

tension gates 150

thank you notes 63

thermometer 123

thrift stores 86

toddler bed 165

toothbrush 130

Tots in Motion 218

toys 61, 212

Tranquil Massage 35

transportation 186

Triple Paste 91

trust funds 33

U

used items 18

V

videos 215

W

wagon 170

Wal-Mart 57, 99, 177

walkers 207

wall hangings 60

wall stickers 181

Walsh, Andrea 113

WIC 74

wipes 58, 93

wires 141

Wiser, Kimberly 218

Thank you

To all the families who shared their parenting experience in the case studies throughout this book. Also, thank you to the parents who submitted photos of babies and children. Some of the children featured were:

Monika Diane Stasiak
Luke Blue (with parents Lance and Neisha)
Lane, Vin and Silas Buchner
Emily and Henry Toth

More Great Titles from Atlantic Publishing

101 Businesses You Can Start With Less Than One Thousand Dollars: For Stay-at-Home Moms & Dads

Most parents today have a tough time economically: They have to be at home raising their children so they cannot work much, and the jobs that are out there are often part-time and low paying. Yet most families need two incomes today to get ahead. Detailed in this new book are over 100 business ideas that can be started for very little money and yet may provide parents with a lot more money than they would be paid by the hour.

This is a collection of businesses selected especially for stay-at-home parents who are interested in augmenting their income. These businesses can be started with minimum training and investment and are all capable of producing extra income.

Starting and managing a business takes motivation and talent. It also takes research and planning. This new book is intended to serve as a roadmap for starting your business. It is both easy to use and comprehensive. Thousands of great tips and useful guidelines will help you keep bringing customers back, give you low-cost internal marketing ideas, low- and no-cost ways to satisfy customers, and sales building ideas.

ISBN-13: 978-0-910627-88-7 • 288 Pgs • $21.95

☆ ☆ ☆ ☆ ☆ "I'm a stay at home mom of six kids. My husband works two jobs and I have been desperately searching for a way to help. This book was a godsend. I was able to organize my ideas and get a clear understanding of which direction to take them. It wasn't hard to take the principles outlined in this book and apply them to my own circumstances and abilities and see what would be most profitable and logical way for me to go. I like the way this book was straight forward, listing businesses with start up costs from zero to $1000 in an easy to read format. There were also things I hadn't thought of like writing a business plan, setting up a home office and advertising. The Internet is chock full of scam companies promising nonexistent home job offers but after reading this book I can stop looking. I feel a little more informed about business ownership and issues like taxes, insurance and permits. Need to know stuff before you jump in head strong."
— *Customer Review from www.barnesandnoble.com*

To order call toll-free 800-814-1132 or visit www.atlantic-pub.com

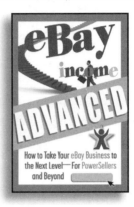

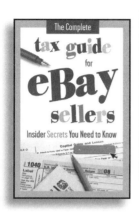  

The Complete Tax Guide for eBay Sellers: *Insider Secrets You Need to Know*

Learn how to take advantage of legal tax loopholes and how to choose the proper business structure. This brand new, up-to-date book covers everything you will need to know to balance the books, including assets and liabilities, keeping track of transactions, payroll, sales tax, balance sheets, keeping a ledger and journal, financial statements, operating accounts, and complete tax information.

ISBN-13: 978-1-60138-124-8 • 288 Pgs • $24.95

The eBay Success Chronicles: *Secrets and Techniques eBay PowerSellers Use Every Day to Make Millions by Angela C. Adams*

"An important part of success on eBay is learning to cross market merchandise between stores and auctions and to find a niche and brand your name. This assures return customers, which is what every business thrives on. Angela's book is a serious lesson on how to do both. From cover to cover it teaches you success on eBay from those who are successful. Highly recommended for anyone who hopes to have a business on eBay — part-time or full-time." — Joyce Banbury, eBay Certified Education Specialist   **ISBN-13: 978-0-910627-64-1 • 408 Pgs • $21.95**

eBay's Secrets Revealed: *The Insider's Guide to Advertising, Marketing, and Promoting Your eBay Store — With Little or No Money*

This book is for those already operating on eBay who want to know how to make more money. Uncover closely guarded strategies for selling products like the pros. Learn dozens of methods to automate your business, including inventory, preventing fraud, payments, accounting, taxes, and fulfillment. Learn new ways to find products and get positive feedback. You will learn pricing strategies, creative methods of writing powerful ad copy that really sells, how to obtain products below wholesale, and ways to make your business work smarter while decreasing your work load.

ISBN-13: 978-0-910627-86-3 • 288 Pgs • $24.95

To order call toll-free **800-814-1132** or visit **www.atlantic-pub.com**

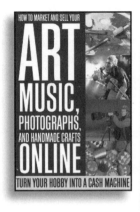
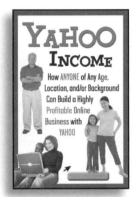

The Online Identity Theft Prevention Kit: Stop Scammers, Hackers, and Identity Thieves from Ruining Your Life

Reduce online identity theft with this up-to-the-minute book. You will find valuable expertise to evaluate and determine your, your family's, and your business's risks. The books has a detailed plan so that you can take action for prevention now. There is also a step-by-step program detailing what to do if your identity has been stolen, plus numerous letters, templates and forms.   ISBN 13: 978-1-60138-008-1 • 288 Pgs • $24.95

How to Market and Sell Your Art, Music, Photographs, and Handmade Crafts Online: Turn Your Hobby into a Cash Machine

Learn the exact steps you need to take to successfully sell your artwork or crafts online — even if you have no experience with marketing and even if you hate to sell. This specialized book will demonstrate, step by step, how to inexpensively market and promote your artwork — easily and, most important, profitably.
ISBN 13: 978-1-60138-146-0 • 288 Pgs • $24.95

Yahoo Income: How ANYONE of Any Age, Location, and/or Background Can Build a Highly Profitable Online Business with Yahoo

A Yahoo! listing is as important as one in the phone book. Yahoo! has evolved into a multinational Internet and communications phenomenon. If you are in business, you need a Yahoo! storefront. This book will provide you with everything you need, including sample business forms, contracts, worksheets, checklists, and dozens of other valuable, timesaving tools of the trade. This expertly written new book will show you how to take advantage of this business phenomenon and arm you with the proper knowledge and insider secrets. Filled with actual examples and anecdotes from real Yahoo! entrepreneurs, this book is as engaging as it is informational.
ISBN 13: 978-1-60138-254-2 • 288 Pgs • $24.95

To order call toll-free 800-81   **NOV 2008**   antic-pub.com
MAIN LIBRARY